Pressing Problems in the Law
Volume 1

CRIMINAL JUSTICE & HUMAN RIGHTS

- Reshaping the Criminal Justice System
- Fraud and the Criminal Law
- Freedom of Expression

Edited by P. B. H. BIRKS

OXFORD UNIVERSITY PRESS · 1995

This book has been printed digitally and produced in a standard specification in order to ensure its continuing availability

OXFORD
UNIVERSITY PRESS

Great Clarendon Street, Oxford OX2 6DP

Oxford University Press is a department of the University of Oxford.
It furthers the University's objective of excellence in research, scholarship, and education by publishing worldwide in

Oxford New York

Athens Auckland Bangkok Bogotá Buenos Aires Cape Town Chennai Dar es Salaam Delhi Florence Hong Kong Istanbul Karachi Kolkata Kuala Lumpur Madrid Melbourne Mexico City Mumbai Nairobi Paris São Paulo Shanghai Singapore Taipei Tokyo Toronto Warsaw

with associated companies in Berlin Ibadan

Oxford is a registered trade mark of Oxford University Press in the UK and in certain other countries

Published in the United States
by Oxford University Press Inc., New York

Reprinted 2001

ISBN 0-19-826042-3

EDITOR'S PREFACE

Many people in the United Kingdom still react strongly against the notion that we might have to carry identity cards. Our traditions incline us to freedom and we shy away from even small advances in the power of the state. We all carry cards which do identify us, but we must not be made to carry and produce identity cards. It is a healthy instinct, but whether it is as strong as it used to be is a matter of doubt. How far can the state go in the fight against crime? The present Home Secretary, although himself a lawyer, seems prepared to go further than most common lawyers would be able to accept. And one trouble is that there is no fundamental law which tells him what line he may not cross. We have taken too much for granted. In Scotland there was no legislation against trading on a Sunday. One supposes that nobody thought that legislation could be needed. Ten years ago Sunday trading began to flourish there, well ahead of the same phenomenon in England. We have certainly supposed that freedom needed no special protection. Erosions now threaten. Among others, sadly, one of the leads which we have lost is the lead we thought we had in the defence of the great freedoms. The contents of this volume serve to illustrate that in human rights as in so many other matters we are now in danger of falling behind Europe. We must be sure of keeping up.

In 1992 the Annual Conference of the Society of Public Teachers of Law chose as its theme 'The European Law School.' That theme has been taken up again and again in different countries, most recently in Metz in October 1994 under the aegis of the European Commission itself. This reflects the reality and depth of the change that has overtaken the law of every member state by virtue of belonging to the European Union. At Metz the consensus was that no more needed to be done to make law schools aware of the need to respond to the impact of the law of the Union, because all were vividly aware already and vigorously responding. What was needed now, it was thought, was more awareness and activity on the private law front. Lawyers must know more about the domestic arrangements of neighbouring European legal systems. That must be right, and that kind of opening to Europe is also under way. At the same time it is not to be forgotten that the enduring foundation of our common European legal culture is chiefly in the keeping of the sister organization, the Council of Europe and, in particular, the Court of Human Rights. Professor Roy Goode was President of the S.P.T.L. in 1992. In his Presidential Address, later published in (1993) 13 *Legal Studies* 1, he urged a packed and distinguished audience to recognize the centrality of the protection of human rights in the new Europe. The Convention represented at once the best of our common legal inheritance and the heart of the lawyer's contribution to a civilised, humane and secular society.

This message needs to be driven home. In some not too distant day when legal education has been emancipated from the dictatorship of the practising professions, the jurisprudence of human rights will move to the very centre of the law school's activity, forming a natural core of the curriculum. This process too is already under way, at least in the intellect of the university lawyers. Unfortunately, the same cannot be said of the most recent professional prescriptions for legal education in England, in which human rights have barely a toe-hold on the edge of something grandly called the Foundations of Public Law. That will be a course taught, alongside two others, in a single semester. When that kind of minimalism has had its day, the study of human rights will begin to pervade many other areas of law. It must have more space to itself, but from that space of its own both the values which it teaches and the techniques for balancing competing interests which it uses will extend through large areas of the curriculum. Nowhere will the effect be more obviously felt than in criminal law and procedure.

The three seminars which are covered in this volume were designed as a triplet to achieve that juxtaposition and interaction. Each part of the book can stand alone, but the intention is and was that, taken together, the volume should be a study in the practicalities of reconciling the vigorous protection of fundamental freedoms with the exigencies of repressing wickedness and vice. The common law has traditionally inclined at every choice to the protection of freedom, but the nature of our constitutional arrangements is such that that has been a matter of unentrenched legal culture. As Dr. Smith says of the right to silence (p.87, col.2), 'Rights are not treated by the British Courts as imperatives, let alone as absolutes . . .' He then goes grimly on: 'When the suppression of serious fraud is the objective, the experience is that the right counts for virtually nothing.' Finally, it is to Strasbourg that he looks for a possible ne plus ultra: 'Whether European jurisprudence will permit that stance to prevail remains to be seen.'

Editor's Preface

Our criminal law has had to face very grave problems in the past decade, some arising from the special intractabilities of serious fraud, others from the emotions whipped up by terrorism. Thus far the only contribution of the professions on the educational front has been to cut the quantum of criminal law required of the aspiring lawyer. The official organs of the professions—as distinct from many individual practitioners and many firms—seem constitutionally incapable of recognizing the relation between problems in the legal system and inadequate provision of legal education. As from October 1995 in England and Wales a one-semester course in criminal law will suffice, one eighteenth of a three-year course, a reduction from the one fifteenth previously required. That is a backwards step, but merely to reverse it would not suffice. Something more radical will have to be done to enlarge the understanding of the matter and spread that understanding more widely about.

One thing which became sadly apparent in the Lord Chief Justice's seminar was that the law schools, strong on substantive doctrine as also on criminology and penology, are weak on procedure. That is not to say that there are not some great experts. But there are not enough, and there is not that wide dispersal of expertise through the system which alone can keep a subject healthy. The law schools are at fault if any subject cannot maintain that critical mass of learning. It cannot go unsaid that the Chief Justice came to the seminar looking for serious practical help with procedural reforms but by and large his questions left us flat-footed. Nor was it obvious that we were just the wrong people. It was evident that he had found out an institutional weakness in the system.

It is not difficult to trace the history of that weakness, nor to mark its limits. Evidence, for example, is excluded. Professor Tapper's paper in this volume belongs in a strong tradition, secured in modern times by, above all others, Professor Sir Rupert Cross. But there is no doubt that procedure, both civil and criminal, has been systematically neglected. The work of Neil Andrews in Cambridge and of Adrian Zuckerman, Nicola Lacey and Lucia Zedner in Oxford serves to bring out the difference between systematic and absolute neglect. The former admits of bright pools of light. Several other examples could be given of individuals and groups who have managed to swim against the system. Nevertheless the systematic neglect is a fact evidenced by the poverty of the law library in procedural matters. It is at least partly explained by the damaging division between a so-called 'academic' phase and a so-called 'vocational' phase. Procedure had fallen into the latter, from which no research emerges. Somehow the institutions responsible for that phase have managed to dispense themselves from the costly obligation to promote research and publication. This is a serious matter. It points to the need to run the two phases of legal education together. Scotland has the institutional framework in which that is possible. England and Wales do not.

It is encouraging that in the recent Consultation Paper put out by the Lord Chancellor's Advisory Committee—the forty-nine questions which all law schools were busy answering at the end of 1994—the first phase was called simply 'the initial phase'. That strikes a blow against the notion of a gulf between academic and practical. If we take 'academic study' to mean study which seeks to get to the truth about something, no subject needs more to be studied academically than does procedure. And one by-aspect of its truth is that it cannot be ignored even by those who purport to be interested only in substantive law. The study of legal doctrine is itself diminished and impaired when it ignores procedure.

The Society of Public Teachers of Law set out to make its annual seminar programme a point of contact between academics, practitioners and judges. The Society owes a particular debt of gratitude to those practitioners who have helped to bring that intention to fruition. Those who have attended and those who have written papers have helped these seminars to bridge a gap which once seemed almost too wide to cross. The health of our law requires it to be bridged effectively and often.

Without the judges who have added the chairmanship of one of these all-day seminars to their other burdens, the programme would not have enjoyed anything like the same success. We are very conscious of the degree to which senior judges are now overworked, and we are all the more grateful to those who have been willing to read even more papers and to guide the discussions at these seminars. Lord Taylor of Gosforth, the Lord Chief Justice, chaired 'Reshaping the Criminal Justice System' on 19th March 1994; Lord Justice Henry chaired 'Fraud and the Criminal Law' on 30th April 1994, and The Hon. Judge Rolv Ryssdal, President of the European Court of Human Rights, chaired 'Freedom of Speech' on 15th October 1994. The Society is deeply grateful to each of these very distinguished judges.

Peter Birks
9 January 1995

The Contributors

Andrew Ashworth, Professor of Law in King's College London and a Fellow of the British Academy, is an authority on criminal law and sentencing; **Profes-**

sor E.M. Barendt, Arnold Goodman Professor of Media Law at University College London, is a leading author on freedom of speech and on social security law; **Sheriff G.H. Gordon, Q.C.**, in addition to his judicial duties is the author of Scotland's leading treatise on criminal law; **Paul Mahoney**, barrister and author on human rights, has for many years been a senior official of the European Court of Human Rights; **Dr. Christopher McCrudden** is a Fellow of Lincoln College, Oxford, with special interests in public law, human rights and anti-discrimination; **David Pannick, Q.C.**, Fellow of All Souls College, Oxford, is a practising barrister who is also a well-known author and regular commentator on the problems of the legal system; **Jeremy Roberts, Q.C.**, is a leading barrister who sits as a Recorder of the Crown Court; **Dr. A.T.H. Smith** is a Fellow of Gonville and Caius College, Cambridge, with special interests in criminal law and civil liberties; **Professor Sir John Smith, Q.C.**, Professor Emeritus in the University of Nottingham and Fellow of the British Academy, has long been one of England's greatest authorities on criminal law; **G.R. Sullivan** is a Senior Lecturer in Law at the University of Durham with special interests in criminal and public law; **Colin Tapper**, Professor of Law at Oxford University and Fellow of Magdalen College, is an authority on the law of evidence and the law in and relating to computers; **Peter Thornton, Q.C.**, formerly chairman of the NCCL, is a practising barrister with many publications in the field of civil liberties; **Colin Warbrick** is a Senior Lecturer in Law at the University of Durham with special interests in international law and human rights.

TABLE OF CONTENTS

TABLE OF UNITED KINGDOM CASES

Table of United Kingdom Cases

TABLE OF CASES FROM OTHER JURISDICTIONS

TABLE OF UNITED KINGDOM LEGISLATION

TABLE OF LEGISLATION FROM OTHER JURISDICTIONS

TABLE OF INTERNATIONAL INSTRUMENTS

PART I

RESHAPING THE CRIMINAL JUSTICE SYSTEM

1. The Report of the Royal Commission: A view from Scotland

SHERIFF G. H. GORDON, Q.C.

As someone who was a member of the Thomson Committee on Scottish Criminal Procedure, I should like to start by expressing my admiration for the speed with which the Report of the Royal Commission was prepared, as well as for the comprehensive detail of its content, and the amount of research material which was available to its authors. I note, too, that the Report (like Thomson) accepts that systems of criminal procedure are born, not made, so to speak, and that every system is the product of its own distinctive history and culture, which makes attempted transplantation liable to failure. I accept, too, the implications of the comment that the Royal Commission has not found, either in Scotland or elsewhere, 'a set of practices which has so clearly succeeded in resolving the problems which arise in any system of criminal justice that it furnishes the obvious model which all the others should therefore adopt'. I have not come here to convert you all to the Criminal Procedure (Scotland) Acts, but merely to offer some comments from the point of view of an alien from another country, albeit one whose system is not all that unlike your own.

I should also make it quite clear that the views I am about to express are my own personal views, and are not to be taken as representing those of any other Scottish judges, far less of even the inferior Scottish judiciary as a group. Perhaps the only thing which all sheriffs will agree about is that if any ten of them are asked a question they will come up with at least eleven answers.

The answers which one does come up with for any of the difficult problems which are the topic of this meeting, like those for any difficult and controversial problem, may depend on where one starts from. To be more precise, in this case they may well depend on the picture one has of the typical accused person, which in turn is likely to be influenced by the actual characteristics of the last four or five accused persons one came across. Is the typical accused a confused innocent youngster, quite bemused or even terrified by police officers and police stations, is he a confident and impudent hooligan who is guilty of far more offences than he will ever be brought to book for, is he a sophisticated criminal, or is he a respectable member of society caught up in a web of unfortunate circumstances? We have to ask ourselves which of these we are legislating for, and to what extent we are prepared to sacrifice the rights of one in order to enable us to deal effectively with the others. Another factor which will affect the result is our view of the police, and in particular whether we think we can trust them to deal fairly with suspects who come into their hands, and honestly with evidence which comes to their notice, and also perhaps, in a subtler way, on the extent to which we think we can rely on them to catch the right people. It is, of course possible to construct a system which will greatly increase the number of guilty persons convicted, at the cost of increasing also the number of innocent people convicted: we could simply create a presumption of guilt, or even an irrebuttable presumption that all confessions are true and reliable, and are sufficient evidence of guilt. We can, conversely, construct a system which has such strict rules of evidence that hardly anyone will ever be convicted. Since, however, neither of these is a practical proposition, we must just accept that at best we are going to arrive at a compromise, which may not even be internally consistent, but which we hope will work not too badly in most cases.

Our system of criminal procedure will also depend to some extent on economics, as the Report recognises. There may be a principle which requires that justice be done though the Heavens fall: there is no practical rule which requires that justice be done even if it bankrupts the Treasury. There are a number of ways of dealing with this difficulty. The one I favour is to limit the number of prosecutions to a level at which they can be carried out properly and efficiently: if you can't prosecute the man properly then don't prosecute him at all. But we live in a world of performance-related rewards, and performance tends to be assessed in quantity rather than in quality. It may therefore be unrealistic to expect those whose performance is being assessed to prefer to prepare and prosecute five cases thoroughly, rather than 10 adequately, or even, as pressures increase, 20 inadequately.

All of which is a rather ponderous way of saying that criminal procedure does not exist in a vacuum, that it is not an ideal construct, but something which is necessarily affected by all sort of extra-legal considerations. After all, changes in the treatment of offenders have been greatly influenced by the comparative costs of the different disposals, and in particular by the reluctance of governments to spend money on building prisons; and much of the impetus behind moves to settle issues at pre-trial hearings comes from a desire to reduce the cost of trials. We live in a different world from that in which 'Always plead not guilty, the Crown witnesses may die', or in modern terms, 'The prosecutor may make a hash of it', or 'The police witnesses will not impress the jury', were regarded as assertions of morally and socially unassailable rights. We cannot afford a system in which fingerprints are sought even when the accused were caught in the act, just in case the jury don't believe the police officers who caught them, or in which identification parades are held in every case even where the victim has identified his assailants by name to the police, just in case he gives evidence that the people who attacked him were not the accused, although they had the same names.

Since I am looking at English law from a Scots point of view, it may be useful to give a very brief general outline of Scots criminal procedure. But it is perhaps worth making one more obvious preliminary point first. What any person regards as an obviously necessary part of any system of criminal evidence or procedure will often depend on what he is used to. I cannot expect English people to view the rule of corroboration with the same sort of religious awe as do the Scots, and conversely I hope that you will not expect me to believe that the right to jury trial is a law handed to Moses on Sinai (as the law on corroboration was, as it happens!)—Magna Carta is not in the Scottish statute book.

An accused in Scotland who is to be tried on indictment first appears before a sheriff in private for judicial examination. And that immediately emphasises the quasi-inquisitorial nature of the system, albeit more in theory than in practice. During most of the 19th century such an accused emitted a declaration before the sheriff, and was examined on it, and on the evidence which was presented to the sheriff by the prosecution, as represented by the procurator fiscal. Witnesses were originally interviewed by the sheriff, but later by the procurator fiscal. This investigation took place within the eight days following the accused's first appearance, during which time he was normally remanded in custody 'for further examination'. At the end of that period the fiscal presented his 'precognition' to the sheriff: the 'precognition' being the evidence in the case, gathered mostly in the form of 'precognitions' of particular witnesses. The sheriff then decided whether or not to commit the accused for trial. If he was committed for trial he was either detained in custody for up to 110 days, or was released on bail. The precognition was sent to Crown Office where it was considered by Crown counsel, who were advocates in private practice, appointed by the Lord Advocate to act under his general direction as public prosecutors on a part-time basis and who considered the precognition, decided if it was to be prosecuted on indictment and, if it went to the High Court, themselves conducted the prosecution, sometimes under the leadership of the Lord Advocate or Solicitor-General. Things began to change at the end of the century, partly because for the first time accused persons were entitled to consult their solicitors before they appeared for examination, and to have them present at the examination, and partly because of the introduction of the Criminal Evidence Act 1898 which gave the accused an opportunity to tell his story in court, and so did away with much of the point of a declaration. From about 1900, right up to 1980, the first appearance for examination became a formality, whose only importance was as an opportunity for the accused to seek bail. Indeed, if he gets bail at that stage, nothing further happens until service of the indictment, even though the minute said that he had been committed for further examination. If he does not get bail at that stage, he appears a week later and is fully committed, unless the fiscal has decided in the interim to deal with him summarily. But the only purpose of the full committal hearing was, once again, to allow for an application for bail. No sheriff even saw a precognition after 1945, and I doubt very much if there is ever a precognition in existence at that stage nowadays. (These committal proceedings are not totally meaningless—a sheriff may refuse to commit for trial because he thinks the proceedings are oppressive or because they are time-barred, but such instances are extremely rare. And apart from cases which are time-barred (and these are probably limited to retrials) the absence of committal proceedings is not a bar to raising an indictment.)

Since 1980, or to be more accurate since the coming into force of the appropriate provisions of the Criminal Justice (Scotland) Act 1980, 'the 1980 Act', the accused's appearance for examination has been the stage at which a judicial examination takes place, and I shall return to that later. Thereafter it is still the case that a precognition is prepared by the fiscal and submitted to Crown counsel for their decision. When an indictment is served on the accused, it will contain a list of Crown witnesses and productions. Since the 1980 Act, too, it has been open to either party go give notice of preliminary matters which they wish to be determined before the trial starts, and which, since the Prisoners and Criminal Proceedings (Scotland) Act 1993, may include notice of any documents the truth of whose contents any party thinks ought to be admitted or any matter which he thinks ought to be agreed. The decision of the court at a preliminary diet may be appealed prior to trial, thus hopefully avoiding the expense of a long trial which will turn out to have been legally flawed for one reason or another.

It should be noted that throughout this process, apart from the preliminary diet procedure, the initiative is in the hands of the Crown, or, as we say, the Lord Advocate is master of the instance. It is for him, or for Crown counsel acting on his behalf, to say whether an accused is to be prosecuted, in what court and on what charges; it is for him to decide what pleas to accept and what to reject. Although the High Court retains the right to stop a prosecution which it regards as oppressive, this is a power rarely used, the court having traditionally a great deal of faith in the integrity of the Lord Advocate, who has the constitutional responsibility for prosecution, and is answerable to Parliament. The court will not even refuse bail if the Crown are agreeable to bail; apart from anything else to do so would be pointless because the Crown have the power to release the accused anyway. A judge has no right to refuse to accept a plea which the Crown are prepared to accept, unless perhaps the subsequent plea in mitigation is inconsistent with guilt. The conduct of any case is therefore very much in the hands of the Crown, i.e. of whoever represents the Crown in court, and not in the hands of the judge. One incidental result of this is that there is no question of the judge having any power to call a witness, although he can recall one for the purpose of clearing up ambiguities. Nor has he any control over the way in which even a long fraud trial is conducted.

Statements by suspects

I must confess that the Scots lawyer's first reaction to the mass of material on police interrogations contained in PACE and the Codes is a combination of bewilderment and an unjustified feeling of superiority. The English, it seems, need pages and pages of words to deal with matters which we in Scotland deal with by a couple of sections of the 1980 Act, taken together with a rule that the police have to behave fairly. [Cf the reply of a distinguished Scottish judge to an English lawyer's astonishment at the lack of any Scottish Theft Act: 'It doesn't need an Act of Parliament to explain to a Scotsman what stealing is.'] That reaction is itself unfair, however. We are back here at the old dispute between certainty and flexibility, between codes and rules on the one hand, and an amorphous concept of fairness on the other, and we must recognise that while the Scots have a leaning towards the amorphous the English prefer to know where they stand. It is also perhaps worth pointing out that, generally speaking, the Scots courts were, for a time which went right up to the 1950s at least, not so much concerned with police tactics as with whether they were entitled to question suspects at all. Once it was settled that they were so entitled, the courts tended simply to leave any question of the fairness of their methods to the jury, the judge being empowered to exclude evidence of statements to the police only if the circumstances were such that no reasonable jury could regard the police as having behaved fairly, unfairness meaning something like 'unfair means which place cross-examination, pressure and deception in close company'. [*Jones* v. *Milne*, 1975 J.C. 16.] This approach rests partly on the view that where there are conflicting accounts of what happened in the police station, as there usually are, it is for the jury and not the judge to determine which is the true account, and partly on the view that questions of fairness depend on what would nowadays, I suppose, be called community attitudes, and that juries are the embodiment of the community, rather on the lines taken by Lord Devlin in the Hart-Devlin controversy. As it happens, about the only formal rule left is one which the Royal Commission would apparently dispense with, the rule that once the police have charged a person, they may not continue to question him: or at least that if they do continue to question him his answers will not be admissible in evidence. The Royal Commission Report suggests that since the police are also involved in preparing the case for the prosecution, which may involve further inquiries, they should be entitled to question the accused after he has been charged, and that this will have two advantages. The first is that since the police will question him anyway, it is better that that questioning be regulated (which is one reason why detention was created in Scotland). The second is that there are often 'legitimate' reasons for such questioning, the only examples given being the possibility of alternative charges arising, or that further questioning may lead to an explanation from the suspect which exonerates him or her, or to information or evidence against other suspects. The position in Scotland is not crystal clear, but the emphasis has always been on what is admissible in evidence rather than on what the police may ask the suspect, and it is probably the case that questioning after charge, designed for example to trace stolen property, is perfectly proper, but that what the suspect said is not admissible in evidence. The protected position of the charged suspect has recently been affirmed in a number of cases in Scotland, and it is unlikely that such questioning will become allowable, or at least that the answers to it will be admissible in evidence. The Scottish approach may depend on the view that different rules apply at different stages of investigation, and perhaps also on a persistent feeling that there is a limit to the extent to which the police should be allowed to encroach on the traditional role of the procurator fiscal and the sheriff (even if the sheriff's role is now pretty formal), if only because such an encroachment would involve blurring the distinction between investigation and the preparation of the prosecution case, which is still the responsibility of the fiscal and not of the police, although I accept that in practice much of the work is done by the police. As late as 1913 it was said that the police had no right to act as examiners and that it was improper for them to examine accused persons in the absence of the safeguards provided by judicial examination, which by that time had virtually ceased to exist. [See *Hodgson* v. *Macpherson*, 1913 S.C. (J.) 68.] It should be remembered, too, that despite the fact that most of the 'leg-work' is done by the police, the preparation of a case is the responsibility of the fiscal and not of the police, and that the function of the police in questioning suspects is to investigate the situation and not to prepare a case. They are limited to what the Report describes as investigative interviewing, but within that limitation they are fairly free to ask what they want, provided they behave fairly. It is, in any event, a little surprising to read a suggestion that the preparation of a case for prosecution should include questioning of the accused by the police.

I am impressed by the emphasis which is given in the Report to the presence of the suspect's solicitor at the police station. The Scots suspect has a right to have his solicitor informed of his arrest, and of course may decline to say anything until his solicitor is present, but there is nothing to prevent the police asking questions in the absence of the solicitor, the answers to which will be admissible, and interviews commonly take place without the presence of a solicitor. Scots solicitors are likely to tell their clients to say nothing, and we are not keen to see police questioning go the way of judicial examinations. The safeguards which are provided are the six-hour limit on detention, and the tape-recording of interviews. It is up to the jury, having heard the tape, to decide if the questioning was fair. It is an odd feature of the differences between our two systems that while jury trial is an article of faith in England, Scotland seems much more ready to entrust matters to juries than is England. There is something almost antinomian in the way in which we leave what are arguably questions of general law to be decided by juries on the circumstances of particular cases. But on the other hand if you can't trust juries, why have them? And if you do have them, what right do judges have to impose their views of fair conduct on juries? The practical problem these days is not that juries are prone to convict, or to believe all police officers, but that on the contrary a perfectly good prosecution case can be lost by the introduction of unnecessary evidence of statements to the police, which are hotly denied, or, where they have been tape-recorded, are said to have been made only because 'the police told me what to say', and where they consist of signed entries in a police notebook are alleged to have been signed on the instructions of the police without the accused being given a chance to read what he was signing. But I do accept the dangers of letting a jury hear a confession and then asking them to disregard it, not because they don't believe it was true, but because they think it was unfairly obtained. There are still cases in Scotland where we hold the equivalent of a voir dire, and the judge excludes the evidence, but they are rare and not encouraged.

I note, incidentally, that the Commission were concerned at the problem of summarising taped interviews. One of the problems with such interviews is, of course, their length, another is that they include a lot of inadmissible material, such as hearsay or references to previous convictions. I do not think there is any way out of supplying the Crown and the defence with the complete tape and transcript. Once that has been done, however, it should be possible in many cases for parties to agree the gist of the interview, and to incorporate the relevant and important parts of it into a minute of agreement, or at least to produce an agreed edited text. There will obviously be cases in which one side or the other wants the jury actually to hear what was said, but there are many others in which all that happens is that the jury are bored by having to listen to the prosecutor and a police officer engage in a poorly rehearsed piece of amateur dramatics as they reenact the interview from the transcript.

It may be worth mentioning here that the Scots have always been fairly permissive when it comes to real evidence, perhaps on the view that it is less likely to be tainted than confession evidence. Scots judges have no power to exclude competent evidence on the ground that its prejudicial effect outweighs its probative value. But they do have power to admit real evidence obtained improperly if the police methods are excusable, the normal excuse being by reference to a widely defined concept of 'urgency'. We have, however, just enacted specific rules allowing the police to take samples of a detainee's external hair from any part of his body, by cutting or combing, to take material from or from under a nail, including the nail itself, and to take blood or other body fluids or tissue, or any other material, from an external part of the body by swabbing or rubbing, provided they do so with the authority of an officer of the rank of inspector or above. [Police and Criminal Proceedings (Scotland) Act 1993, s.28.]

The effect of silence

At this point I must put my cards on the table and stick my neck out. I belong to the camp which can see no reason why an accused should not be expected to explain his position and give his answers to the allegations made against him. It seems to me to be artificial, to put it no higher, not to ask the person who knows most about his involvement or non-involvement in the offence what he has to say about it, and unrealistic not to take into account his failure to provide an innocent explanation of circumstances which seem to point to his guilt. I would have no conscientious objection to a continental-type system in which the trial opened with the accused being judicially examined, but I do not think that such a system would fit into our adversial trial procedures. (Nor do I favour the dramatics of solemnly calling on the accused to give evidence and recording his negative response). Within the context of our adversarial procedure, I see no reason why an accused's silence should not be relevant at the stage at which the Crown have proved that there is a case for him to answer. The majority recommendation in the Report appears to be based partly on the absence of any evidence that to remove the right would make much difference, and partly on the view that it is only when the prosecution case has been fully disclosed that defendants should be required to offer an answer to the charges made against them at the risk of adverse comment if they fail to do so. I think, with respect, that that may confuse the preparation of a defence or the giving notice of a defence, with refusing to answer simple factual questions put by police officers. As I have indicated, I have never myself been able to understand why a jury should not be allowed to take account of silence at this stage. I am not suggesting that it is proof of guilt, or corroboration of other evidence, but only that it is relevant in assessing evidence, and in particular credibility. Nor am I suggesting that inferences should be drawn from the fact that the accused made no reply when cautioned and charged. What I am talking about is a refusal to answer specific questions, or to explain suspicious circumstances when such an explanation is asked for. If the suspect has a genuine explanation to offer, why should he not offer it when asked? I appreciate that some people may prefer to hang rather than, for example, proffer a true explanation which will show they have been unfaithful to their wives [See Laurence Dowdall, *Get Me Dowdall* (Edinburgh, 1979), chap. III], but that is a choice they have a right to make, and there is nothing the legal system can do to prevent them making it. This has nothing to do with the burden of proof, which remains, as it does on the Continent, with the prosecution. It may be connected with a different proposition, namely, that an accused has no duty to help the Crown to prove the case against him, to provide evidence against himself. On that I would say two things. The first is that there is a difference between forcing an accused to provide evidence against himself, and allowing the jury to make the normal inference from an unanswered and unexplained Crown case. The second is that there is no inalienable right not to be required to assist the Crown to make out its case. Apart altogether from the use which can be made of silence, there are situations in which the accused is under a duty to provide the authorities with information which may incriminate him, in which failure to provide the information is itself an offence, and in which the information may be used in evidence against the provider. The best known examples arise under the Road Traffic Acts, where an allegedly drunk driver is obliged to provide a sample of breath, and any person believed to be the driver or owner of a car when an offence was committed in connection with it is obliged to disclose to the police who was driving the car at the relevant time. There are also cases, of the kind to which the Report refers, in which persons suspected of certain frauds are required to provide information to government inspectors, and in some examples of which the information may be used as evidence. [See e.g. *Styr* v. *H.M. Advocate*, 1993, S.C.C.R. 278.]

The Report's response to the fraud cases is to point out that 'suspects in such cases are persons in responsible positions with ready access to legal advice, charged with sophisticated offences which might otherwise go not merely unpunished but undetected.' But that hardly applies to motorists. And in any event, serious fraud is not the only crime committed by sophisticated persons in white collars, or by experienced criminals in no collars at all. In the end of the day whether or not suspects are obliged to provide evidence against themselves does not depend on any great constitutional principle, but on the needs of the moment. So far as mere silence is concerned, I am not saying that it is proof of guilt, nor even that there should be any duty to speak in most cases, but only that it is a relevant circumstance. It will always be for the jury to consider whether any particular accused's silence is significant. It is true that some accused persons are flustered and make bad witnesses, etc., but the same is true of many Crown witnesses, and juries are expected to be able to deal with such situations.

I note that the Report is quite happy with comments on the failure of an accused to give evidence, so that once again the 'right to silence' is not absolute. I note, too, however, that the comment of which the Report approves, which is also about as far as Scots judges would be permitted to go, is really pretty anodyne, not to say self-evident.

There seem to be two reasons for objecting to comments about an accused's silence in answer to police questioning in particular. The first is one of principle: that he should not be required to give an explanation until he knows the strength of the Crown case. I can see that there is an argument that the police have no right to require explanations unless they have some evidence against the suspect, and it may be that silence in the face of what one might call 'fishing interrogations' should be protected. But, generally speaking, to allow the suspect to keep quiet until he knows what evidence the police have, seems to me to be somewhat quixotic. After all, the only result of waiting for an explanation until the suspect knows the full prosecution case is to give him an opportunity to tailor his response to the evidence, instead of telling the truth. This, however, is a matter on which there is not a great deal of room for discussion.

If, however, the main objection is related to the position of the police, there is room for compromise. It may be said that the police have no right to pry into a man's secrets, and that conversely it is not right that the citizen should be required to bare his soul to a police officer. It may also be said that the fact that a police officer has suspicions should not be enough to impose on the citizen anything that could be seen as a requirement to answer questions, although it is enough to impose on him a requirement to submit to arrest and search in many circumstances. It may even be said that despite all the safeguards provided by PACE evidence of statements allegedly made to the police is so inherently unreliable that the wisest course is always to say nothing, and nobody should be put at risk by taking that course, although in that case things said to the police should not be admissible either. These objections can be met by having the accused questioned in the presence of his solicitor whom he has a right to consult, in a judicial setting, the judicial examination. I accept at once the comment of the Report that the judicial examination experiment in Scotland has not been very successful, because the accused can just parrot, and I mean parrot, 'On the advice of my solicitor I have nothing to say'. (Or, to quote one not very bright accused, 'I have nothing to say on behalf of my solicitor'.) The courts have, somewhat belatedly, come round to holding that that stock response is open to critical comment from the bench, but as in all cases of comment on an accused's silence, they have stressed, some might suggest over-stressed, the need for restraint on the part of the judge. It is also very difficult to assess that kind of response without knowing what information the accused gave to his solicitor, and that kind of inquiry might be regarded as improper. If, however, solicitors were aware that 'on the advice of my solicitor' was not an all-purpose get-out, they might change the advice they give, or at least make sure that the accused knows the risks involved in keeping quiet.

It should be noted, too, that comment on silence at judicial examination is permissible only where the accused leads evidence on the matters about which he kept silent, and that the scope of the examination is itself somewhat restricted, being fairly well limited to inquiring as to any positive defence the accused has, and whether he wants to challenge any admissions he allegedly made to the police, or complain about the circumstances in which they were extracted from him. (It is even thought by many prosecutors to be improper to ask him if he denies it.) I still think that there is room for a somewhat more wide-ranging interrogation of the accused at this early stage, and I would accept that it is only fair for the prosecutor to put his cards on the table, and to invite the accused to respond to the evidence the prosecution claim to have. It is worth noting, too, that the judicial examination can work to the advantage of the accused; early investigation of an honest alibi, for example, should lead to an early discharge. The other way in which judicial examination can work to the advantage of the accused is by enabling him to give his side of the story without being subjected to cross-examination, thus avoiding the need to give evidence at his trial. That, however, as you will appreciate, is something I should like to see prevented, but that is another matter. So far as judicial examination is concerned, I would simply say that I see no reason why silence in these circumstances, away from the police, in a court, after advice from and in the presence of one's solicitor, should not be taken into account, provided that the Crown have established that there is a case to answer, whether or not the accused leads evidence. If he does lead evidence, then the only significance of the earlier silence is in relation to the credibility of the later answer, and that again seems reasonable enough.

Corroboration

I do not propose to say very much about this. As you would expect, I think that confessions should require to be corroborated. They are such peculiar things in themselves, and the circumstances in which they are made are likely to be so unusual (in at least the sense that for at least many accused police cars and police stations are not their normal habitat) and so controversial, that they should not be enough in themselves for conviction. I think too that the notion of the 'special knowledge' confession has been carried too far in Scotland, and that such confessions should be 'self-corroborating' only where it is clear that the only explanation of the accused's knowledge of the relevant facts is guilt, and only where none of these facts was known to the police. I am, frankly, also somewhat chary about cases which depend on an admission in a police car, or some other type of 'blurt' as the only corroboration of not very much other evidence, but that situation probably has to be left to the good sense of the jury. I would, however, strongly favour the Report's suggestion that any such blurt should be put to the accused at the start of his taped interview. It is normally put to him at judicial examination, although I have to concede that it is not necessary to put it then in order to lead it in evidence, whether or not the accused has been judicially examined. In any event, the judicial examination may be a bit late, since by then the accused is unlikely to be willing to admit having made an unrecorded confession.

I would also quite like to see some requirement of corroboration of identification evidence in many cases. One good identification supported by a poor one, or perhaps even two not very good identifications, may well be enough in Scotland, [See e.g. *Ralston* v. *H.M. Advocate*, 1987 S.C.C.R. 467.] where the judge does not have the power to withdraw a weak identification case from the jury which I understand he has in England; all he can do is to give a warning on the dangers of such evidence. The objection to my proposal might well be, however, that in these days of masked robbers, it is difficult enough to catch dangerous criminals without putting yet another obstacle in the way of the Crown—but that of course assumes that the police know enough to catch the right people even if they can't get together more than a minimum amount of evidence to prove it, which takes us back to my introductory remarks. Once again, I strongly favour the recommendations in the Report on identification evidence generally, on the recording of parades, and on the duty of the police to provide the defence with the descriptions originally given by the witnesses (Shades of Oscar Slater!)

Disclosure

So far as disclosure by the Crown is concerned, it has always been the position in Scotland that the indictment is accompanied by a list of witnesses and productions, and that the productions are available for examination by the defence. That, of course, covers only material which the Crown propose to use; so far as other material is concerned, there are no formal rules. It has, however, always been the attitude of the Crown that it is their duty to present to the court, or at least make available to the accused, all relevant evidence which is in their hands, despite a somewhat unusual statement by the court not so long ago that they had no duty to do so, a statement on which the Crown have since indicated they do not rely. [Cf. *Higgins* v. *H.M. Advocate*, 1990 S.C.C.R. 268; *H.M. Advocate* v. *Ward*, 1993 S.C.C.R. 595.] The judge in *Ward* refused calls for the provision of all statements taken by the Crown from witnesses on the ground that these were of the nature of 'fishing diligences' of a kind which would not be allowed in civil litigation. In the end, however, the Crown agreed to provide statements which were available to the police at the time they interviewed the accused and which were the source of allegations put to them by the police in an interview the Crown intended to lead at the trial. There have, so far, been no other suggestions that the Crown should hand over their complete file, so to speak, or anything like it, or that there should be any formal mechanism for ensuring that the police pass all relevant information to the fiscal. It may be that these things will come, but so far it seems that the machinery for asking the court to require the Crown to make specified material available has worked satisfactorily in cases where the Crown have not handed over the material voluntarily. (In one recent case they provided the defence with negative fingerprint evidence; i.e. evidence that the fingerprints found on, inter alia, a stolen cash drawer, were not those of the accused but of other, unknown persons.) We have still to develop this area of law. My hunch is that it will be comparatively unaffected by English developments, that there is likely to be a more limited right to disclosure than appears to be the case in England, and that things will by and large work themselves out on the basis of agreements between the parties, but that we may be influenced by the European Court of Human Rights. Short of any decision of that court, however, the Crown will not be required to let the defence see their precognitions. A sort of sanctity traditionally adheres to those not very reliable documents, although in pre-legal aid days it was not unknown for them to be shown to the defence. The need for them to be available to the defence is much reduced, if not removed entirely, by the right the defence have to interview the witnesses and take their own precognitions, which now includes a right to apply to have reluctant witnesses precognosced before a sheriff. It should be added that it is official Crown policy to encourage discussions with, and the provision of information to, the defence, albeit in the hope of getting an offer of a plea of guilty. But the extent to which such discussions occur in practice is a function of the Crown's resources, and these are very limited.

So far as the defence is concerned they, too, are obliged to lodge lists of witnesses and productions. They are also obliged to give notice of a very limited range of so-called special defences—insanity, self-defence, alibi and incrimination, including incrimination of a co-accused where the notice is presumably for the benefit of the co-accused rather than of the Crown. That being so, it is difficult for a Scot not to feel that the Report makes rather heavy weather of this matter. There is no good reason why the categories of special defence should be closed, but they seem to be so in practice. They could well extend to the other matters referred to in the Report, and indeed there would be much to be said for a requirement to state one's general line of defence in any case, even if it is only that the Crown can't prove the charge. I should add that there is no question of a speciaL defence, such as self-defence, involving an admission of guilt, and so helping the Crown prove its case. The plea is one of not guilty, 'and specially and without prejudice to said plea that on the occasion libelled he was acting in self defence'. If the Crown do not set up a case to answer then the plea becomes otiose. The only way in which a departure from a special defence could help the Crown would be in cross-examining the accused if he gives evidence. Of course, it is a little difficult to combine a plea of alibi with one of self-defence, but the law of criminal procedure cannot change the nature of the world. Even so, if the Crown evidence discloses that whoever carried out the assault acted in self-defence, I do not see why the accused should be convicted, even if his alibi was rejected by the jury. The Crown can object to the defence leading evidence of self-defence unless they have lodged a special defence, but that need not prevent the Crown leading such evidence, intentionally or otherwise. But that is uncharted territory, and I could be wrong, as I usually am in my efforts to prophesy what the courts will do.

Pre-trial hearings

I sense a feeling of war-weariness, as well as of a somewhat resigned determination to have one last push, in this part of the Report. I also feel, if I may say so with respect, that many of the recommendations are more pious exhortations than anything else. Similar proposals have been made by the Scottish Office, and their motive is, of course, purely economic. The Scottish Law Commission have recently issued a response to the Scottish Office proposals for pre-trial hearings at which the judge will take what it is now fashionable to call a 'pro-active role', in which they point out that this will involve a radical change in the philosophy which underlies current criminal procedure, and in which they regret the absence of any discussion of that philosophy and the absence of any research material to support the policies the Scottish Office seek to introduce. They then point with approval to the relevant material in the Royal Commission Report and Professor Zander's dissent. The principal objection taken by the Scottish law Commission is to the proposed role of the judge, which they see as compromising both the fact and the appearance of judicial impartiality. They point out also that judges (in Scotland if not in England) have no information about the case on which to base an interventionist role (Scottish judges do not get copies of the precognition; at most they may see copies of documentary productions prior to the start of the trial.) Moreover, any attempt by the judge to jolly things along would lead to an appeal on the ground of oppression which would probably be successful.

I think that in the end of the day, we have to accept that there is no way of forcing the Crown and defence to agree anything, if only because there is no effective sanction for failure to disagree. It is tempting to suggest that the judge should be able to order a reduction in legal aid fees in respect of time spent at the trial on matters which are not really in dispute, but that would be unfair in cases where the client's instructions were not to agree those matters. And it should be remembered, too, that one of the functions of a trial is to provide a way of ensuring that the executive cannot interfere with an individual on the ground that he has committed a crime unless it is able to prove that crime in a way acceptable to the laws of evidence.

Despite all that, I am in favour of pre-trial diets. They have proved useful in Scotland in determining questions of relevancy and competency prior to trial, and they can also be used to determine questions of the admissibility of evidence. I do not see, incidentally, why there should not be an appeal from such decisions. There is not much point in wasting time on a long trial in which any conviction will be quashed because it proceeded on the basis of evidence wrongly held at a preliminary diet to be admissible, or for that matter in which the accused will be acquitted because the Crown were wrongly prevented from leading certain evidence, when the matter could have been settled by an appeal before the trial. It is possible, at least in theory, to ensure that these matters are determined prior to trial by making it incompetent to raise them later. This is more or less the position in Scotland, although they can be raised later with leave of the court, and the general attitude of both court and Crown is to allow them to be raised late, at least if they appear to be of any substance. (Cf. the English attitude to late alibis, which can be found in Scotland as well.) In addition, as I mentioned earlier, it is now possible for either party to seek a preliminary diet for the purpose of seeking agreement on specified matters. It is far too early to say what use will be made of that provision, which was slipped rather quietly into the Prisoners and Criminal Procedure (Scotland) Act 1993, or how effective it will be, given particularly that there are no sanctions attached to refusal to agree, but it could prove to be an interesting experiment. And it is worth bearing in mind that while you can't make the horse drink, taking him to the water will at least put the idea of drinking into his head.

Any developments in this area must, I think, be voluntary, and will, I agree, depend to some extent at least on a change in outlook on the part of the bar. It may be possible, however, to make some progress by relying on inertia. There is provision for various matters, such as the analysis of substances believed to be controlled drugs, to be proved by certificate, and for those certificates to be sufficient evidence of their contents in the absence of prior intimation of objection. These provisions seem to work, and by and large no objection is taken to evidence of this kind unless there really is some point to be made. I think that it would, therefore, be worth trying a system in which the Crown presented the defence with a list of facts they thought they could prove, and the defence were required to state their position in respect of each of them. This would, of course, involve a little extra work on the part of the Crown, but they should be in a position to perform this exercise fairly easily if they have prepared their case properly, and it would be a useful by-product of such a system if it led to better preparation by the Crown. I am intrigued in that context by the suggestion that the defence might make a submission of no case to answer before the trial. I doubt whether such a submission would have more than a very rare chance of success, but it too might help to concentrate the mind of the Crown. (Incidentally, I would challenge the view stated in the Report that Scots indictments contain a lot of detail: some of them are very short indeed, although it is true that fraud indictments should contain a statement of the alleged false pretence and of the allegedly true situation.)

Talking of concentrating minds, I am highly pessimistic about any proposals to encourage early pleas of guilty, short of large discounts on penalty. I think we just have to accept that it is only the knowledge of imminent hanging which concentrates the mind, and that there is no reason for an accused to plead guilty if there is any chance that the trial will not go on for a while yet. I think we just have to accept that the presence of potential jurors and witnesses is a necessary price to pay for a plea of guilty; and that it is better to get a plea on the day of the trial than not to get it at all. Preliminary diets may increase the number of pre-trial pleas, but there will, I think always be lots of pleas on the day of the trial.

Sentence bargaining

If there is one aspect of the English system which shocks the Scots lawyer it is the involvement of the judge in plea and sentence bargaining. Scots judges are not involved in such matters. And this is not because the Scots judge does not have a copy of the depositions, or because there is no tariff against which to measure discounts, or even because it is thought to be wrong that the gambler should be allowed to postpone placing his bet, so to speak, until he knows the likely result. It is because such things are just not done. Bargaining is just not seen as part of the judge's function. Apart from anything else, trials are public, and not even dress rehearsals should be held in private. I accept that this is not very pragmatic, and that it perhaps pays too little attention to the fact that experienced practitioners who know their judges can probably give the client a good idea of the likely result of a plea anyway, or even in some cases decide whether or not to plead only when they know who the judge is. But there is a feeling that there is an appropriate sentence for any particular instance of an offence, depending on the circumstances of the offence, and that that sentence should be the same whether it follows on a plea of guilty or a hotly contested trial. Allowance can be made for a plea as a sign of remorse, or even as showing consideration for the victim and avoiding the necessity of her (usually) giving evidence, but not simply for the fact of a plea, or even of an early plea. My own heretical view is that this is an area where we are better without rules, whether they are in the form of tables of discounts on a kind of shop early and get a good price basis, or a prohibition on all discounts such as has been imposed by the High Court in *Strawhorn* v. *McLeod*, [1987 S.C.C.R 413]. All that is needed is a general feeling that an early plea will get some sympathetic consideration from the bench, and permission for defence counsel to seek such consideration.

What does go on in Scotland, and goes on a lot, is what we like to call plea negotiation, whereby the Crown accept pleas to part only of a charge, or to some of a number of charges, the resultant plea being often to very much less than was originally charged. This is, of course, often done on the basis that the reduced charges will attract a reduced sentence, and sometimes on the basis that the Crown will take out charges to keep the accused happy, knowing that it will make little or no difference to the sentence because, for example, the normal discount for wholesale means that it makes not much difference whether you plead to five or ten housebreakings. But none of this involves the judge. He is obliged to sentence on the basis of whatever pleas the Crown have accepted, but the accused must take his chance as to what that sentence will be.

Appeals

Finally, a few words about appeals. I have a feeling, as I have already indicated, that Scots courts have more respect for jury verdicts than do English, and are less ready to disturb them. This may be a rare example of judicial humility: why should the impressions of three judges who have not heard the evidence be preferred to the decision of some eight to fifteen citizens who have? Or it may just be some built-in inertia. I think, however, that it does recognise the difficulty of having a system of jury trial, and then allowing the verdict to be over-ridden by judges. True, the ground of appeal is miscarriage of justice, but that tends in Scotland to be seen as meaning some error in the trial (which, paradoxically perhaps, can include the absence of sufficient corroborative evidence), rather than an 'unsafe' conviction, far less a doubt which is sometimes described as 'lurking' and sometimes as 'serious'. There was one case [*Reilly and Ors* v. *H.M. Advocate*, 1981 S.C.C.R. 201] in which the appeal court quashed a conviction because it was dissatisfied with the 'character, quality and strength' of the evidence, which was as it happened identification evidence, but that case must be regarded as a bit of a maverick [See e.g. *Rubin* v. *H.M. Advocate*, 1984 S.C.C.R. 96]. The idea that the appeal court should allow a retrial where they have a feeling that there might have been a wrong conviction and should quash a conviction if they are sure there was a wrong conviction, all on the basis of the same evidence as the jury heard, strikes a Scots lawyer as extraordinary. (This is perhaps partly because we are unused to retrials generally—they were introduced only in the 1980 Act. The existence of the majority verdict avoids any question of retrials because of hung juries, and we do not have anything like the English appeal by way of retrial in our summary procedure, a fact which shocked Lord Hailsham in the debates on the 1980 Act.) Apart from anything else, facts are for juries, and not for judges. Contrary to what were once my views, I would suggest that the appeal court should be restricted to dealing with questions of law, except for fresh evidence cases. Fresh evidence cases are different, and I agree that they should be dealt with by retrial, and that retrial should be refused only when the fresh evidence is clearly without value.

All of which means, of course, that there has to be other machinery for dealing with cases which juries have got wrong, and I welcome the Report's proposals for a review body to deal with them, though I am not sure that the last word should normally lie with the appeal court.

Note: Parts of this paper appeared in an article in the October 1993 issue of the Journal of the Law Society of Scotland

2. Trends and Techniques in the Law of Evidence

COLIN TAPPER

THIS paper is designed to address a number of fundamental questions relating to the law of evidence many of which are ignored by the standard sources, and even by specialised articles. Consideration has been inspired by the recent flurry of reform suggested by the reports of the Law Commission on Corroboration,[1] and on Hearsay,[2] and of the Royal Commission on Criminal Justice,[3] though it is not restricted to points relevant to those documents. The paper will challenge some general perceptions about the coherence and unity of the law of evidence, before going on to examine the diversity and volatility of the techniques available and eligible for use, both from the point of view of the analysis of the substance of the law, and from that of proposals for its reform.

I. Coherence

This section of the paper will first present the conventional view of the coherence of this area of the law, and then go on to suggest that any such coherence has been exposed to such centrifugal pressures as to dissipate any such stability.

A. *Conventional Notion of Coherence*

The law of evidence is part of the law of procedure, and prescribes the way in which facts are to be proved. Legal rules consist of antecedent generalities of fact within which the facts of a given dispute must be subsumed in order to attract the dependent remedy prescribed by the rule. Fact finding is thus essential to the operation of all other legal rules, and so lies at the very heart of the rule of law, and it can be said, without exaggeration, at that of all civilised social life. The techniques employed to accomplish it have, in this jurisdiction, come[4] largely[5] to be developed by those mainly responsible for implementing it, namely trial judges. Much of this development has taken place *ad hoc* in the decisions of individual cases, themselves frequently arrived at *ex improviso* in the hurly burly of the trial without reference to authority in the instant resolution of unanticipated events. Such a system both depends upon, and fosters, a compact and easily understood body of interlocking material. Where legislation has intervened, it has often amounted to little more than the endorsement of a position already determined at common law. It further follows that in order to achieve satisfactory results in the conditions thus described the law must be slow to change, and to this end the incremental operation of precedent is ideally suited as the means. Because so much depends upon the common understanding of practitioners, both advocates and judges, the law is parochial and develops differently in different jurisdictions, and under different legal systems. One further consequence of this context in which the law of evidence has developed is that because it is a law governing lawyers, and not laymen, it has been able to indulge in legal technicality to a much greater extent than branches of the substantive law, which have to be capable of large measures of self-application by lay people. All of these factors contribute to a perception of the law of evidence as one of complex technicality, but so integrated and founded on pragmatic principle as to be capable of being known and understood instinctively by experienced practitioners. It is no surprise that this guild craft is highly local.[6]

B. *Centrifugal pressure points*

While these views have much truth in them, especially from a historical point of view as explaining the development of the modern law, they do not embody the whole truth, and they have been exposed to countervailing pressures from a number of different directions.

1. *Substantive law*

The first, and perhaps most obvious of these is the pressure exerted by the substantive law. To a certain extent the means of proof must depend upon the nature of what it is that has to be proved. Here one tendency has been to transform the procedure into the substance of the offence. There may thus be an original offence of drunken driving, and the obviously appropriate evidence is some showing of the ingestion of alcohol and of its effect. This may allow

[1] 'Corroboration of Evidence in Criminal Trials' Law Com. No. 202, Cm. 1620 (1991).

[2] 'Hearsay in Civil Proceedings' Law Com. No. 216, Cm. 2321 (1993).

[3] Cm. 2263 (1993).

[4] After early attempts at the invocation of divine intervention by way of ordeal etc., though even then mediated to a considerable extent by human judicial assistance.

[5] But not entirely, legislators and higher courts have played their part, as more indirectly have writers and commentators.

[6] Procedural rules are in private international law invariably those of the forum.

ingenious defences extremely difficult to prevent from being regarded as raising a reasonable doubt, so the definition of the substantive offence is changed, and the ingestion of alcohol which was at first merely evidence of the commission of the offence becomes the substance of a new offence of driving with a certain proportion of alcohol in the blood, itself supplemented and supported by the creation of another new offence, here of refusing to provide a specimen from which the blood alcohol level can be calculated. The same determination to prevent evasion leads to the strengthening of the purely evidential inference of blood alcohol level at a prior time by reference to current levels. Gradually the originally purely common law of evidence is transformed into an entirely statutory procedure, no longer having an evidentiary role but becoming a substantive offence.

2. Procedure

Another way in which the established law of evidence can become undermined is by changes elsewhere in procedural law. It had become the law that in order to take advantage of some statutory exceptions to the hearsay rule notification should be given to the party against whom the evidence was to be tendered, so as to prevent surprise, and to provide an opportunity for the maker to be requisitioned as a witness if available. Under the modern law of procedure it has become[7] obligatory to provide to the opposing party, in advance of the trial, proofs of all evidence which will be tendered at the trial. If there is such a universal obligation to provide copies of such statements the whole force of the notice system in relation to hearsay is undermined.

3. Foreign Systems

Although as noted above each jurisdiction has tended to develop its own law of evidence quite independently,[8] it has become exceedingly difficult to sustain such individuality in the face of modern conditions in which trade increasingly crosses jurisdictional boundaries, and is ever more governed by international treaties and conventions. In many case such treaties envisage identical effects wherever their provisions are enacted. It is, after all, worse than pointless to legislate for different jurisdictions in identical substantive terms if the adjectival laws differ. Such a situation will not promote the same effects in the relevant states, but on the contrary will promote different ones. It is too much to expect that those drafting such international instruments should draft subtly different variants for each participating state so as to achieve identical effects, given the different procedural régimes.[9] By far the easiest solution in such a case is to insist on identical procedural, including evidential rules, so as to ensure uniform application.

4. Developments

Some of the most potent forces compelling the dissipation of the erstwhile coherence of the law of evidence are to be found in the different dimensions and forces for change which have emerged over the years. A selection of influences is developed below, but it is not suggested that the list is either exhaustive or exclusive. Other influences could be mentioned, and those which are mentioned overlap and interact with each other.

i. Attitudes

The law of evidence has always had to reflect a consensus of view among lawyers, and the views of lawyers naturally enough change as the views of society change. In a number of respects highly relevant to the development of the law of evidence attitudes have changed substantially, and are now changing faster than ever. At one time religious belief could be assumed to be more or less, universal, and perhaps even more importantly could be assumed to govern the lives of those holding the beliefs. Consequently the swearing of an oath assumed huge importance in assessing the reliability of a witness. Unless the witness was prepared to swear a Christian, even denominational, oath his testimony would not be received. For similar reasons his out of court statements could not be taken into account since they would rarely have been given an oath, though conversely if there were something equivalent to an oath, such as imminent death, then on the assumption that a man would not wish to go before his God with a lie on his lips, his dying declaration would be accepted.[10] In more modern times similar changes in attitude have had their evidential reflections. As children and women have been accorded increased respect, so the evidential rules have raced to respond. The evidence of young children has moved from being totally inadmissible, to becoming admissible but requiring corroboration, to requiring a warning of convicting in the absence of corroboration, and now increasingly to being accepted even though not cross-examined, to being positively shielded from cross-examination, to being taken out

[7] Rules of the Supreme Court, Order 38 rule 2A.

[8] In civil law countries the law of evidence, such as it is, is merely part of more general procedural law.

[9] It is indeed probably impossible because some peculiarities of a given jurisdiction's procedure may just not be reproducible by any combination of substantive law with another jurisdiction's procedure.

[10] Though this widely accepted rationale hardly explains the limitation of the acceptance of such evidence to the issue of identity of the killer of the deceased.

of court in advance of the trial, and to being capable of being bolstered by expert evidence.

ii. Psychology

As a means of establishing belief in the past existence of certain facts and circumstances by, in large part, the oral questioning of human beings by other human beings, and in drawing inferences from the appearance of objects and the contents of documents, the law of evidence must rely to a considerable extent on the contemporaneous state of the discipline of psychology.[11] This has been an area of rapid development in modern times, and has imposed its own pressures on the traditional attitudes of the law of evidence. It may be approached from the point of view of the evidence given to the trier of fact, from that of the means of eliciting the evidence for presentation to the trier of fact, and to the mental processes of the trier of fact, and especially the jury. In the first area there is now more scepticism about such matters as the reliability of a witness's memory, of his perception of the identity of another human being, and of the link between bad conduct in one respect and unreliability of testimony.[12] Similarly there is much less readiness to accept without question a general proposition that criminals are likely to re-offend, or that no one will confess to crimes which he did not commit. At the level of means there is now much greater reluctance to accept inferences from the demeanour of witnesses, and a better understanding of the effects of particular ways of posing questions. A particularly striking example of the effects of greater awareness of the psychology of decision making may be seen in the recent moves to abolish corroboration warnings.[13] One of the features contributing to this decision was limited empirical evidence[14] that the warning might sometimes be counter-productive and make the jury concentrate more on the evidence of the suspect witnesses to whom the warnings related, with the result that where the warnings were given the jury was inclined to give greater rather than less weight to such evidence. Some judicial scepticism has also been expressed as to the assumption that the reasoning processes of jurors is able to suppress evidence simply because they are told to disregard it by the judge in his summing up, or to use it only for one purpose and not for another.[15] It is to be hoped that the Royal Commission's recommendation[16] that direct research be undertaken into the operation of juries will, this time[17] be implemented.

It is even possible that in due course non-human branches of psychology will invade the law of evidence now that dogs are so widely used for tracking, for sniffing out drugs, and as guards.[18]

iii. Business

Law is essentially a tool for resolving disputes and providing facilities so as to improve the smooth running of society. As such it is necessarily influenced by the operations which that society seeks to undertake. In other words the structure of the law is determined ultimately by the environment in which it operates. It is clear that the environment is changing, and changing at an ever-increasing rate. This has its effect on the law of evidence in two main ways. It may operate indirectly through the influence of the substantive law, or it may operate directly upon the rules of evidence themselves. Thus as society has become more industrialised, and people work together in larger groups, so new wrongs of discrimination and exclusion from associations and employment have been created, which require tools of a statistical character which the traditional law of evidence was ill-equipped to handle. In more direct fashion, changes in the structure of business have meant that fewer and fewer people deal with more and more information of a more and more routine and unremarkable character, so that personal knowledge must be relied upon less than systematic recording to reconstruct past dealings. Another example is that modern society in its complexity has created large corporate entities dealing with the public, but details of their internal operation are opaque. In such circumstances it may be difficult for someone suffering injury to know precisely how an injury has occurred, and so there has been a need to develop ways of escaping from an evidential impasse, in this case achieved by manipulation of rules about presumptions and the burden of proof.

[11] And so far as perception is concerned, to a lesser extent on physiology also.

[12] Almost no one would now think someone with sexual experience outside marriage more likely to lie than one without, though this appears to have been widely believed in the past, and was incorporated into the law by invariably allowing corss-examination as to the sexual immorality of the witness whatever the issue.

[13] Criminal Justice and Public Order Act 1994 ss. 33, 34.

[14] See 'Juries and the Rules of Evidence' [1973] Crim. L.R. 208 at 220.

[15] See *R* v. *Watts* [1983] 3 All E.R. 101, at 104.

[16] Cm. 2263 ch. 1 para. 8, and recommendation No. 1.

[17] See Cretney Times 1st February 1994 for an account of the fate of the previous proposal to this effect, and see also the remarks of the Lord Chief Justice on this issue in his Tom Sargant Memorial Lecture reproduced in the New Law Journal for 28 January 1994 at p. 125.

[18] See McCormick 'The Admissibility of Tracker Dog Evidence' [1985] Crim. L.R. 202.

iv. Technology

One particular specialised area of change is in the technology which society employs, and which also affects the law of evidence both indirectly and directly. Indirect effects are to be seen in such technological developments as photography, telegraphy, typewriting, photocopying, and computing. As such technologies become more and more common in everyday use, so the law of evidence has to adapt to accommodate them. As the pace of such developments increases so does the pressure for change, and this is made more complicated by the interaction of new developments, and changes in the internal direction of such technologies preventing any simple linear development. For example, the move from reliance upon personal testimony to reliance upon documents became distorted when the advent of typewriting prevented easy personal identification of the authorship of particular passages in documents, and the replacement of the typewriter by the word processor has further distorted the position by weakening the possibility of reliance upon the form of an 'original'.[19] Other areas directly affected by the advent of modern technology include identification of actors by reference to fingerprinting, and more recently by DNA analysis. Here too the line of development is not linear, and courts are gradually realising that the considerations which applied to the reception and weight of fingerprints cannot be transferred without further adaptation to DNA 'fingerprinting.[20] The use of recording techniques both by audio and video tape are gradually being assimilated, and new techniques for their creation, reception and appraisal developed. Lastly it should be noted that technology has now appeared in the courtroom itself with the increased use of filmed evidence, and of computer simulations. Here again a whole new approach to the use of such technologies has had to be developed.

5. Consequential change

It might be thought that the preceding considerations do no more than show that like every other area of the law, evidence has had to adapt to the modern age. This is quite true. The only unique feature is that evidence has traditionally been thought of, as noted in the previous part of this section, as a tightly integrated, well-understood and slowly changing area of the law. It has been argued that this is no longer the case, if it ever was, and that there is considerable pressure, sometimes quite irresistible, and certainly unresisted, for change in particular areas. These have been implemented piecemeal, sometimes by particular pieces of legislation, and sometimes by the decisions of the courts. In this jurisdiction[21] there have, as yet,[22] been no general codes.[23] This is particularly disruptive in so tightly integrated a subject as evidence. If the rules relating to, say hearsay in civil proceedings, are changed, anomalies will immediately begin to crop up elsewhere. Because many activities are capable of giving rise both to civil and to criminal proceedings, and because the decisions of each can in certain circumstances be relied upon in others, the whole balance of the law can be disrupted by such piecemeal change. Similar difficulty can arise from the interdependence of pieces of legislation, no doubt for considerations of economy, so it can be argued that cross-reference between statutory definitions, or between such a definition and the common law, can lead to anomaly.[24] As will emerge more clearly later this effect is particularly significant where the change takes the form of a complete change of technique, for example the shift from rules of admissibility to guidelines on weight which has occurred in relation to hearsay, or from rules resting upon the application of legal concepts to those resting upon judgments of balance, as many supposed to have taken place in relation to the admissibility of similar fact evidence, or from the predominant governance of mandatory rules to considerations governing the exercise of judicial discretion, as in relation to the admissibility of illegally obtained evidence.

[19] Indeed in the context of the computer the whole conceptual foundation of many areas of the law of evidence dealing with documents breaks down completely, see Tapper 'Evanescent Evidence' 1 International Journal of Law and Information Technology 35 (1993), 'The Impact of Computers upon Law in an International Context' Proceedings of 1993 Biennial Computer Law Conference.

[20] See *R* v. *R* [1994] 4 All ER 260; Cookson 'DNA: the case for the prosecution' Financial Times 5 February 1994.

[21] In contrast to many parts of the Commonwealth, especially the Indian sub-continent, and other parts of the common law world, especially the United States, where the Federal Rules have been almost universally adopted by the states.

[22] Though such codification was prominent on the agenda of the Law Commission in its early days.

[23] Despite the efforts of Jeremy Bentham, and his disciples in the Nineteenth Century, though not for lack of trying, see the plethora of draft Codes in the 1870s.

[24] See e.g. *R* v. *Shephard* 93 Cr. App. Rep. 139 at 142 (1991) where the Court of Appeal refused to accept the effects of the incorporation of the definition of a computer in the Civil Evidence Act 1968 into the Criminal Justice Act 1988, unaffected on this point when the decision was affirmed by the House of Lords [1993] A.C. 380; and *R* v. *Beckford and Daley* [1991] Crim. L.R. 833 and 834 where Watkins L.J. refused to accept the operation of the apparently literal meaning of sect. 76 of the Police and Criminal Evidence Act 1984 in its modification of the hearsay rule.

II. Unity

Another perception, perhaps more of an implicit assumption, in most accounts of the law of evidence, is that it is universal in extent applying across the whole range of fact-finding. Such a belief is no doubt fostered by the idea that the principles of logic, scientific reasoning and common-sense are universal, and can be applied to any attempt at reconstructing the events of the past from the evidence of the present. Such a view is, of course, fundamentally inconsistent with the notion that evidence is a parochial discipline. If the rules differ in different jurisdictions it would be most surprising if they were the same in every different context within any given jurisdiction. For a number of reasons they are not.

A. Types of Tribunal

In the first place the particular combination of evidential rules to be applied to a dispute seems to depend upon the nature and process of the tribunal charged with the responsibility of finding the facts.

1. Variety of tribunal

The most fundamental difference is between curial and non-curial tribunals, but within each there are a number of variants. In relation to courts the most fundamental differences are between those where trial is by judge and jury, and those where it by judge alone, though there are other possibilities, for example where trial is by a lay judges, or where judges sit with assessors, either lay or expert. It is probably no accident that the hearsay rule is the same in both civil and criminal proceedings where the mode of trial is the same, whether in both cases by judge and jury as in the United States, or by judge alone as in South Africa; but different in England and Scotland, where the form of trial is quite different in civil and criminal proceedings. It is however arguable how rational the arguments are for adopting different procedures in jury and non-jury trials. In the case of hearsay the argument is that professional judges will be able to assess it better than juries. This may not be the case, nor in accordance with the normal justification for having a jury, namely that it can inject its own popular common-sense, reflecting the abilities and attitudes of the community at large. But in everyday life we assess the value of hearsay as a normal, and indeed inevitable, part of the business of making our minds up about what has happened. On the other hand if the hearsay rule is adhered to in its classical form, the judge must instruct the jury what falls within and what falls outside the rule, what exceptions are allowed, which uses of evidence count as hearsay and which do not, against whom such evidence can be counted and against whom it cannot, and how the jury not only may, but must, in some circumstances arrive at conclusions which are inconsistent with each other, for such reasons. Needless to say no one reasons in such a way in ordinary life, yet it is conceived that such artifice should be imposed on the jury in the name of shielding its members from the responsibility of doing what they do as a matter of course every day of their lives.

Outside the courts the range of fact finding tribunals is enormous, each adopting its own idiosyncratic combination of rules as to the pre-hearing supply and requisitioning of evidence, the range of reasons for resisting such claims, the competence of witnesses, the possibilities of cross-examination, the range of exclusionary rules to be derived from the law of evidence as applied in fully-fledged courts, the application of public policies, the use of findings of other tribunals, the availability of discretions to dispense with or add to the rules, and the burdens of proof to be borne.

2. Style of tribunal

Quite apart from varying with the type of tribunal involved, the combination of evidential rules and practices to be applied may vary according to the general style of the tribunal, and in particular how inquisitorial or adversarial it might be.[25] It is, of course, the case that even in cases governed by the strict rules of evidence, judges are sometimes free to appoint their own expert assessors, to call witnesses not called by the parties, to question witnesses, and to sum up on both the law and the facts. They also have extensive powers to interfere with the presentation of the case by the parties, disallowing certain lines of argument or evidence, restricting cross-examination and rebuttal, and offering heavily persuasive guidance on the general conduct of the suit. The extent to which these powers are employed is largely a matter within the discretion of the judge, and subject only to a weaker form of control than that which governs judicial application of mandatory rules.

B. Types of issue

It is now becoming increasingly common for the operation of evidential rules to vary according to the particular issue which is in dispute. The most obvious such area is that affecting the welfare of children, where the paramount interest of the welfare of the child has led to the abrogation of a number of

[25] As the Royal Commission itself remarked no system seems to be wholly adversarial or inquisitorial, but rather all are a mixture of both in different degrees, Cd. 2263 para. 1.11.

otherwise applicable evidential rules, especially those relating to the use of hearsay, the availability of the witnesses for cross-examination, and the privilege applying to various documents compiled at different stages of the proceedings. Similarly the rules relating to cross-examination vary according to whether the witness is, say a victim in a sexual case, or the accused when testifying at his own trial. Occasionally variations are introduced *ad hoc* to meet specific situations, such as the rule excusing banks from producing their working ledgers, or allowing computer output to be used in magistrates' courts in cases relating to local taxes.

C. Stage in process

The final variable to be mentioned here is the stage in the process at which the finding of fact occurs. Sometimes a finding of fact is required to establish a point of pre-trial procedure. In a civil case this could concern a notice under the Civil Evidence Act 1968 in relation to hearsay when it might be decided by a Master at a summons for directions; or in a criminal case it might arise on arraignment in relation to a plea in bar, when it will be decided by a jury. When such an issue arises in the course of a trial as to the competence of a witness, or as to the admissibility of a piece of evidence, it may be decided by the judge alone on a voir dire, or sometimes simply on the basis of the evidence adduced at that point on the basis of the submissions of counsel. The rules relating to such exercises in fact finding are somewhat exiguous, and some use is made of the judge's inherent discretion to control the course of the proceedings before him, and especially his power to hear evidence on a provisional basis *de bene esse*. Different rules apply also at the post-trial stage, when the judge is considering sentence, some ancillary order such as confiscation of property, or on appeal when some further issue of fact is raised. In relation to none of these issues does the full panoply of evidential rules which applies at the standard trial apply in quite the same way.

III. Techniques

It has been argued so far that the law of evidence is far from the coherent and unified entity it is sometimes assumed to be. It might nevertheless be thought that it is merely the combination of exclusionary rules that changes from time to time, and differs from context to context. What is less well understood is the range of techniques which the law of evidence employs to achieve its ends, and precisely how these are changing. In a very broad and crude way the law of evidence can be seen to have passed through several technical phases. At first there were few explicit rules, and jurors could use whatever material they chanced upon to decide the questions of fact before them. When the more modern form of adversarial procedure became established with the parties first entitled, and then obliged, to call their own evidence, the law developed in such a way as to put the main emphasis on the competence of witnesses, especially in the construction of the disqualification of witnesses interested in the outcome of the proceedings. It was not until the middle of the nineteenth century, in the aftermath of the Evidence Act 1843[26] that the law took a new turn, and became predominantly a law relating to the admissibility of evidence. It came to be seen as a law which in principle admitted all relevant evidence, unless it were excluded on the basis of some policy or another. This remains the prevailing orthodoxy, but it is arguable that a further change has occurred, and the emphasis shifted from exclusionary rules to procedures for assessing weight, from what the judges *do* to what the judges *say*.[27] Some attempt will be made in what follows to consider the different techniques of the law in evidence as they are used in modern practice. Since this approach has rarely been attempted there is no canonical way in which to order consideration. Some attempt has been made to follow the chronological order of a trial, but it is not intended to be applied rigidly. In particular the categories reflect different perspectives and cut across one another.

A. Process

This part will deal with the basic thrust of the tools which are operated in this area of the law, and in particular the objects at which they are directed, which are here described as controlling the parties, manipulating the jury, and directing the jury. In the first two the form of control is, in general, mandatory; in the last, persuasive.

1. Controlling the parties

The parties may be controlled in a number of ways before the trial, first incentives and constraints may be provided in relation to the creation of evidence, to its disclosure to the other side, and to its being withheld from the other side.

i. Creation of evidence

It has sometimes been said that the law has a horror of the manufacture of evidence, but this refers to

[26] Which abolished the general disqualification on the ground of interest.

[27] Including in the case of trial by judge alone, what they say they do.

false evidence, and in the interests of efficient trial process the law positively encourages the creation of reliable evidence. A number of examples can be adduced.

a. Experiments
If experiments are to be conducted by the parties and the evidence adduced in a subsequent trial, the law is generally concerned to prevent long-drawn out contests between experts, and leans towards early co-operation between the parties, so that experiments are conducted under joint supervision of the parties, in the hope that their outcome can be agreed, and such evidence removed from the area of dispute.[28] If the experiment is to take place after the trial has begun, then it may be regarded as a view, and need to be conducted in the presence of the judge, trier of fact,[29] and the parties.

b. Samples
One of the most common techniques for the compulsory creation of evidence is by the taking of samples from suspects in criminal cases. In such cases it is common for there to be an elaborate set of rules for taking the samples, made under statutory authority. The general object here, as with experiments, is to ensure that the trial is not taken up with elaborate scientific argument. To this end such rules will generally prescribe a procedure starting with the grounds for compelling the provision of a sample, the means by which it may be secured,[30] the technique for analysis, its provision to the subject for independent analysis, the way in which it is to be reported to the court, and sometimes its disposition after use. Such regulations are a fertile ground for dispute. It is further necessary, as noted above, to ensure that samples are forthcoming, by providing for the creation of independent offences of failure to provide the relevant sample when it has been properly demanded.

c. Documentation
One of the most beneficial aspects of the Codes of Practice made under the provisions of section 66 of the Police and Criminal Evidence Act 1984 has been the requirement upon the police to set up and operate systems for the documentation of the events taking place during the apprehension and interrogation of suspects. It has been pointed out that only if such documentation is forthcoming can the reliability of conflicting claims about the methods of obtaining evidence and the treatment of suspects be satisfactorily elaborated. Such documentation is regarded as of such vital importance that evidence obtained in its absence may for that reason be excluded from a trial.[31]

Nor is the requirement of such documentation limited to evidence to be adduced at a criminal trial. For example in order to admit evidence of scientific devices the law requires evidence of their checking and calibration to justify their reception, and in relation to output from computers there must be evidence of satisfaction of an elaborate series of conditions.[32]

d. Compulsion to answer
This is the most dramatic way in which the law compels the production of evidence, and one which has become the battlefield on which attempts at comprehensive reform of the law of evidence in criminal proceedings have so far been defeated. It should be noted however that there have been statutory incursions into the general area of protection going back for many decades, and in recent years increasing in number as business becomes increasingly regulated. It has also always been the case that equity has fostered compulsory pre-trial provision of evidence, and, in part, of its creation by way of answers to interrogatories.

1) *Right to silence* This slogan has been the rallying call of those most opposed to pre-trial compulsion of the accused in a criminal case to answer questions posed by the investigating authorities, and especially in modern times by the police. It has been the subject of innumerable reports in many jurisdictions, and here modern consideration stems from its treatment at the hands of the Criminal Law Revision Committee in its Eleventh Report.[33] It has now been re-examined by the Royal Commission,[34] and analysed by the House of Lords.[35] Its terminology is redolent of the issues addressed by this article. It suggests that the issue is whether the accused can be forced to provide answers to police questions. In fact, of course, it is concerned with the quite different question, of the extent to which the jury may be advised that they can draw adverse inferences from the accused's reaction to events which take place in the

[28] See in relation to experiments by a Court witness R.S.C. Ord. 40 r. 3, and to experiments by parties to patent proceedings, R.S.C. Ord. 104 r. 12.
[29] If different.
[30] Including any necessary explanations to the subject.
[31] *R* v. *Delaney* (1989) 88 Cr. App. R. 338 at 342; *R* v. *Canale* [1990] 2 All E.R. 187.
[32] Though their number will be dramatically reduced if the recommendations of the Law Commission in its Report No. 216 'The Hearsay Rule in Civil Proceedings' are enacted, see paras. 4.37–4.40, recommendations 5.12–5.15, and draft bill cll. 8 and 9.
[33] 'Evidence: General' Cmnd. 4991 (1972).
[34] Cm. 2263 Ch. 4, paras. 1–30.
[35] *R* v. *Serious Fraud Office ex parte Smith* [1993] A.C. 1.

presence of the police[36] before his trial. These circumlocutions are necessary because of the ambiguity of terms such as 'right', 'silence' and 'question'. There is any number of ways in which such a situation could be governed. Suspects could be tortured to make them speak, conclusively presumed to be guilty unless they did, have statements prepared by the police conclusively presumed to be true except so far as specifically denied, have the burden of proof cast upon them at trial in respect of any statements subsequently made by them, including statements at such a trial, be prosecuted for a separate offence of remaining silent, be encouraged to speak by banning any direct use in evidence of anything that they said, or have the jury instructed in any variety of ways, by judge or prosecutor as to the inferences which they may or must draw from the failure or refusal in whole or in part to provide evidence. In fact, as is now notorious, the Criminal Justice and Public Order Act 1994 ignored the recommendations of the Royal Commission, and adhered to the recommendations of a Home Office Working Party in 1989,[37] in choosing to permit adverse inferences to be drawn.

2) *Statutory investigation* It is not at all uncommon for new investigatory bodies to be established as part of the regulatory régime for an area of business or commerce which has created concern. In order to operate effectively such provisions sometimes need to confer compulsory powers of investigation upon designated classes of person. It is then a matter of debate exactly how far such powers should extend, how they should be regulated, and in particular how far they can be permitted to derogate from the privileges against self-incrimination and in favour of confidential communications between lawyer and client. In some cases provision is made for compulsory investigation, but at the same time in order to encourage compliance the use that may be made of such compelled evidence is strictly limited.[38]

3) *Interrogatories* The law of evidence always operated differently in Chancery,[39] especially in its attempt to secure documentary evidence in advance of the trial, and to that end it permitted the service of interrogatories whose sole purpose was the creation of evidence from the opposing party in advance of the trial. With the assimilation of procedure in Chancery and at Common Law in the latter half of the nineteenth century such a procedure became more widely available, and exists to the present as part of the arsenal of procedures securing the compulsory creation of evidence.

ii. Disclosure

A second aspect of the coercion of the parties relates not so much to the creation of evidence as to disclosure and production. Such disclosure may be of the case, and thus of the subject-matter of evidence, or of the evidence itself. In part because of the differences in pre-trial procedure[40] these techniques apply differently in civil and criminal cases, and between parties and witnesses. Some of these differences are reflected in the pattern of what follows.

a. Case

1) *Civil Proceedings* In civil proceedings the case of each party is presented well before the trial, and is encapsulated in the pleadings, sometimes after reference to the Court in the usual shape of a Master. It is an axiom of pleading that law is pleaded and not evidence. If a party fails to disclose its full case in advance of the proceedings various sanctions are available, ranging from disallowance of any part not so pleaded, to various sanctions by way of costs.

2) *Prosecution* In criminal proceedings the matter is much more controversial, especially so far as disclosure by the defence is concerned. This may itself be conditioned, as may a number of other rules, by the extent of compulsory disclosure imposed upon the prosecution. Here timing may be critical. Different degrees of disclosure are required at different stages. In order to justify any interference with the conduct of a member of the public, for example by stopping in order to ask questions or to search, it is incumbent on a policeman to inform that person of the nature of the suspicion which the policeman entertains and which motivates the proposed interference.[41] So too if a person is to be arrested he must be informed of the charge made against him,[42] and so on at every stage, including committal, until an indictment is drawn setting out the various counts. Problems may occur in relation to late amendment of the prosecution case, especially if the accused has

[36] Or others with the duty of investigating offences or charging offenders, see draft bill cl. 32(4).

[37] 'Report of the Working Group on the Right to Silence' 13 July 1989, for commentary see Zuckerman 'Trial by Unfair Means' [1989] Crim. L.R. 855.

[38] See, for example, the powers conferred upon the Director of the Serious Fraud Office to obtain evidence, and the limitations imposed upon its use when obtained by the operation of sect. 2 of the Criminal Justice Act 1987.

[39] See Williams 9 Civil Justice Quarterly 139 (1990).

[40] Though these themselves are, of course, symptomatic of more fundamental differences.

[41] See Code of Practice for the Exercise by Police Officers of Statutory Powers of Stop and Search para. 2.4.

[42] Police and Criminal Evidence Act 1984 sect. 28.

been required to disclose his defence in advance, as proposed by the Royal Commission as indicated below. More specific provision has been made for some areas, such as serious fraud where the Judge may require the prosecution to supply a 'case statement', containing, inter alia, any propositions of law upon which the prosecution proposes to rely, and any consequences from the interaction of such propositions with the details of the evidence which is also required.[43]

3) *Defence* Disclosure of the defence case is much more controversial. The absolute old rule that the accused need do no more than plead not guilty and let the prosecution seek to prove its case so as to rebut every possible defence,[44] was abandoned as long ago as 1967,[45] when the accused first became obliged to serve advance notice of his intention to rely upon a defence of alibi.[46] One of the issues on which the Royal Commission divided was the desirability of extending this requirement.[47] It seems that the majority's recommendation is merely for the broad disclosure of the nature of the defence,[48] and the sanction is not to be disallowance of an inconsistent defence, but rather the permission of adverse comment.[49] These recommendations have not yet been cast into legislative form, but it seems likely that the recommendations will be accepted, thus imposing an obligation on judges to say something rather than to do something.

b. Evidence

The classic view of English law as developed in civil proceedings at common law was that the parties had to reveal their case in advance,[50] but not the identification of their witnesses and still less the substance of their evidence. This was changed in relation to the parties themselves by the assimilation of relevant parts of Chancery procedure in the nineteenth century, and has very recently been changed in relation to witnesses by legislative endorsement of changes in procedural rules.

1) *Civil parties* The parties have for more than a century been under an obligation to discover all of the material in their possession or power relevant to the matters in issue.[51] Once discovered such evidence is made subject to inspection and to production to the opponent. This obligation is however limited to parties, and does not extend to mere witnesses.

2) *Witnesses* So far as witnesses are concerned the situation has been transformed by the gradual extension of the requirement of pre-trial disclosure of evidence to be given at the trial,[52] with an obligation originally strictly limited to particular courts and to particular forms of evidence having burgeoned into a universal requirement.[53] This extension received the imprimatur of parliament in section 5 of the Courts and Legal Services Act 1990.

3) *Prosecution* Criminal proceedings have a completely different set of pre-trial procedures, and the law has developed differently. It has for centuries been the case that the prosecution must disclose the material upon which it proposes to rely in order to seek the committal of the accused to trial. Unfortunately it proved to be the case that the prosecution[54] sometimes withheld material which would help the defence, and for that reason guidelines to secure the disclosure of 'unused' material were issued in 1982,[55] and tightened in subsequent holdings, notably in *R* v. *Saunders*[56] and *R* v. *Ward*.[57] This proved quite drastic both in the burden thrown upon the prosecution in terms of the amount of material involved, and delicate in that it needed to be vetted to prevent difficulty and embarrassment, with the result, so it was claimed, that viable prosecutions had to be abandoned rather than comply. This has led to some retrenchment, at least where the reason for declining to produce the material has been a

[43] Criminal Justice Act 1987 sect. 9(4).

[44] Mitigated only to a minor degree by manipulation of the burden of proof in relation to matters peculiarly within the knowledge of the accused, or in reliance upon an exception or proviso.

[45] Criminal Justice Act 1967 sect. 11.

[46] Advance notice of an intention to rely on expert opinion was added by the Police and Criminal Evidence Act 1984 sect. 81, and provision for the Judge to require notice of the defence in general terms in the case of serious fraud by the Criminal Justice Act 1987 sect. 9(5).

[47] The Committee's view is contained in paras. 6.57–6.73, and Professor Zander's dissent in his Note of Dissent paras. 1–12.

[48] Recommendation No. 134. In para. 68 they suggest the use of a standard form.

[49] Recommendation No. 136, see para. 70.

[50] By pleading it.

[51] *Flight* v. *Robinson* (1844) 8 Beav. 22, now enshrined in terms of documents in the Rules of the Supreme Court, Order 24 rule 1.

[52] See also the procedure endorsed in *Khanna* v. *Lovell White Durrant* [1994] 4 All ER 267 whereby a *subpoena duces tecum* can require production to an opponent prior to the trial, thus approaching closer to the situation of the United States where extensive depositions are customarily taken in advance from all of the potential witnesses.

[53] See the remarks of Lord Donaldson M.R. in *Mercer* v. *Chief Constable of the Lancashire Constabulary* [1991] 2 All E.R. 504 at 508, 509.

[54] Or the investigating authorities.

[55] Practice Note [1982] 1 All E.R. 734.

[56] Independent Newspaper 17 May 1991.

[57] [1993] 2 All E.R. 577.

ground of public policy immunity, or possibly[58] sensitivity falling short of public policy.[59]

4) *Defence* It is virtually axiomatic that the accused is not compelled to testify in criminal proceedings, and very unusual to introduce any form of compulsory process, even by statute.[60] The accused is however required to give advance notice and particulars of witnesses in relation to alibi defences and expert evidence, but even then not to supply witness statements themselves. The Royal Commission decided not to extend such disclosure of names and addresses to defence witnesses in further cases.[61] It remains to be seen how far this will be accepted by the government. As an incentive to the defence to disclose more of its evidence the Royal Commission recommended a two stage procedure for the disclosure of prosecution evidence, with the second stage triggered by defence disclosure of its case, whereupon more extensive disclosure would be required from the prosecution in response to the particular defence indicated.[62]

iii. Prevention of access to evidence

This is the converse of control by way of compulsory disclosure, and relates to situations in which the disclosure of relevant material either cannot be compelled, or more unusually, is prohibited.

a. Privilege

The classic case of justification for refusal to disclose evidence is when it is subject to privilege. There has been a tendency in modern times for the number of cases where privilege operates to be reduced,[63] and against the creation of new privileges. Even those few to remain, of which the privilege against self-incrimination and legal professional privilege are the most important, have been criticised.[64] This stems from the anxiety of the courts to consider all relevant and credible evidence in the interests of accurate fact-finding. Such privileges as remain have to be justified on the basis of compelling ancillary policies, such as that of providing an inducement to testify in the case of the privilege against self-incrimination, and an inducement to settle in the case of the privileges connected with litigation relating to the provision and receipt of legal advice, materials for the conduct of litigation and without prejudice statements. Such general hostility to the evidential effects of such privileges has also led to their restrictive construction, and to the limitation of their effect as to be the prevention of compulsory disclosure, rather than as bars to the use of evidence, once it has been obtained.[65] Interestingly enough there is in some Commonwealth jurisdictions some sign of an altogether different and more expansive approach converting what had hitherto been regarded as a strictly procedural immunity into an evidential emanation of a more fundamental human right.[66]

b. Public interest

If the public interest is more directly engaged resistance to compulsory production may move from the realm of privilege to that of duty. The orthodox position here is that resistance is better protected, first by excluding secondary evidence, and then by providing that the protection may not be waived, and if not claimed by a party, should be invoked by the court on its own initiative. This is not always as straightforward as it might appear, given a tendency to expand the categories of public policy immunity. When so extended, for example to information relating to the behaviour of children or complaints against the police, there is evidence of some desire on the part of the relevant institution to have the best of both worlds, both an absolute bar on disclosure and prohibition of the use of secondary sources where the institution is defendant, but a desire to use such records when the institution or some of its members are plaintiffs. To some extent this is accommodated by manipulation of the status of the information, which may be subject to restrictions based on public policy when the institution wishes to suppress its use, but holding it not to be so, when the institution is anxious to use it in a public forum. Given the vagueness and uncertainty of the definition of the public interests involved, this tactic has had some success. Sometimes these rules are manipulated by concentrating far more on the reason for the rule, than upon the effects of the rule. This has permitted extension of the rules by somewhat false analogy. The rule protecting the police from being

[58] See Royal Commission para. 6.47.
[59] See *R* v. *Davis* [1993] 2 All E.R. 643.
[60] Though not completely unknown. For example the Criminal Justice Act 1987 sect. 2 gives powers of compulsory process to the Director of the Serious Fraud Office both in relation to interrogation, and to the production of documents, from the person under investigation as well as others.
[61] Para. 6.69.
[62] Para. 6.52 and Recommendations 124–126. See also *R* v. *Keane* [1994] 2 All ER 478 at 484.
[63] See, e.g. Civil Evidence Act 1968 sect. 16; Police and Criminal Evidence Act 1984 sect. 80(9).
[64] See the remarks of Lord Templeman in *Istel Ltd* v. *Tully* [1993] A.C. 45 at 53.
[65] Secondary evidence of privileged matters is generally permitted in England, though not everywhere, cp. *R.* v. *Tompkins* 67 Cr App Rep 181 (1977) with *R* v. *Uljee* [1982] 1 N.Z.L.R. 561.
[66] See the views expressed by the High Court of Australia in *Baker* v. *Campbell* 153 C.L.R. 52 (1983) and by the Supreme Court of Canada in *Descoteaux* v. *Mierzwinski and Att.-Gen. of Quebec* [182] 1 S.C.R. 860.

obliged to reveal the names of their informers is dictated by the policy of enabling the police to offer immunity in return for information. However if the information does not lead to sufficient evidence to mount a prosecution, the authorities are faced with the dilemma of either calling the informant to testify, and having his evidence tested in cross-examination, or of abandoning this prosecution. Because the same protective policy is involved, this reasoning has been extended to concealing the location of police observation posts. In this case however the police are also allowed to use the evidence of observations from such posts, without revealing their location, and thus insulating it from the very tests which are a means of validating oral testimony.

c. Statutory provision

Numerous statutory provisions are designed to prevent the disclosure or use of certain information by particular parties, for example there are restrictions on the disclosure or use of such things as census information at the hands of census officials, or personal data in the hands of operators of databases. The generic class of official secrets has always constituted a controversial example. One of the most stringent of modern provisions in this respect is the Interception of Communications Act 1985 which prohibits in section 9 any evidence or questioning in the ordinary courts[67] which might even lead to the inference of a breach of the Act by government employees.

2. Manipulating the jury

There are many ways in which Judges can influence the decisions of the jury, here divided into those things which the Judge can do, and those things that the Judge can say. The former clearly have a more direct and certain effect. They include in rough chronological order the withdrawal of issues from the jury, the exclusion of witnesses, the control of the questioning of witnesses, and the exclusion of evidence.

i. Withdrawal of issue

This is the most powerful tool of all for manipulating the jury. It can decide only those issues which the Judge leaves to it. In order for an issue to come before the jury, it will normally have been raised in advance in the pleadings, or in the indictment in criminal proceedings. In criminal proceedings the evidence may have been tested for sufficiency at the committal proceedings, or in civil pursuant to a motion to strike out the cause of action. In either case at the trial no issue is decided in the absence of sufficient prima facie evidence, that is evidence which if believed and uncontradicted would be sufficient to discharge the burden of proof borne by the relevant party. The converse of this is where there is insufficient evidence not to establish, but to deny a fact, and a party may choose to make a formal admission. Another situation of withdrawal is one where the Judge withdraws an issue, not because there is insufficient evidence, but because it has already been decided, and as a matter of policy there has to be an end to litigation. This doctrine of estoppel operates more freely in civil than in criminal proceedings. Then there are some issues which the Judge takes upon himself to decide by way of the doctrine of judicial notice which dispenses altogether with evidence.

ii. Exclusion of witness

This includes cases where the Judge decides that the witness is totally incompetent,[68] and those where he decides that a witness shall not testify in the exercise of his discretion. The first category is now rather depleted, especially in civil proceedings, and in criminal its main application is in relation to the insane and those too young to understand the need to tell the truth. It also operates there in respect of a co-accused who can testify for the prosecution only in a restricted range of circumstances.

iii. Control of questioning

There are some matters and some methods of questioning which the judge will prevent from being raised or pursued. Thus witnesses may not be asked about matters irrelevant to the issues, or to their credibility.[69] Sometimes the latitude of the permission of the common law in the latter respect has had to be modified by statute, principally in relation to criminal proceedings, where there are restrictions both upon questioning the accused,[70] or more unusually of witnesses for the prosecution.[71] In addition to regulating the matters upon which witnesses may be questioned, the Judge may determine also the way in which they are to be questioned, and in particular whether leading questions, or refutation by reference to previous statements are to be permitted. The Royal

[67] This does not apply to proceedings in the special tribunal set up by sect. 7 of the Act.

[68] Including a case where a witness is tendered for a special purpose, for example, to testify as an expert when there is an insufficient showing of expertise.

[69] Although as indicated above the law has traditionally taken a broad view of the latter.

[70] Principally by way of the operation of the Criminal Evidence Act 1898 sect. 1.

[71] See the Sexual Offences (Amendment) Act 1976 which restricts the permissible range of cross-examination of complainants of rape.

Commission has further proposed that Judges should act more robustly to prevent intimidatory styles of questioning.[72] Finally the judge may decide the circumstances in which questioning is to take place, such as within the Court room or outside it.[73]

iv. Exclusion of evidence

Traditionally the most important means of controlling the jury is by the exclusion of evidence from its consideration. This is most effective when done as a preliminary matter. Once the jury has heard the evidence, although it is possible to instruct the jury to disregard it, it is impossible to determine whether or not this has happened, and in the opinions of many is of somewhat dubious possibility. The most important cases where this occurs are in relation to prejudicial or unfair evidence in criminal proceedings, but there are many large categories of evidence excluded for one reason or another in many types of proceeding. In one respect the Royal Commission has recommended a substantial addition to such powers in its proposal that the English judge be given a wider power of discretionary exclusion similar to that available to an American judge under rule 403 of the Federal Rules of Evidence.[74] Indeed the orthodox view is that the law of evidence overwhelmingly consists of rules of this character. It is the theme of this article that this is no longer true, and that increasingly the law is turning to rules relating to the direction to be given to the jury which constitutes the next category. While there are many reasons for welcoming such a development it is perhaps worth noting that it may sometimes be used as a refuge from the more demanding task of formulating workable rules, which do have the advantage of providing more guidance for the parties in advance of the trial. If the rules are sufficiently well-defined it should be easier to determine how they will be applied by a judge, than how a jury will react to a set of directions about weight, after hearing not only the evidence and the directions of the judge, but also the arguments of counsel, the whole suffused by the drama of the trial. The outcome of the proceedings is liable to become much less predictable, early settlement less likely, and trial on indictment more eligible. Such disadvantages should not too lightly be disregarded.

3. Directing the jury

So long as there have been juries, judges have had to direct them. In this jurisdiction such intervention has always been rather extensive,[75] and largely consists of reminding the jury of the evidence which has been tendered, and relating it to the issues which the jury has to decide. The tenor of such direction has become increasingly subjected to rules, and appeals are commonly made, often successfully, on the basis of a defective direction on the treatment of evidence. There are broadly two views on the proper approach to the direction of juries. The first is that it is better to stick to a well-established formula, since any attempt to vary or gloss it is likely to attract an appeal. The disadvantage of this is that such formulae have to be relatively short if they are to be repeated verbatim by every judge, and they become more a ritual incantation than a real direction. This often leads to attempts at a vernacular explanation of the formula, and any advantage from the fixed form is lost. The other extreme is to permit the judge some latitude in the terminology but to insist that it be related very clearly to the facts of the case. The difficulty with that approach is that the direction can be controlled only by a virtual rehearing of the whole case before the Court of Appeal. So critical is the form of direction now conceived to be, and so productive of appeals, that model directions have been devised to save trial judges from the most egregious errors. The intimate connection between the grounds of appeal and the form of direction to be given to juries demands further attention within the context of the change to an emphasis upon considerations of the weight of evidence. It seems also an area which would benefit greatly from some easily undertaken empirical research. A few examples can be given of areas where the form of direction to the jury has already created problems.

i. Burden of proof

One of the best-known sagas in this area relates to Lord Chief Justice Goddard's attempts in the middle of the century to replace the traditional description of the burden of proof in criminal cases, as proof beyond reasonable doubt by reference to satisfaction so as to be sure. This attempt to replace one formula with another did not succeed, and the current view is that the form of direction is less significant than its effect, though how in the absence of knowledge of

[72] Rec. Nos. 182 and 201.

[73] For example in the case of witnesses who may be intimidated, ill or overseas.

[74] Royal Commission para. 8.13 and Rec. No. 181.

[75] See per Lawton L.J. in *R* v. *Sparrow* [1973] 2 All E.R. 129 at 135g. Indeed it is common for United States lawyers to distinguish between trial by jury in that jurisdiction and trial by *judge and* jury in this.

the jury's reaction this can be ascertained otherwise than by reference to the words which have been used is obscure. Particular difficulty has been experienced in some jurisdictions in recent years in directing as to the proper resolution of cases depending upon an accumulation of circumstantial evidence. It has been only after initial descent into the abyss of prescribing the reasoning process in detail that courts have finally extricated themselves to the terra firma of the traditional generality of requiring no more than that the jury consider whether the prosecution has proved its case.[76] It is arguable that some of the traditional difficulty in handling similar fact evidence stems from the fact that it is essentially a form of circumstantial evidence.

ii. Presumptions

Here the emphasis is on the proof of individual facts, rather than on the evaluation of the case as a whole. The whole point of presumptions is to authorise or direct the jury to find one set of facts, when a different set has been adduced. It may be questioned why the jury which is the sovereign finder of facts should need any authorisation. How are matters advanced by directing the jury that it *may* find some presumed fact upon the proof of a basic fact. It is conceived that the function of such a direction is to pre-empt the barrack-room juror's pedantry in the jury room insisting that the prosecution had to prove *A*, but have in fact proved only *B*, and that the criminal process requires strict proof. It is fortunately relatively rare for presumptions to be used in criminal cases to the disadvantage of the accused, and it is relatively easy for a judge in a civil case to handle them.

iii. Corroboration

This is an area where the problems of directing the jury have been influential in changing the whole emphasis of the law. Because judges felt that for corroboration rules to work properly they had to be explained in detail to the jury in terms of the facts of the particular case, it gradually came to be accepted that the trial judge was obliged to go through all of the evidence tendered at the trial by all parties, explaining which pieces could, and which could not, amount to corroboration. This led to the accrustation of the rules with layers of fact to such an extent that it became virtually impossible to direct a jury accurately, except in the most simple of cases with few counts and a single defendant. Once the counts and the defendants multiplied, as they have tended to do in response to financial pressure on the court system, the burden upon trial judges became intolerable, and more informal directions were preferred in new situations.[77] Such a policy is now proposed in relation to the two principal areas where corroboration is currently required in criminal cases, those of accomplices and the victims of sexual crimes.[78] It is interesting also that in the case of confessions to the police, where it was felt a new safeguard was required, the Royal Commission's recommendation again opted for an informal warning, rather than anything resembling the old mandatory requirement.[79]

B. Means

This section will deal with the variety of means to effect its purposes which is available to the law of evidence. The principal means are the testimony of witnesses, the contents of documents and the appearance of objects. For centuries the common law[80] leaned towards principal reliance upon the testimony of witnesses, and an oral process.

1. Witnesses

As noted above the law of evidence could be described until the mid-nineteenth century as mainly a law of witnesses, with most of the questions relating to the qualifications and competence of witnesses.

i. Competence

While it is true that some witnesses still are incompetent, it is a diminishing number, and in parallel with the movement from admissibility of evidence to the weight of evidence, so there has been a movement from the competence of witnesses to the credibility of witnesses. In part this reflects some of the changes mentioned earlier which discriminate much more minutely between different individuals, and abjure the common treatment of broad classes.

ii. Compulsion

The old rule was that any witness who was competent was also compellable, and it was only after the abolition of the disqualification of parties and spouses that the concept of witnesses who were

[76] For the current view, see in Canada *R* v. *Morin* [1988] 2 S.C.R. 345; and in Australia *Shepherd* v. *R* 170 C.L.R. 573 (1987).

[77] For example in relation to identification where *R* v. *Turnbull* [1977] Q.B. 224 provided a model for a different sort of approach.

[78] Criminal Justice and Public Order Act 1994 ss. 32 and 33, implementing recommendation No. 195 of the Royal Commission on Criminal Justice, itself referring to the recommendations of the Law Commission in Law Com. No. 202 (1991) 'Corroboration of Evidence in Criminal Trials'. Cp. *McKinney* v. *R*; *Judge* v. *R* (1991) 171 C.L.R. 468 illustrating the different approach taken in Australia.

[79] Recommendation Nos. 89 and 90.

[80] But not equity.

competent but not compellable came to be established. There may be signs now that the emphasis is shifting to the use of documents and witness statements, that compulsion may occupy a place in a new context, and that a body of law will grow up relating to the circumstances in which those who have provided documents, or other forms of prepared evidence, in advance, will be compelled to appear for the purposes of cross-examination.

iii. Corroboration

One consequence of the widening categories of competence was that it became necessary to provide some means of evaluating the weight of the wider class of witnesses who could be heard. So far as the evaluation of some of the witnesses was concerned the law decided that juries needed special guaranties of truthfulness. The precise operation of these rules was not always fully understood, as may be illustrated in the case of accomplice evidence. The law developed a rule that a corroboration warning was necessary in the case of an accomplice called by the prosecution, but not in relation to a co-accused testifying on his own behalf. Some argued that this was the wrong way round because the co-accused being still in jeopardy was *more* suspect a witness than an accomplice testifying for the prosecution who would not be permitted to testify unless he were not in jeopardy. This reasoning fails to appreciate however that the whole point of a corroboration warning is to assist the jury by preventing them from giving too much credit to a suspect witness. In the case of an accomplice called by the prosecution the danger was that the jury might not appreciate the increased plausibility of his testimony given that any lie could be insulated from detection by being embedded in a mass of quite truthful detail, and that the jury might not see why such a witness should want to lie. In the case of the co-accused it would be obvious to the jury that the witness was fighting for himself, and that he would be familiar with the detail of the events in question, and hence there was much less need to remind them of it.

iv. Credit

The main weight of the direction of change towards wider categories of competence is that the means of evaluation becomes much more important. To some extent this has been assisted by advances in knowledge and expertise of the sorts mentioned earlier. As medical knowledge has advanced it has become possible to distinguish more precisely between different categories of mental impairment, and to adduce expert evidence on the effects upon reliability of different mental conditions. Unfortunately much of the law relating to the limits of cross-examination as to credit goes back to earlier times when cruder views were held as to the reliability of different types of witness, thus allowing witnesses to be discredited by reference to unpopular characteristics, such as immorality or criminality in very general terms unrelated to the subject-matter of their testimony. Some attempt has been made to modify the worst examples of such engrained prejudice, but there is still a long way to go.

2. *Documents*

As indicated above changes in the environment to which the law has to be applied has determined a change in the balance between oral and documentary evidence. It is often the case that modern labour-saving business practice has eliminated personal knowledge as a means of proving particular transactions. At one time, no doubt, with local banks used by only a few prominent local citizens banking transactions could perhaps be proved by the genuine recollection of employees. As banking grew in scale so more and more was committed to paper, and such employees, who may indeed have been involved in the relevant transactions, could do no more than 'refresh' their memories of them by reference to the relevant documents. Nowadays it is increasingly the case that no human being is involved at all, and automatically engendered records are the only evidence of what has taken place. Such changes have indeed rendered a fundamental change in approach quite unavoidable.

i. Admissibility

Business transactions have now achieved a size and complexity which demands considerable division of labour, and such replacement of human input by automated procedures that it is inevitable that documents[81] have become the primary means of proof. While the common law has in this jurisdiction[82] found itself largely unable to make the necessary fundamental accommodation so far as documents in conventional form have been concerned, leaving it to statutory change,[83] it have been able to accomplish the assimilation of records in unconventional form.[84]

[81] In an extended context, including records in electronic form.

[82] See *Myers* v. *D.P.P.* [1965] A.C. 1001, but cp. in Australia *Walton* v. *R* 166 C.L.R. 283 (1989), and in Canada *Smith* v. *R* [1992] D.L.R. 4th 590.

[83] See e.g. Civil Evidence Act 1968 Part I; Criminal Justice Act 1988 Part II.

[84] See e.g. *Grant* v. *Southwestern and County Properties Ltd.* [1975] Ch. 185.

ii. Authenticity

Once documentary evidence, especially in the wider sense, becomes the primary form of evidence it achieves its cogency not through the credibility of its maker, but through the reliability of the system which utilises it. If the system is defective, then the documents produced by that system cannot be relied upon so strongly. This means that the law of evidence has to concern itself much more with the foundation testimony about the system from which the document emanates It will be necessary to explain the procedures for collecting information, for checking it, for storing it and for retrieving it. These in turn require different procedural stages, since these matters need, if they are to be tested thoroughly, to be brought to the attention of the opponent in detail at an early stage. Even if they are, the logistical problems may be immense.[85]

iii. Weight

In this situation the question of weight becomes more important. Even if a documentary system is defective in many ways it is highly unlikely that all of the documents it produces are inaccurate, so the trier of fact has to try to make a judgment about the sort of errors which are likely to occur in relation to which documents, and then to translate what may end up as a statistical probability into a judgment. At this point the reasoning process becomes clouded by consideration of the consequences of the decision, since there is understandable reluctance to 'transmute a mathematical probability into a forensic certainty'.[86] Nevertheless such a determination is now demanded in all cases where the reliability of documentary systems is in issue.

3. Novel Means

Many of the older rules dictated by the social and business environment of the past have become outmoded by recent developments, and some of these can provide useful supplements to the means employed in the past. A few examples are indicated below.

i. Electronic forms

The most dramatic example of the assistance afforded to the law of evidence by the spread of electronic devices is in the now widespread use of tape recording in the capture of police interviews. While there may remain some scope for chicanery, it still seems that the advent of such recording, and the increasing move to video-recording is greatly beneficial in establishing with greater certainty exactly what has taken place.[87] The Royal Commission, while fully supporting audio recording, felt that more research was needed into possible disadvantages of video recording, though the tenor of the Report is still very favourably disposed towards its introduction, at least when the current technology and the expertise of the police in operating it has improved.[88]

Textual information is increasingly held in electronic form, sometimes by initial generation in that form,[89] sometimes by translation into it,[90] and sometimes by a combination of such forms.[91] While such forms have significant advantages for their users, they do present new dangers in the forensic context, largely on account of their ready volatility, and ease of convincing falsification. The converse of this however is that the effort to overcome such dangers may lead to the employment of new methods of verification. It is so easy and cheap to copy and to store vast quantities of information nowadays, that it is becoming feasible to provide neutrally owned databanks to which vital information can be copied as a matter of course at the moment of creation in electronic form. If such receipt is time-stamped, it can provide a ready check on the authenticity of such information when tendered by a party. The end result may well be that such information will so achieve much more credibility, just because its obvious vulnerability has compelled the introduction of better methods of authentication.

ii. Reconstruction

Another area where novel means can assist the forensic process, is by the use of reconstruction of events in the courtroom itself. Sometimes the output of surveillance cameras can be adduced in court to assist the tribunal, so that the jury can observe the events that occurred, rather than rely upon the evidence of witnesses. Even where this is not possible it is often the case that the acting out of the events of the crime by its participants will supply much more information than could have been supplied by oral testimony. There are, of course, dangers, in that those untrained as actors may unwittingly give a misleading impression, or conversely that those who are accomplished actors will wittingly do so, but in

[85] *Derby* v. *Weldon (No. 9)* [1991] 2 All E.R. 901 is a particularly dramatic example, showing the system very close to the limits of possibility of proof on account of such logistical problems.

[86] *Re J.S. (a minor)* [1981] Fam. 22 at 29, in relation to a determination of the paternity of a child.

[87] See Baldwin New L.J. 31 July 1992 p. 1095.

[88] Paras. 3.65–3.72, and Recommendation No. 70.

[89] For example in the case of telephone bills.

[90] For example by image processing techniques.

[91] *R* v. *Shephard* [1993] A.C. 380 is a good example in the everyday context of a chain store till receipt.

accordance with the modern tendency to secure as much information to the tribunal as possible, and then to sift and weigh it, it seems that such dangers are better explored by searching cross-examination and submissions than by exclusion. There is already a considerable amount of guidance on the best way of preparing and presenting this sort of evidence in relation to child victims of abuse. Such evidence has also been considered by the Privy Council in the context of the reconstruction of a crime by those admitting participation in it.[92]

iii. Charts

Another area where modern techniques of presentation is making an increasing impact is in the use of charts, and other non-verbal representations of information to help the jury. Such innovation was enthusiastically recommended by the Roskill Committee,[93] and provision made for its preparation and introduction, first in cases of serious fraud,[94] and then in all criminal cases.[95] While research for the Roskill Committee showed that the presentation of evidence in such a form increased comprehension, it will be necessary for counsel to develop new realms of understanding and techniques of cross-examination and expertise to ensure that evidence is not by such methods presented in a misleading way.

iv. Simulation

Very similar remarks apply to new techniques of simulation by way of computer graphics. These are really no more than the automation of the techniques mentioned in the previous section. It is however worth mentioning them separately since their use presents special problems of pre-trial procedure. Such techniques will be most beneficial when the underlying data is agreed between the parties, and prepared in a common format. It will also be useful for the simulation programmes to be provided to the other side at as early a stage as possible so that they can be tested, and counter-programmes prepared if necessary. If such accommodation is refused it will be a legitimate ground for complaint, the adverse allocation of costs, and may well lead to the drawing of adverse inferences as to the weight to be ascribed to the evidence. There remains plenty of scope for the development of the most appropriate techniques to make the most of the new opportunities which are offered.

C. Discretion

The modern law of evidence works the concept of discretion so hard as to find earlier expressions of disquiet,[96] totally misplaced. It seems to have become the modern criminal lawyer's equivalent of the mediaeval practitioner's concept of equity, measured now apparently by the length of the Lord Chief Justice's foot. It is not an easy concept to grasp in the context of the law of evidence.[97] Its invocation is so pervasive in the modern law that it is possible here to do no more than indicate some of the more salient problems involved in its application and to mention one area where its use has created some confusion.

1. Judgment and Discretion

Professor Dworkin has distinguished between stronger and weaker conceptions of discretion, according to the degree of constraint imposed upon the exercise of the discretion. At one extreme the holder is able to exercise an arbitrary choice, and at the other is required to do no more than determine the application of a standard not susceptible of completely objective application. While few, if any, judicial discretions reside at the arbitrary end of the spectrum, there is certainly some uncertainty at the other, where it has proved necessary to remind judges that some decisions are better described as applications of judgment, than exercises of discretion.[98] While this may seem a merely semantic problem, it does have repercussions in relation to the form of review adopted by higher courts.[99]

2. Balancing

A technique often associated with the exercise of discretion is that of balancing one set of considerations against another is the process of arriving at a disposition of an issue. It is not at all clear exactly what mental process is involved in this exercise. The basic problem is that in everyday life balancing involves the comparison of two different objects by reference to one common factor, that of weight, so as to determine which is the heavier. It commonly includes the use of a precise technique, for example scales, to establish the comparison when cruder forms of comparison may be inappropriate or inaccurate. It is far from clear how far this model applies to forensic balancing. It may be true that the things to be compared are similarly apparently diverse, but it is far from

[92] *Li Shu-ling* v. *R* [1988] A.C. 270.
[93] 'Fraud Trials Committee Report' (1986) paras. 6.64–6.66.
[94] Criminal Justice Act 1987 sect. 9(4)(b).
[95] Criminal Justice Act 1988 sect. 31.
[96] For example the remarks of Channell J. in *R* v. *Cargill* (1913) 8 Cr. App. Rep. 141 at 149.
[97] Its complexity and variety can be assessed by the depth of scholarship revealed in Dr. Pattenden's searching analysis in her seminal work *Judicial Discretion and Criminal Litigation* (1990).
[98] E.g. the determination of the fairness of refusing the right to cross-examine the complainant of a sexual offence about her previous sexual history, see *R* v. *Viola* [1982] 3 All E.R. 73 at 77.
[99] See *Yates* v. *Thakeham Tiles Ltd.* (1994) Times, 19 May.

clear that they possess a common element, or that the forensic process of comparing them is in any way more precise than that which would have been accorded without reference to balancing at all. The problem is admirably illustrated in relation to the admissibility of similar fact evidence.

3. Similar Facts

This is the rubric customarily attached by English commentators to the rules governing the admission in chief of evidence of the accused's discreditable disposition, especially when inferred from his actions on occasions other than those constituting the offence in issue. Such evidence is now regarded as being admissible only when the probative force of the evidence exceeds its prejudicial effect.[100] Neither of these concepts seems to be very precisely defined. It is difficult to see how the determination of whether or not to admit the evidence is much advanced by advocating that they should be balanced against each other. It is possible, and may well be beneficial to suggest that they should be further analysed, but it is hard to see how the concept of balancing is going to help, given that one seems to operate in the logical world of relevance and other more in the emotional one of moral attitude. It is certainly unclear what common measure the forensic process provides for their comparison.

A subsidiary problem here is that although such balancing is thought of as determining the admissibility of the evidence as a matter of rule, such a rule has for some years been qualified by a discretion to exclude evidence the probative weight of which exceeds its prejudicial effect. The precise scope of such a discretion after the operation of a rule of admissibility cast in identical terms has yet to be satisfactorily elaborated. If the only evidence to be admitted at all is that which the judge has determined to be more probative than prejudicial, it is difficult to see much scope left for the exercise of a discretion by the same judge to exclude the same evidence on the basis that it is more prejudicial than probative.[101]

As a final consideration in this context it is perhaps worth pointing out that the rules relating to similar fact evidence provide an excellent illustration of just how inapposite the terminology of discretion is in a context truly requiring no more than judgment. It would be absurd, and rather offensive, to suggest that if a judge determines that evidence is more prejudicial than probative that he should still retain a discretion to admit it.

D. Guidelines

It has become increasingly common for both judges and statutes to lay down considerations which should be considered in making determinations, usually of admissibility, in the law of evidence. Such guidelines usually rehearse the factors relevant to considerations of weight. It seems that in part they are intended as a checklist to remind the judge of the matters he should take into account if sitting without a jury, and to include in his directions in a jury trial. Such guidelines can sometimes be very unclear in their effect. In the Australian decision of *Bunning* v. *Cross*[102] one of the factors mentioned in the guidelines propounded by the High Court as requiring consideration in determining the admissibility of illegally obtained evidence, was the seriousness of the crime. It would have been more helpful if the Court had been more explicit about the effect of this factor. It is possible to argue perfectly reasonably on the one hand that if the crime is not very serious, and the consequences to the accused are likely to be trivial, that illegality does not matter too much. It is also possible to argue equally reasonably that in a case where society has not been seriously injured by the crime it is more important to signal the importance of observing the strict letter of the law in obtaining the evidence. Converse considerations may apply at the other end of the spectrum. While one may make a reasonable guess about the intention of the Court it is not impossible that different combinations of the other considerations might influence reaction to this one.

If it be argued that no further guidance is necessary than that the relevant factors be considered in some fashion, but without any indication of how the trier of fact is to be influenced, then such guidelines begin to look more like the terms of an insurance policy against a successful appeal.

E. Credit

A further concomitant of the switch of emphasis from admissibility to weight is a greater concentration upon factors which affect the credibility of evidence, whether of witnesses or documents. As indicated above much of the substance of this sector of the law of evidence bears the mark of cruder and more credulous attitudes to truth-telling. More attention was paid to falsification and fabrication than to mistake and forgetfulness. Evidence was seen in black and white terms, all true or all false. This was

[100] *D.P.P.* v. *P* [1991] 2 A.C. 447.

[101] The only logical possibilities seem to be either than the decisions are taken at different stages, and so on the basis of different considerations, both of knowledge of the relevant issues and of the reception of other evidence and material, or that the discretion and rule operate on different material.

[102] (1978) 141 C.L.R. 54.

indeed reflected by the crude blanket rules of competence, later mitigated by rules of admissibility. It was still largely[103] all or nothing, Modern notions of psychology and the stress on the weight of evidence require some modification of these approaches. A few illustrative examples may be given.

1. Hearsay

Hearsay is now much more freely admitted than hitherto. One of the traditional reasons for the rule was that the original supplier of the information was not present in Court to swear an oath and to be cross-examined so as to validate and test the information adduced. It has accordingly been suggested that one of the considerations underlying the creation of exceptions to the rule of inadmissibility has been the presence of some extrinsic guarantee[104] of truthfulness. It is accordingly no surprise to find that the statutory removal of restrictions upon the admissibility of hearsay similarly garnished with provisions relating to the credibility of the supplier of the statement.[105] It is perhaps disappointing to find that these provisions do not purport to change the basic rules relating to the testing of credit, but merely apply so far as possible in respect of the absent supplier of the information, the rules which would have applied to test his credit had he been present.

2. Character

The rules relating to the effects of character upon credibility are particularly well-established, and are thoroughly unsatisfactory. The rules permit convictions for any offences however remote from that charged, or from dishonesty, to be used to discredit a witness, and proclaim the view that character is indivisible. They appear to assume that sexual promiscuity is indicative of a propensity to lie on oath.

On the other side of the coin when the accused has a good character, and chooses, to testify there is an enhanced obligation to direct the jury not only that possession of such a character enhances the credibility of the witness's testimony, but also makes it less likely as a substantive matter that he should be guilty of the offence charged against him.

3. Documents

Rules relating to the authenticity of documents and their wider admissibility carry their own endorsement of the weight to be accorded to such evidence. When relied upon as hearsay, documents, and their authors, are susceptible to their credibility being impugned in the ways mentioned above. In addition the Court often has statutory authority to draw inferences from all circumstances from which any inference can reasonably be drawn as to its accuracy of statements in documents admitted under relevant provisions.[106]

4. Special witnesses

Some categories of witness have traditionally been made the subject of special rules as to the weight of their evidence, usually by way of corroboration requirements, though here too it would seem largely on account of traditional prejudices, or anecdote,[107] rather than upon the basis of any scientific research.

i. Complainants in sexual cases

It is now notorious that the rules relating to the need to corroborate the evidence of those complaining of sexual offences were based on inadequate grounds, and that the form of the rules even then failed to match the justifications that were advanced to support them. While mandatory requirements are now recommended for abolition as indicated above, it seems that Judges will still be permitted to issue such warnings, and the terms, circumstances and regulation of such warnings in the future may require careful attention from appellate courts.

Quite apart from such considerations it has to be remembered that the credibility of such complainants is as central to the issue to be decided as is the credibility of the accused, and to the extent that the accused is traditionally shielded from attack on the issue thinly disguised as attack upon his credit, so should special consideration be given to similar attack upon complainants of sexual offences.

ii. Children

As indicated above it can be argued that the law has, in the case of the evidence of young children vacillated too wildly from almost total disbelief as a matter of law to almost total acceptance. It seems from such empirical evidence as exists,[108] that children vary widely in their ability and inclination to tell the truth, and that, except perhaps, at the very lower end of the age range, generalisations are as likely to be as unsatisfactory in their case as in that of any other witnesses. It remains to be seen how far special rules, whether generally more unfavourable than

[103] Mitigated only by rules of corroboration in relation to the status of witnesses, and of privilege in relation to the admission of evidence.

[104] This is the conventional description, taken from Wigmore, though it might be thought something of an overstatement. It is really no more than some factor conducing towards the likelihood of truthfulness.

[105] E.g. Civil Evidence Act 1968 sect. 7; Criminal Justice Act 1988 Sch. 2 cl. 1.

[106] See the general provisions in the Civil Evidence Act 1968 sect. 6(3), and the Criminal Justice Act 1988 Sch. 2 cl. 3.

[107] If thought to be different.

[108] See Spencer and Flin *The Evidence of Children* (1993) ch. 11.

those applying to others as in the past, or more favourable, as now, are justified.

iii. The accused

The accused in a criminal case is placed in a difficult position, in which the distinction between questioning going to issue and credit diminishes to vanishing point. It was largely for that reason that the accused was accorded a measure of special protection from cross-examination as to his commission of other offences, convictions, charges and bad character by section 1(f) of the Criminal Evidence Act 1898. Where such questioning was allowed, its relevance was conventionally believed to go only to the accused's credit.[109] It naturally followed that no evidence of the matters which could have been put to the accused if he had testified was permitted in cases where he had not.[110]

There has always been some scepticism as to the extent to which these rules relating to cross-examination to credit were more than a façade concealing the true purpose of prejudicing the accused in the eyes of the jury. The Royal Commission's report seems to confirm such scepticism in its recommendations on this point. Although not completely explicit it seems not to disagree[111] with the current view that the test for the admissibility of evidence of the accused's bad disposition is that such evidence should be more probative than prejudicial. This makes its recommendations on the admissibility of evidence of the accused's previous convictions quite unacceptable. It proposes to extend admissibility beyond the range of the similar facts rule, and thus to admit some evidence despite its being at least as prejudicial as it is probative. It also endorses the current procedure whereby cross-examination, when permitted under the provisions of section 1(f)(ii) of the Criminal Evidence Act 1898 is not limited by considerations of probative value in a way similar to the rules governing the admission of evidence in chief. Such cross-examination is supposed to go to credit, and it might perhaps, though most unconvincingly, be argued that this purpose is present whenever the accused testifies, even though there is clearly a serious danger of prejudice to the accused on the issues in the case. Even this figleaf of justification is absent in relation to the proposal to permit evidence in chief, even though as prejudicial as probative, whenever the defence attacks the prosecution witnesses.[112] This is justified by reference to the almost equally objectionable rationale of the second part of section 1(f)(ii). Not only is that provision preserved, it is extended. This is done in the name of equity. It is argued to be wrong for the jury to hear the prosecution witnesses discredited when the accused is not, whether or not he chooses to give evidence. It is conveniently ignored that the position of witnesses for the prosecution and that of the accused in terms of jeopardy on the issues is quite different; and nothing is heard of the inequity of permitting prosecution witnesses to attack defence witnesses without any danger of prejudicial consequence, though any retaliation by the defence is liable to meet with the consequences described above.

IV. Reform

The aim of this paper thus far has been to demonstrate both that the law of evidence is changing and must change further, and the range of techniques which is available to implement such change. The nature of any reform must depend upon an assessment of the defects which need reform, and consideration of the policies which should guide the direction which that reform should take.

A. Assessment

One of the most striking changes to have occurred in modern times is the widespread commitment to systematic analysis of legal problems before an attempt is made to solve them. Some of the means of analysis are mentioned below.

1. Commissions

Commissions of enquiry into the operation of the legal system have flourished since the time of Bentham, and may be his most enduring memorial. The methods of such Commissions have however changed beyond recognition. The membership of such Commissions has been widened from leading practitioners to include academic lawyers, members of other professions and representatives of the lay public. Commissions work less on an *ad hoc* part-time basis, and now in some cases employ full-time permanent[113] research staff. Proposals are often worked up to the stage of draft legislation, though this sometimes creates difficulty when the draft legislation is designed to interlock and to cover a whole

[109] Except under the provisions of sect. 1(f)(i) where its relevance to the issue is made explicit, and to which it is probably so limited.

[110] *R* v. *Butterwasser* [1948] 1 K.B. 4.

[111] *R* v. *P* [1991] 2 A.C. 447 where this view is explicitly adopted by a unanimous House of Lords is cited in para. 8.30 without apparent disapproval.

[112] Para. 8.34. The only protection proposed is that the leave of the Judge be obtained.

[113] Perhaps more accurately, no more impermanent than research staff employed elsewhere.

range of issues, some of which fail to command support.[114]

2. Foreign systems

It has become extremely common to examine foreign systems in an effort to detect problems, and to evaluate solutions. Some of the reasons for adopting this attitude were explored earlier in this paper. It must always be remembered however that evidence and procedure interlock to a considerable extent, and that it is often difficult to adopt and adapt part only of a foreign system. It is also the case that the full effects of the environment within which a foreign system operates will not always be apparent to outsiders. Sometimes it is the legal environment, for example the operation of constitutional provisions which makes comparison with the law of the United States always so hazardous. Sometimes it is the more subtle influence of extraneous factors, such as the practices of insurers, or the logistics of social security systems. While comparison with foreign systems can be beneficial, it is a prime example of the cautionary precept that a little learning is a dangerous thing.

3. Commentary

Legal rules are now subjected to more minute scrutiny than ever before. More law is published to more people, and more is written about it than ever before. One way in which such commentary is stimulated is by the practice of reform bodies to publish tentative proposals in the shape of working papers during the course of their work, and to solicit evidence and responses to specific questions from those interested in the area under investigation.

4. Research

Alongside the public input stimulated in the ways described above, it has become common for reform bodies to commission their own research studies. The Royal Commission on Criminal Justice can be proud of the lengths to which it has taken this practice. It really is nonsensical to try to analyse the defects of the system of criminal justice without attempting to gather as much knowledge as possible of the operation of the system. The argument that to permit scrutiny of the innermost workings of the system will destroy confidence in it is utterly incoherent. Even if it were the case that the system were found by such scrutiny to be working very badly, and that no better system could be devised, such results would simply demonstrate that the existing system for all its defects was the best that could be managed. It is, of course, extremely unlikely that the second of these propositions would be supported. Given, as argued above, that the emphasis of the law of evidence is switching to the directions given to jury on the assessment of the weight and credibility of evidence, it is submitted that there can be no rational objection to the examination of the effects of directions on real juries. It should be easy to devise systems for accomplishing such research without in any way prejudicing the security of individual jurors.

B. Policy

Once problems have been identified in the ways indicated above, it is necessary to set about seeking a solution. The most obvious way of doing this is to identify the values which caused the problem to be so identified, and to employ them to devise a relevant remedy. While this may well serve as a generally acceptable approach, it should be recognised that it will not always be appropriate, and even to the extent that in an ideal world it would be, more pragmatic factors may compel some modification of the ideal.

1. Rules and reasons for rules

There is always a temptation to seek to substitute for a rule which occasionally works badly, a less structured statement of the reason for the rule, which is then itself substituted in an attempt to cure the problem. It is arguable that this has happened in relation to 'similar fact' evidence. It was felt that the rule had become rigid, and that categories had been created, membership or non-membership of which was an automatic passport to admission or exclusion. Since it was rightly believed that the reason for the rule was to admit such evidence only when its probative force exceeded its prejudicial effect, the rule was first softened by the overlay of a discretion to exclude evidence when that condition was not fulfilled, and then to harden that discretion into a restatement of the rule of admissibility.[115] It is invariably the case that the reasons for a rule are cast in vaguer terms than the rule itself. The greater latitude so conveyed is indeed the reason for recession to such reasons. The danger is that such greater latitude may provide an opportunity to change the effect of the rule, without any overt change in its formulation. Here too it is

[114] The implementation of part only of the draft proposals appended to the Eleventh Report of the Criminal Law Revision Committee 'Evidence: General' is a good example of this. Section 74 of the Police and Criminal Evidence Act would certainly have been much more acceptable had it been enacted within the intended context of more radical reform of the hearsay rule.

[115] In so doing squeezing the scope for the exercise of the discretion to vanishing point.

arguable that such a consequence has occurred in relation to 'similar fact' evidence.[116] Almost immediately advantage was taken of the looser formulation to water down the stringency of the rule of exclusion, and it is depressing to note that in *D.P.P.* v. *P*[117] the Lord Chancellor was able to adopt the formulation in *Boardman* without so much as a nod towards the need for stringency in admission, and to apply it to facts very much weaker than those present in *Boardman* itself, which were said at the time to lie right on the borderline of admissibility.

Nor is the danger of adopting the reason for the rule confined to judicial innovation. Section 76 of the Police and Criminal Evidence Act 1984 enacted new criteria for the exclusion of confessions, using as one criterion the unlikelihood of unreliability. Here one of the reasons for the old rule excluding confessions obtained by the threats and promises of persons in authority had been the danger of unreliability. The legislature realised that simple reference to the likelihood of unreliability was likely to be unsatisfactory, since that would have the contingent disadvantage of forcing the judge to make a preliminary decision on the very issue that the jury would have to decide at a later stage. In an effort to avoid this consequence the unlikelihood of unreliability was insulated from the confession in issue, by reference to a hypothetical confession made by that accused person in those very circumstances, the distinction fortified by reference to the possibility of the real confession being true despite the hypothetical one being false. It is hard to believe that this artifice has had the slightest effect on the course of trials, and that judges are studiously averting their gaze from the confession before them, and instead concentrating on what might have been said falsely, however much they believe this one to be true. The reality is that when the test for admissibility was divorced from the rule for admissibility it was much easier to prevent the conditions for admissibility, which it was for the judge to determine, from coalescing with the reasons for the ultimate decision, which it was for the jury to decide.

2. Conflicting policies

Sometimes the problem is not that the rule cannot easily be reformulated in a workable way, but rather that policies conflict, and point to different solutions, which may be quite inconsistent with each other. One of the best known such areas is that of illegally obtained evidence. It is the policy of the law that relevant and material evidence should wherever possible be put before the court, but also that some methods of obtaining evidence are so objectionable that every deterrent should be put upon their use. As is well-known this has led to the development of quite different rules in different jurisdictions, and to attempts to blur the conflict by a smokescreen of discretion. Similar recourse has been made in the different evidential context of the use of previous convictions to discredit the testimony of the convicted person. Here the general policy that all such convictions go to discredit, runs up against the policy of rehabilitation of offenders, especially in relation to 'spent' convictions.

3. Economic constraints[118]

It has long been clear that the desirability of arriving at the most accurate determination of fact must sometimes bow to economic reality. As Rolfe B. once said,[119]

> if we lived for a thousand years instead of about sixty or seventy, and every case was of sufficient importance, it might be possible and perhaps proper . . . to raise every possible inquiry as to the truth of statements made. . . . In fact mankind finds it to be impossible.

Such considerations determine many aspect of criminal procedure and evidence, from the order of presenting evidence, to the use of estoppels and other means to prevent the relitigation of matters once they have been determined. Similar considerations dominate the rules relating to the matters which may be appealed, and the procedures for dealing with the admission of fresh evidence on an appeal.

4. Political constraints

It is perhaps unrealistic to distinguish between economic and political constraints on truth-finding, since they are so intimately intertwined. Nevertheless criminal law is something of a political football, and some evidential issues, especially matters such as the role of the jury, the 'right to silence', the privilege against self-incrimination and public interest immunity, all have a clearly political dimension, which it would be misleading to suppress. It must not be forgotten that fundamental reform of the law of evidence in this jurisdiction is nowadays[120] the prerogative of the legislature, and that the legislature is populated by politicians who require periodic

[116] Despite the efforts of the architects of the change, Lords Cross and Wilberforce in *D.P.P.* v. *Boardman* [1975] A.C. 421.

[117] [1991] 2 A.C. 447.

[118] See Dworkin 'Principle, Policy, Precedent' in Tapper (ed.) *Crime, Proof and Punishment* (1981, and Fox 'Expediency and Truth Finding in the Law of Evidence' in Waller and Campbell (eds.) *Well and Truly Tried* (1982).

[119] *Attorney-General* v. *Hitchcock* (1847) 1 Exch. 91 at 105.

[120] Certainly since Lord Reid's remarks in *Myers* v. *D.P.P.* [1965] A.C. 1001, at 1021.

re-election. The influence of such constraints is shown by the readiness to abridge the right of silence in Northern Ireland where political pressure was most acute, before attempting to do the same in England and Wales. It will be interesting to observe the reaction to the report of the Scott Inquiry so far as it relates to public interest immunity, and it is submitted naive to expect that such reaction will be dictated only by formal technical considerations, unaffected by wider political influences.

3. Righting the Wrongs: How Best to Remedy Miscarriages of Justice

PETER THORNTON QC

To no man will we sell, or deny,
or delay, right or justice.

THE present system of criminal justice provides no satisfactory way of dealing with alleged miscarriages of justice. Its defects include the weaknesses of the Home Secretary's 'reference', the limitation of 'fresh evidence' appeals, judges who are reluctant to overturn jury verdicts and a Court of Appeal averse to ordering retrials. The result is a haphazard appellate system which is more likely to remedy a technical defect than to uncover an injustice.

What is sorely needed is a bold legal step which removes fact-finding from the Court of Appeal and places it first with an independent body and last with a jury in a fresh trial. Unfortunately the opportunity has been lost. The Royal Commission on Criminal Justice has proposed (and the Government will implement the proposal) that a new body be set up to investigate miscarriages of justice, but it will not make decisions or even recommendations. Instead the Court of Appeal will have still wider powers than at present to decide the issues in such cases. More retrials are encouraged, but the Court of Appeal will be given stronger subjective powers to decide whether a conviction 'is or may be unsafe'. In short the Royal Commission's proposals will not provide an effective 'safety net' for miscarriages of justice.

In the Queen's Speech in November 1994 the Government affirmed its intention to carry out the Royal Commission's proposals and set up a new independent body to investigate miscarriages of justice. As the Bill to implement these proposals has at the time of writing yet to be published, this article will refer to the detail of the Royal Commission's proposals.

The new body: composition

The Royal Commission proposes the establishment of a new independent body to consider allegations of miscarriage of justice (11/1[1]). It calls the new body the Criminal Cases Review Authority ('the Authority').

The Chairman of the Authority will be appointed by the Queen on the advice of the Prime Minister, as with the present system of Lords Justice of Appeal (11/14). The Chairman should be chosen for his or her 'personal qualities rather than for any particular qualifications or background' (11/20). To emphasise the independence of the Authority from the courts, the Chairman should not be a serving member of the judiciary (11/20). This proposal is somewhat weakened by not excluding past members of the judiciary.

The members of the Authority could be appointed by the Lord Chancellor. Both lawyers and lay persons should be represented; not all need be full-time (11/20). The lay element is particularly important. Almost all of those who gave evidence to the Royal Commission suggested that a new body should be set up and that it should include lay members. Those who preferred not a new body but a change to the courts' existing powers also insisted on increasing the lay element. For example, the Criminal Bar Association favoured an increase in the Court of Appeal's powers and the introduction of lay assessors to sit with the judges. The Crown Prosecution Service argued for a new intermediate court. This court would sit with lay assessors and assist the Court of Appeal in fresh evidence cases by deciding issues of fact. However, the Royal Commission was rightly persuaded by the vast majority of the evidence that the new body should lie outside the structure of the courts. The lay element could also be reinforced by a Chairman without a legal background.

The Royal Commission further proposes that the Authority should be supported by a staff of lawyers and administrators, with access to specialist advisers, such as forensic scientists (11/21).

Role of the new body

The Royal Commission proposes that the role of the Authority should be to consider allegations put to it that a miscarriage of justice may have occurred, and to launch an investigation where necessary (11/12). It sees the Authority as a body of last resort, available only when all avenues of appeal have been exhausted. It does not suggest that the Authority should be able to take cases of its own motion, preferring the reference provision in terms similar to the current Home Office reference procedure. This is a

[1] References, for example 11/1, are to chapter and paragraph of the Royal Commission's Report, Cm 2263.

weakness. There may be cases of injustice which require investigation but where no applicant comes forward. Judith Ward's case lay buried for many years before she was persuaded to protest her innocence. The purely reactive approach of the Home Office, responding only to the specific representations made to it, was criticised by Sir John May in the Maguire inquiry.

Abolition of Home Secretary's reference

The setting-up of the new body will inevitably replace the role of the Home Secretary's reference (11/10). The function of the Home Office as 'gatekeeper to the Court of Appeal', as the Home Office describes it, will therefore be abolished. Section 17 of the Criminal Appeal Act 1968 will be repealed. This is to be welcomed.

The Home Secretary currently receives about 800 petitions a year claiming wrongful conviction. Once a case has been through the appellate system and failed, the only avenue is by way of petition to the Home Secretary who may refer the whole case to the Court of Appeal 'at any time'. The Court must then treat the case as an appeal in the ordinary way. The petitions are dealt with in the Home Office by a department known as C3 Division. About 16 per cent of petitions result in a request to the Court of Appeal for further papers. About 18 per cent result in further inquiries. Only a tiny percentage of petitions reaches the Court. Most of the high profile cases proceed through this channel after unsuccessful appeals. In the cases of the Birmingham Six and Judith Ward, for example, the Home Office commissioned the reviews of the forensic evidence. In the Bridgewater Four case—the killing of Carl Bridgewater, the newspaper boy—there have been two unsuccessful appeals, one on a Home Secretary's reference. A recent further petition to the Home Office has not been referred back to he Court, although it is expected that this case will eventually makes its way back to the Court of Appeal.

The role of the Home Secretary's reference has long been in question. Support for it is almost non-existent. The Home Office is not considered to be an appropriate body for investigating miscarriages of justice. In theory it is not seen to be sufficiently independent of the institutions against which serious complaint is most often being made. In practice it is not sufficiently successful in identifying true miscarriages of justice, and, conversely, those cases which are referred are often dismissed by the Court. Douglas Hurd, a former Home Secretary, told the May Inquiry that the reference provision should be removed from the executive. He had learnt that any 'lurking doubts' a Home Secretary might have were not necessarily welcomed by the Court. Others see C3 as woefully inadequate. Chris Mullin, MP and campaigner, summed up his disregard for C3 in his evidence to the RC:

'The House of Commons library contains a long memorandum, presumably drafted by C3, explaining why the Maguire convictions are safe. It was written not long before the Maguire convictions were quashed. I recommend this to anyone who is convinced that the present arrangements are satisfactory.'

The Royal Commission does not criticise the work of C3. But its reasoning reflects some of the concerns expressed:

'. . . the role assigned to the Home Secretary and his Department under the existing legislation is incompatible with the constitutional separation of powers as between the courts and the executive. The scrupulous observance of constitutional principles has meant a reluctance on the part of the Home Office to enquire deeply enough into the cases put to it . . .'

Selecting cases for investigation: the criteria

The Royal Commission has decided not to put forward specific criteria for the selection of cases requiring further investigation:

'In practice [the Authority] will need no further justification for investigating a case than a conclusion on the part of its members that there is, or may be on investigation, something to justify referring it to the Court of Appeal.' (11/24)

The early sifting process will be vital, particularly with the rush of cases in the early days. But the Royal Commission gives no further guidance other than to warn of the dangers of too narrow a remit, citing the limitations of the fresh evidence provisions under which the Home Office currently acts. It repeats the words of Sir John May in the Maguire inquiry: '. . . there is no doubt that the criterion so defined was and is a limiting one and has resulted in the responsible officials within the Home Office taking a substantially restricted view of cases to which their attention has been drawn'. The Royal Commission also proposes to exclude cases pending in the courts except those specifically referred to the Authority by the Court of Appeal (see below).

The new body: powers of investigation

When the Authority decides that a case requires further investigation it may instruct the police to conduct the investigation. The Authority will have similar powers to those given to the Police Complaints Authority. It will be responsible for supervising the investigation (11/12), and it will be able to order that a police force different from the one that investigated the original offence should carry out the investigation (11/28).

There has been general agreement that the new body should have the power to carry out investigations. The Law Society, for example, suggested that police inquiries should be conducted through the Director of Public Prosecutions. The Bar Council prefers an inquisitorial process, based upon a Department of Trade inquiry under the Companies Act.

Others, more persuasively, have suggested that the new body should be able to make inquiries through its own 'police' force. This would be a group of experienced investigative officers who are not necessarily police officers, such as Post Office and Customs & Excise officers. They would have extensive powers of investigation and would be empowered to enlist the help of police forces where necessary. This would avoid the problem of police officers reluctantly investigating other officers in their own or in another police force.

Relationship with the Court of Appeal

The most important feature of the new body—and also its greatest weakness—is its proposed relationship with the Court of Appeal. The Royal Commission recommends that where the Authority concludes that there are reasons for supposing that a miscarriage of justice may have occurred, it will refer the case to the Court of Appeal. The Court will then consider it 'as though it were an appeal referred to it by the Home Secretary under section 17 now' (11/12). The Royal Commission has therefore deliberately chosen not to imbue the new Authority with the power to decide cases or to grant leave to appeal, or even to make recommendations to the Court. The scope of the new body's powers will be limited to taking up a case (but only one which is referred to it), supervising an investigation into the case and referring the case back to the Court of Appeal for the Court to make its own decision. Apart from being independent of the executive, the proposed body looks remarkably like the unmourned C3.

This proposal is one of the central provisions of the Royal Commission's report. As a remedy for miscarriages of justice it fails in two respects. First, it will inevitably perpetuate the uneasy relationship between the Court of Appeal and the non-judicial body (currently the Home Office) which refers cases to it. Over the years there has been a palpable resentment that a body outside the criminal justice system should presume to suggest that the Court of Appeal reconsider its earlier decisions. As one appellate lawyer has put it, the present system suffers from 'the odium that the Court of Appeal plainly attaches to a [Home Secretary's reference].' This was best expressed by Lord Lane, then Lord Chief Justice, in his incautious remarks in the unsuccessful first appeal of the Birmingham Six: 'As with many cases referred by the Home Secretary to the Court of Appeal, the longer this case has gone on, the more this court has been convinced that the jury was correct.' Times are undoubtedly changing, and so are attitudes both on the bench and off. But there is more than a lingering suspicion that the Court of Appeal still harbours a deeply-felt reluctance to overturn convictions.

Secondly, and more significantly, the decision-making process remains in the hands of the Court of Appeal, the very forum which for many years has failed to deal effectively and consistently with miscarriages of justice.

There is no doubt that the Court of Appeal has often proved to be an adequate forum for correcting errors of law. It has been notably less successful in identifying miscarriages of justice. It is true that there have been famous successes in recent years. Convictions have been quashed, for example, in some of the high profile cases such as the Birmingham Six, the Guildford Four, the Maguire Seven, the Tottenham Three and in Judith Ward's case, in cases involving the West Midlands Police Serious Crime Squad, and in other cases such as those of the Darvell brothers and Stefan Kiszko.

But while these decisions are to be welcomed there is much still to cause concern. These cases have taken years to put right, long years of imprisonment for innocent people accused of some of the worst crimes in our history. Many of them suffered earlier setbacks with unsuccessful appeals. It is not enough that the wrong was corrected in the end. It must be corrected sooner if public confidence in the appeal system is to return.

In some successful appeals the judgment of the Court of Appeal has been seen as reluctant or providing only a partial vindication. The Court of Appeal's decision in the Maguire case was seen by many as grudging. Alastair Logan, solicitor-campaigner involved with the case, has said:

> 'The real verdict of the court was 'Guilty but we cannot prove which one of them it was', so, reluctantly and with ill grace, they acquitted them all.'

The Birmingham Six appeal was decided on the narrow issue of the forensic evidence; the appellants are still trying to prove that the confessions were beaten out of them by the police. Indeed, many of these convictions centred on false confessions, an area of criminal justice which the Royal Commission has left more vulnerable with its proposals on police questioning; silence may be frustrating, it may sometimes hide the truth, but at least it is safe.

And there are yet more cases to come. The Bridgewater Four case has yet to return to the Court of Appeal for a third hearing, now 15 years after conviction. The convictions for the M25 murders were upheld, with the Court of Appeal propounding its own theory for events in order to justify the convictions. Jeremy Bamber's conviction in 1985 for killing his family may be unsafe, according to new scientific evidence. His appeal against conviction was turned down. Many other cases, less well-known, are now coming to light, cases in which the conviction has been upheld by the Court of Appeal and many years have passed by. *Liberty* and the *National Association of Probation Officers* have submitted to the Home Office a dossier of 170 cases of possible miscarriages of justice.

The Court of Appeal has without doubt looked uncomfortable in the role of re-assessor. As *Justice* has pointed out: 'The Court of Appeal is currently too concerned with legalities and is loath to address the wider question of guilt or innocence.' One reason for this may lie in the fact that the Court of Appeal spends little of its time reviewing alleged miscarriages of justice. Most of its time is spent on appeals against sentence. Less than ten per cent of appeals against conviction are brought under the 'fresh evidence' provisions of the Criminal Appeal Act 1968 and only about 7 per cent of those cases succeed, about one per cent of all cases before the Court.

Perhaps the judges lack experience in this field. Perhaps some still feel that to declare a miscarriage of justice is too much of an admission that the system has failed. The Home Office has pointed out that any system will have 'a natural reluctance' to reopen issues which have already been addressed. As the *Society of Black Lawyers* told the Royal Commission:

> 'Allowing an appeal may be seen by some as constituting an implied criticism of their colleagues. At times professional loyalty and loyalty to other criminal justice personnel appears to outweigh the commitment to carry out a critical evaluation of the original decision to convict.'

Professor Mike McConville, a Royal Commission researcher, calls it a 'general dispositional problem'.

There still appears to be a commonly held judicial belief that juries acquit too often and therefore rarely wrongly convict. The Bar Council, referring to the 'intellectual dishonesty' of judges, has said: 'There is a tendency, to which many judges who have been advocates seem to become prone, to believe that juries do not convict those who are innocent.'

In the past the Court has openly voiced its reluctance to interfere with the verdict of a jury. The classic words are those of Lord Widgery, then Lord Chief Justice, in 1968: '[This is] a case in which every issue was before the jury and in which the jury was properly instructed, and, accordingly, a case in which this Court will be very reluctant indeed to intervene' (*Cooper*[2]). In the same case Lord Widgery developed the 'lurking doubt' test:

> '. . . whether we are content to let the matter stand as it is, or whether there is not some lurking doubt in our minds which makes us wonder whether an injustice has been done . . . a reaction which can be produced by the general feel of the case as the Court experiences it.'

Since the decision in *Cooper*, in the 20 years between 1969 and 1989, *Justice* found that the 'lurking doubt' test had been applied to quash convictions in only six cases. The 'general feel of the case', as Lord Widgery put it, was that the convictions in the other cases should not be upset. The Luton post office and robbery case,[3] championed by Ludovic Kennedy, returned five times to the Court of Appeal, without success, before the Home Secretary recommended a pardon.

The role of the Court of Appeal in fresh evidence cases was further extended in *Stafford and Luvaglio*.[4] Before then the Court, which had been set up in 1907 to correct a miscarriage of justice, had to ask itself the sensible question: 'Might this [fresh] evidence have led the original jury to have a reasonable doubt?' But in *Stafford and Luvaglio* the House of Lords decided that the Court of Appeal should be allowed to make up its own mind about the evidence; the Court should adopt a subjective approach and put itself in the place of a reasonable jury, even though the Court hears only part of the evidence, the fresh evidence, and not the other evidence which was given and evaluated by a jury at trial. As one experienced appellate lawyer has put it, this decision allowed the Court of Appeal to expand its own jurisdiction at the expense of retrials.[5]

Alternative ideas

The precise relationship which should exist between the Court of Appeal and the new body has produced many varied views and proposals. The range of views extends from an increase in the powers of the

[2] 53 Cr. App. R. 82.
[3] See, e.g., *Cooper and McMahon* 61 Cr. App. R. 215.
[4] [1974] A.C. 878.
[5] See [1990] Crim. L.R. 615.

Court of Appeal on the one hand to a serious reduction of those powers and a corresponding increase in the powers of the new body on the other. The Royal Commission (and now the Government) places itself firmly at the former end of the spectrum.

The Law Society proposed in its evidence to the Royal Commission a model—an impressive and well thought out structure—which would involve the Authority employing a panel of 'rapporteurs', senior legal staff with the status equivalent to the 'single judge' (the High Court judge who under the present system grants or refuses leave to appeal). The rapporteurs would deal with all cases and recommend to the Authority if leave to appeal should be granted. Leave to appeal would then be decided by the Authority. If leave to appeal were granted the case would go to the Court of Appeal. The Court would be required to order a retrial before a jury except where the lapse of time or any other compelling reason would make a fair trial impossible. In which case the conviction would be quashed by the Court. If leave were to be refused by the Authority, the defendant would be able to renew the application for leave to the Court of Appeal.

This radical approach, subsequently abandoned by the Law Society in the light of the Royal Commission's Report, has the merit of removing troublesome issues of fact from the Court of Appeal. It emphasises the importance of the new body's independence from the courts (and the executive), at the same time as developing an effective relationship with the rest of the criminal justice system. The new body would both investigate *and* decide, but only as to whether the case was fit for a fresh trial. As the Law Society puts it: 'The best court of last resort is a jury. The best tribunal for determining questions of fact is a jury.'

In one respect the Law Society's model goes too far. It proposes that the new body should deal with leave to appeal in *all* types of case. This would be too much of a burden for a body which will be inundated with claims of injustice. The new body will have to deal not only with new cases but many old ones which have foundered on the rock of C3. The initial caseload will be daunting. The new body must be allowed to focus its attention on miscarriages of justice; these cases must be given priority. It must confine itself to issues of fact. It must deal with fresh evidence, fresh information, and, where necessary, old evidence as well. It must not be afraid to reconsider old material.

The answer to this difficulty is to permit an application for leave to appeal to be made in either the Court of Appeal or the new body. A miscarriage of justice point may also involve a point of law. The Court and the new body must therefore have linked powers to refer cases at the leave stage to each other. The relationship between Court and body must be sufficiently independent, but the mechanisms which link the two must also be flexible. If the new body refuses leave to appeal, the applicant should be able to renew the application before the full Court. As with the new body's grant of leave, if the full Court grants leave to appeal the case will normally be retried.

It is also clear that the new body would need sound mechanisms for the decision-making process. It would need the power, if it thinks fit, to conduct its own hearing, with evidence and submissions. It should also have the power to grant legal aid for solicitors and counsel where appropriate. It should not be forgotten that some of the notorious miscarriages of justice would not have been unearthed but for the persistent 'digging' of some solicitors and journalists. Gareth Peirce, solicitor, would encourage the new body to be partisan. But even if it cannot be partisan itself, she has said, there must at the very least be a dialogue with somebody who is. Finally, the new body should also have the power to declare that innocence has been proved (as in the grant of a pardon) and refer the case to the Court for the conviction to be quashed.

By contrast the Royal Commission has not only decided to retain the Court of Appeal's role as reassessor, it has also proposed that the powers to be exercised in that role should be increased.

New powers for the Court of Appeal

It is central to the Royal Commission's proposals that the Court of Appeal will have more power than ever before in dealing with appeals against conviction. It will retain its function in deciding fresh evidence cases (except where a retrial is appropriate) and it will have new powers to assess the 'safeness' of convictions (see below). This is a serious weakness in the Royal Commission's overall strategy. It is the very effectiveness of the role of the Court of Appeal 'in considering new evidence on appeal' (one of the terms of reference of the Royal Commission) which has been brought into question.

The Royal Commission accepts that the Court's role is at the heart of its overall proposals: 'The performance of the Court of Appeal is crucial to the early correction of miscarriages of justice . . .' (10/1) Yet it has to concede that the Court has in the past been seriously deficient in this respect: it has not been ready enough to overturn jury verdicts (10/3,46) and it has had 'no means of putting itself in the place of the jury as far as seeing and hearing the witnesses is concerned' (10/3). The Royal Commission has not responded to these defects by an alteration to the decision-making process itself. Its response is limited to the hopeful exhortation for the future that 'the court should be more willing to consider arguments that indicate that a jury might have made a mistake' (10/3). In the view of the Royal Commission the answer lies not in a reduction in the role of the Court of Appeal in fresh evidence cases, but in an increase in the Court's power to deal with them.

The fresh evidence test

As the Royal Commission points out successful appeals based on fresh evidence are 'relatively rare' (10/51). The Donovan Committee,[6] which recommended the terms of section 23 of the Criminal Appeal Act 1968 on fresh evidence, expressed the expectation that the Court would 'exercise its power to hear fresh evidence in such a way as to ensure that any miscarriage of justice will so far as possible be avoided or corrected'. That was a forlorn hope. As the Home Affairs Select Committee of the House of Commons concluded in 1986, the Court of Appeal is an inappropriate body to conduct what are essentially not appeals but inquiries.

The Royal Commission has, however, not sought fit to alter this function of the Court of Appeal. It recommends the retention of section 23 with only one amendment. The test in section 23(2) requires the Court to be persuaded that the evidence is 'likely to be credible'. The Royal Commission proposes that the test be changed to 'capable of belief'. This is, perhaps, no more than a change without a difference. The Royal Commission considers it to be a 'slightly wider formula' (10/60).

Furthermore, the Royal Commission recommends that the much-criticised decision in *Stafford and Luvaglio* should be retained, in part at least (10/62–63). In *Stafford and Luvaglio* the House of Lords decided that the Court of Appeal should make up its own mind about the evidence, a test which Lord Devlin, amongst many, has since argued usurps the function of the jury. The Royal Commission proposes that the Court of Appeal should quash the conviction and order a retrial where it decides that the fresh evidence is 'capable of belief'. But where a retrial is impractical or otherwise undesirable the Court should apply the *Stafford and Luvaglio* test and decide for itself, rather than quash the conviction (10/63). This will undoubtedly be the position in many fresh evidence cases, which will often be brought before the Court years after the original conviction. The Royal Commission concedes that a retrial will not be feasible in a 'significant number of cases' (10/65).

The Royal Commission is right to encourage the greater use of retrials where practicable (see (10/65). Since the amendment to the 1968 Act by section 43 of the Criminal Justice Act 1988 the Court of Appeal is no longer restricted to ordering a retrial in a fresh evidence case. It can order a retrial in any case where 'the interests of justice so require'. After slow beginnings—one ordered in 1988, none in 1989 and three in 1990—the graph is beginning to rise. 23 retrials were ordered in 1992. But the Royal Commission is wrong to permit the Court of Appeal to decide 'for itself' in the 'significant number of cases' in which a re-trial will not be practicable. In those cases the conviction should be quashed, according to the current practice in cases which are not fresh evidence cases. And as we have seen, there are many, including the Law Society, who do not believe that the Court should have the power to decide in this type of case at all.

Re-writing section 2 of the Criminal Appeal Act

The majority of the Royal Commission proposes that the three grounds for quashing a conviction in Section 2—(a) unsafe or unsatisfactory, (b) wrong decision of any question of law, or (c) material irregularity—should be replaced with a single ground. The Court of Appeal should decide whether the conviction 'is or may be unsafe' (10/32). If it *is* unsafe the appeal should be allowed outright. If the Court believes the conviction *may* be unsafe it should quash the conviction and order a retrial. If the defect in the case is an error at trial, such as a legal ruling or defective summing up (about 80% of successful appeals), the conviction will be quashed only if the conviction is or may be unsafe (10/38).

This test has the merit of simplicity, but it leaves too much to the subjective opinion of the judges on appeal. It lets them decide, without having heard all the evidence, whether the jury did or might have come to the wrong conclusion. It will inevitably perpetuate a *Stafford and Luvaglio* approach.

Furthermore, the majority of the Royal Commission could envisage no pre-trial malpractice or procedural irregularity which would be sufficient alone to quash the conviction. The conviction would still have to be unsafe (10/48). The minority rightly point out in a strong dissent that defendants should not be serving prison sentences on the basis of trials that are

[6] *Report of the Interdepartmental Committee on the Court of Criminal Appeal*, June 24, 1965.

seriously flawed (see Professor Zander's note of dissent at para. 64). If the error occurred pre-trial or at trial and was a serious one there should be a retrial if feasible or otherwise the conviction should be quashed (paras. 62–72).

The minority argues that this is much more than mere punishment of aberrant policemen: 'Where the integrity of the process is fatally flawed, the conviction should be quashed as an expression of the system's repugnance at the methods used by those acting for the prosecution.' If it were otherwise the Court of Appeal could uphold convictions where the prosecution had fabricated evidence or the suspect had been beaten during interrogation or the provisions of PACE had been deliberately flouted. As Professor Zander points out, the word 'unfair' has become the by-word for decisions in PACE cases. It is a word that expresses the underlying moral principle that 'the process itself must have integrity'. The Court, it is rightly argued, must therefore have a residual power to quash the verdict no matter how strong the evidence of guilt. The case of *Mason*[7] is one such example. The police decided to trick the defendant into confessing to arson by falsely telling him, and his solicitor, that they had found one of his fingerprints on a fragment of the bottle used to start the fire. He confessed. In quashing the conviction Watkins LJ said that it was not the Court's function to discipline police officers. But he concluded:

'Before parting with the case, despite what I have said about the role of the court in disciplining the police, we think we ought to say that we hope never again to hear of deceit such as this being practised upon an accused person, and more particularly possibly on a solicitor whose duty it is to advise him, unfettered by false information from the police.'

Conclusion

No system of criminal justice is immune from miscarriages of justice. Recent history has proved this with shocking clarity. There is an overwhelming case for a new body to investigate cases of this kind. The Royal Commission's proposal (adopted by the Government) that a new body be set up should be widely welcomed. But the model proposed is too weak and too similar to the existing reference provisions. It leaves too much discretion in the hands of the Court of Appeal, the very body which has been seen by many as being at the heart of the problem. It can only be hoped, but with little optimism, that Parliament in its reappraisal of the Commission's Report and the Government's proposals will adopt a more radical approach, one that takes power away from the Court and places it first with a well-supported, well-resourced independent body and last with what is still the best arbiter of justice, a jury.

This paper is based on an article by the author in *The Criminal Law Review*, entitled *Miscarriages of Justice: A Lost Opportunity*, [1993] Crim. L.R. 927.

The author is chairman of the Civil Liberties Trust, a contributing editor of *Archbold*, and co-author with Anthony Scrivener QC and Ann Mallalieu QC of *Justice on Trial* (1992).

[7] 86 Cr. App. R. 349.

4. Principles, Practice, and Criminal Justice

ANDREW ASHWORTH

IN 1991 the Royal Commission on Criminal Justice was appointed to consider and to make recommendations on a number of issues in criminal justice. Its report, published in the summer of 1993, provided the impetus for this seminar.[1] Already the Government has filleted the report for its purposes, adopting some recommendations straight away, putting others out for further consultation, and rejecting those that it finds politically unpalatable—notably, the recommendation that the right to silence during police questioning be preserved. Academics and practitioners are rightly involved in the here-and-now of the reform process, most obviously in raising both practical and principled objections to some of the provisions in the Criminal Justice and Public Order Bill as it passed through Parliament during 1993–94. The benefit of the seminar is to allow us to stand back from practical politics and to reflect on current approaches to criminal justice reform. The primary question is not *whether* the criminal justice system should be re-shaped, or even *how* it should be re-shaped, but *on what basis* it should be re-shaped.

The terms of reference of the Royal Commission required it 'to examine the effectiveness of the criminal justice system in England and Wales in securing the conviction of those guilty of criminal offences and the acquittal of those who are innocent, having regard to the efficient use of resources.' These terms of reference recognise just some of the conflicts that arise inevitably in any system of criminal justice. Too frequently, the tendency is to move from recognition of the fact that there are conflicts to proposals based on the notion of 'balancing'. Not surprisingly, the Royal Commission took this approach on several issues. Chapter 1 commends the idea of striking a balance, and it re-appears at several stages throughout the report. Defenders of the report may well ask: how can one propose new rules, policies or structures without striking a balance? The question is naive, and it should not be answered as it stands.

Instead, we should begin by reflecting carefully on the factors that should included in, or excluded from, the balancing process. What interests should be secured by the criminal justice system as a whole and, more concretely, by the various stages in the criminal process? This question can only be tackled if one has some kind of theoretical framework or standpoint from which to make judgements. At this point some readers, among them many practitioners, may become apprehensive. Are the academics asking for a treatise on jurisprudence? Must we be dragged through the works of Hart, Dworkin, and others before we can have a sensible discussion on which cases should be tried in the Crown Court and which in the magistrates' courts? The answer to this is the familiar 'yes and no'. Jurisprudence can contribute a great deal to our understanding of the interests at stake in criminal justice and how to evaluate them. One of the tasks of academics is to 'mediate' these insights, by presenting them in a form that can be grasped fairly readily by those who do not have the leisure to plough through the original works. What must be avoided is the fallacy that one can make proposals on re-shaping the criminal justice system without any theory about the interests of those involved—victims, defendants, the general public. Proposals on such topics as plea negotiation, prosecutions, the so-called right of silence, and the taking of samples from suspects always imply a judgement about the relevance and strength of certain interests. To suggest otherwise is nonsense.

Moreover, there is in existence a set of rights that have a direct bearing on criminal justice and which apply to Britain. This is the European Convention on Human Rights and Fundamental Freedoms. Not only is this binding on the United Kingdom, in the sense that there is a right of individual petition to the European Court of Human Rights, but it also provides a short-cut for those apprehensive about the need to delve into jurisprudence. The strength of the European Convention is that it sets out some rights unequivocally. Its weakness is that it covers only a limited range of issues, neglects some interests that ought to be included (e.g. victims' rights), and is not held in high esteem by the British Government (which has tended more towards feet-dragging than towards willing compliance). In any examination of the criminal justice system it would be necessary to supplement the European Convention with wider discussion of the importance of certain interests. Nonetheless, it is staggering that the Royal Commission's report pays no heed at all to this source.

The question about the 'balance' of criminal justice has not been answered yet. I have sought to establish that a first step is to decide what interests are at

[1] Royal Commission on Criminal Justice, *Report* (Cm 2263 of 1993).

stake. Closely connected with this is some attempt to assign weight to the relevant interests at each stage of the criminal process. This task is an excellent example of a sphere in which co-operation between academics and practitioners is likely to be the most productive approach: by exploration of the interests of the parties and discussion of priorities among them, theory and practice can be combined to give a rounded view. In the papers for this seminar, there is ample evidence of how one might develop this approach, since all three speakers were careful to straddle theory and practice in their papers.

Let us take a few examples of how the task might be carried forward. One central principle of criminal justice is the presumption of innocence. This is not the place to essay a justification of that principle and assess the counter-arguments: it is sufficient to record that in the European Convention, to which the United Kingdom is a signatory, Article 6(2) declares that 'everyone charged with a criminal offence shall be presumed innocent until proved guilty according to law.' If one tries to translate this into practice, numerous questions press forward. Some of them can be answered by reference to the jurisprudence of the European Court, but most of them remain for discussion. To enumerate a few:

(i) if the prosecution bears the burden of proof in court, must it always be beyond reasonable doubt? Why?

(ii) are the many statutory provisions that place the burden of proof on the defendant, albeit on a balance of probabilities, contrary to Article 6(2)? Are the arguments offered for these exceptions sufficiently cogent?

(iii) does Article 6(2) support the right of silence during questioning by the police or other investigators? The European Court's decision in *Funke* v. *France* (1993)[2] suggests that it does, but the British Government has gone ahead with the provisions in the Criminal Justice and Public Order Act 1994 to allow courts to draw adverse inferences from a person's silence when questioned by the police.

(iv) does the presumption of innocence have implications for mode of trial? If practitioners believe and statistics show that the acquittal rate is far lower in the magistrates' courts than in the Crown Court, does it not compromise the presumption if defendants are progressively stripped of their power to elect Crown Court trial?

(v) could it be said that pre-trial reviews compromise the presumption of innocence? Practitioners involved in them might suggest that some of the bargaining that goes on may exert pressure on the defendant. This leads into the next question:

(vi) is not the standing inducement to plead guilty offered in English law, in the shape of the sentence discount, incompatible with the presumption of innocence? Surely it is nothing less than inconsistent to proclaim the presumption of innocence and then to tempt defendants to forego their right to trial in exchange for a guilty plea and a lesser sentence.

Any rigorous examination of the criminal justice system should attend to questions of this kind. This is not to ignore the pressure of resource constraints: even academics realise that public money is not limitless, and that there is a need to cut one's coat according to the available cloth. But resource constraints should be taken into account only after it has been decided what the priorities are and why. If desirable changes have to be trimmed for this reason, it is essential to know exactly what concessions to economics are being made. Public expenditure limits are a poor excuse for failing to conduct a proper examination of the principles and the practical possibilities.

One lesson of criminal justice reform that practitioners might tend to emphasise more than academics is the significance of the personnel and institutions of the criminal justice system. Changes in the rules are all very well, but changes in practice may not follow—or may take an unexpected form—if insufficient account is taken of the working practices of those inside the system. The Royal Commission was rightly concerned about the vulnerability of suspects in the police station, even if they were provided with some kind of 'legal advice'.[3] Unfortunately, the Government has brushed aside these concerns in its determination to curtail the right of silence. The practical result of the Criminal Justice and Public Order Act will be to shift even further power from the court to the police station. Evidence from the past suggests that there will be problems with the non-recording of alleged statements by suspects, together with what some practitioners have called 'non-verballing' (i.e. the police stating that when a suspect was accused of the offence he said nothing, even if he did say something, in order to

[2] (1993) A.256.

[3] On the quality of legal advice, see Royal Commission on Criminal Justice Research Reports No. 3, *The Role of Legal Representatives at Police Stations*, by J. Baldwin; and No. 16, *Custodial Legal Advice and the Right to Silence*, by M. McConville and J. Hodgson.

permit the court to draw adverse inferences from silence). Similar concerns have been voiced about the work of the projected Criminal Cases Review Authority and about reliance on the Court of Appeal at the end of the criminal process, when it is a question of the investigation of alleged miscarriages of justice. Ingrained attitudes and practices may not be easy to alter.[4]

Many of the latest changes to the criminal justice system have apparently been motivated by a desire for political popularity, and have not proceeded from a rounded examination of the relevant practices and principles. Although the Royal Commission on Criminal Justice made many welcome recommendations, its report contains no framework for the future, no principled basis that can be used to promote or to criticise subsequent proposals. As a result, academics and practitioners find themselves in a wilderness, in which the task of reconstruction is immense. Important parts of the criminal justice system have been laid waste by the storms following the various miscarriages of justice. The Royal Commission has proposed a few patchwork repairs. The Government sees advantage only in re-structuring a few parts that can be easily seen by voters. Academics and practitioners have to re-examine the whole landscape and its interlocking parts, and should not be deflected from the task of carefully examining principles in the light of practices and practices in the light of principles. The three papers for this seminar give significant pointers, albeit in their different styles, to how this task must be begun.

[4] Readers are referred to four fuller works on the subject-matter of the Royal Commission: S. Field and P.A. Thomas (eds), *Justice and Efficiency: the Royal Commission on Criminal Justice* (Blackwell, 1994); A. Ashworth, *The Criminal Process* (Oxford U.P., 1994); A. Sanders and R. Young, *Criminal Justice* (Butterworth, 1994); M. McConville and L. Bridges (eds), *Criminal Justice in Crisis* (Edward Elgar, 1994).

PART II

FRAUD AND THE CRIMINAL LAW

5. Fraud and the Criminal Law

J. C. SMITH

THIS paper is concerned with the adequacy of the substantive criminal law to deal with fraud. The recent spate of cases involving 'mortgage frauds'[1] shows that all is not well. Convictions are quashed on grounds which have nothing to do with the merits of the case or the adequacy of the evidence but because of a defect in the substantive law or a failure to apply it. Its excessive complication leads to errors by prosecutors and courts. The vagueness and uncertainty of some parts of the law is also subject to legitimate criticism.

The law of theft

It must first be noticed that the basic offence of fraud, theft, contrary to s. 1 of the Theft Act 1968 is very much wider than was once thought. It is not unknown for the Court of Appeal to attempt to restrict the broad effect of unwelcome decisions of the House of Lords but it is assumed in this paper that (as seems probable) the speeches of their Lordships in *Gomez*[2] will be given their full effect. In that case, *Gomez*:

(i) confirmed the opinion in *Morris*[3] that the assumption by a person of *any* of the rights of an owner in property amounts to an appropriation of the property;[4]

(ii) rejected the opinion in *Morris* that an act done with the consent or authority of the owner is not an appropriation. An act may amount to theft from V although V consented to or authorised that act;

(iii) held that there is an appropriation of property belonging to V although the entire proprietary interest passes to V at the instant of the theft; so that all obtaining of property (except land) by deception is theft; and it is immaterial that the passing of the property is *not* induced by deception;

(iv) implied that there need be no intention permanently to deprive by the act of appropriation; it is sufficient that the appropriator has a present intention permanently to deprive, either by that act or by some subsequent act.

The effect is that theft might now be re-defined as follows.

> 'Anyone doing anything whatever to property belonging to another, with or without the authority or consent of the owner, appropriates it; and, if he does so dishonestly and with intent, by that act or any subsequent act, permanently to deprive, he commits theft.'

The elements of the actus reus are minimal. Acts which would once have been regarded as merely preparatory, falling well short of an attempt to steal, have become theft. Consider the question asked by Tucker J. in the *Asil Nadir*[5] case:

> 'If, for example, a Defendant has authority to arrange the disposition of goods in a warehouse and he places certain goods near the door so that his accomplices can come and steal them, is the Defendant's act an unauthorised act so as to amount to appropriation and theft? Or is it merely a preparatory act?'

Tucker J opined that this was a merely preparatory act. Following *Gomez* it is theft. The judge was posing an analogy to the case alleged before him, namely that D, a company director with authority to transfer the company's funds to a subsidiary abroad, did so with the intention of there disposing of the funds, not for the company's benefit but for his own private interests. The transfer of the funds, indeed the mere instruction to transfer them (an exercise of a right of the owner), is, we now know, theft.

The act in relation to the property of another which is capable of amounting to an appropriation must, it is submitted, be subject to one limitation. If, in the civil law, D has an indefeasible right to the property, the exercise of that right can surely not be held a criminal offence. If D could sue V for the price

[1] See *Archbold News*, 26/3/93.

[2] [1993] AC 442, [1993] Crim LR 304. It is assumed that *Gallasso* [1993] Crim LR 459, a case which came before the Court of Appeal on the day judgment was given in *Gomez*, was wrongly decided. See [1993] Crim LR 307.

[3] [1984] AC 320.

[4] Though Lord Keith in *Gomez* thought this proposition in *Morris* is 'undoubtedly right' it is submitted that it is a misconstruction of the Theft Act. See Smith, *Theft* (6th ed.) para [36]; but, for purposes of this paper it is assumed that, right or wrong, it is likely to remain the law.

[5] *R* v. *Central Criminal Court, ex p Director of Serious Fraud Office* [1993] 2 All ER 399, 401. In *Shuck* [1992] Crim LR 209, a case similar in this respect, it was held that D was guilty of theft when he disposed of the property in the Isle of Man. It now seems probable that he committed theft when he transferred the funds to the Isle of Man so that, unless the theft could be regarded as a continuing act, which seems improbable, he was wrongly convicted of theft in the Isle. Cf *Atakpu* [1993] 4 All ER 215, discussed by Sullivan and Warbrick, [1994] Crim LR 650. *Gomez* has many advantages for the prosecutor but it also provides some traps.

of goods sold and delivered, it cannot be theft for D to receive the price, however dishonest a jury might consider his conduct in obtaining it to have been: Cf *Smith* v. *Hughes*.[6] It is arguable that this principle extends further so that no act can be an appropriation unless it is unlawful in the civil law; but the courts have shown no inclination to decide this.[7]

Apart from this, the only limitation on the range of the actus reus of theft seems to lie in the requirement that the appropriation must be of property 'belonging to another'. This concept is widely defined by s. 5 of the 1968 Act. It is sufficient that V has a equitable interest in the property. So in the recent case of *Clowes (No 2)*[8] it was held that money paid to and received by a company for the specific purpose of buying government stock continued to belong to the investors even where it was paid into a mixed account, partly comprised of money belonging to the company. The investors had a first charge on the mixed fund which constituted a proprietary interest within the meaning of the Act.

A change in the civil law may affect the reach of the criminal law. In 1890 the Court of Appeal decided in *Lister* v. *Stubbs*[9] that an employee who received a bribe in the course of conducting his employer's business was merely a debtor; but in *A-G for Hong Kong* v. *Reid*[10] the Privy Council held that that case was wrongly decided. The employer does have a proprietary interest in the secret profit. In that case, it is capable of being stolen from him by his employee.

Apart from the possibility of including temporary deprivations, it is hard to envisage a more comprehensive law of theft. The criticism that is made of it is that it is too broad resting much too heavily on the concept of dishonesty.

> 'Now all of this is to put a weight on the word 'dishonestly' which it is unfit to bear for two quite different reasons. The first reason is that 'dishonestly' should properly be understood, not as adding a positive ingredient to offences in whose definitions it appears, but as having a negative function—as meaning "otherwise than honestly." . . . But, secondly, dishonesty is not fit for this role of crucial inculpating element because of the way in which it has to be identified in any particular case. The law does not declare in advance what conduct is dishonest. Prima facie innocent conduct may, it seems, be theft only because the jury or magistrates as "reasonable and honest people" say after the event that it was dishonest—whatever they may suppose that that means in the context of such conduct—and believe that the defendant will have anticipated their saying so.'[11]

This criticism might be answered by asking, why should a person not be convicted of stealing when, he has acted with the intention of permanently depriving another of his property, knowing that what he is doing is considered by right-thinking people to be dishonest? Whether that is a satisfactory answer is a matter for consideration.

The limitations of theft are that it does not protect interests which are not recognised by the civil law as proprietary interests, such as the right to payment of a debt, an expectation of a proprietary interest, or confidential information. It does not extend to dishonestly causing others to incur obligations which may be just as damaging as the loss of proprietary interests, or dishonestly obtaining advantages which do not involve the loss by another of a proprietary interest. These matters may however be fairly regarded as not falling within the concept of stealing. Hence the law of theft must be supplemented by other offences and we have no fewer than seven general offences in the Theft Acts of getting something by deception. For the purpose of ascertaining the reach of the criminal law, we can now discount obtaining property contrary to s. 15 of the 1968 Act, the most important offence in practice, because everything that it covers (except obtaining land) is now theft. Of the remainder, the most comprehensive, on its face is 1978 s. 1, obtaining services by deception, because this is committed where V 'is induced to confer a benefit by doing some act, or causing or permitting some act to be done, on the understanding that the benefit has been or will be paid for.' More particular in their nature are obtaining a 'pecuniary advantage' specified in 1968, s. 16, the execution of a valuable security, contrary to 1968, s. 20, and the three offences of evasion of liability to make a payment contrary 1978, s. 2. Behind all this we still have the offence of conspiracy to defraud at common law.

The Range of Conspiracy to Defraud

Until recently it was generally accepted that there are two categories of conspiracy to defraud. The first relates to injury to economic interests, the second to inducing a person to act contrary to his duty. The second category, as well as the first, is relevant to commercial fraud because its most likely application is to inducing acts which will lead to economic gain, such as obtaining an export licence. The nearest approach to a definition of the first category of con-

[6] (1871) LR 6 QB 597. Cf Smith, *Theft*, 2–19, 2–20.
[7] *Bonner* [1970] 2 All ER 97.
[8] [1994] 2 All ER 316.
[9] (1980) 45 Ch D 1.
[10] [1993] 3 WLR 1143, noted (1994) 110 LQR 180.
[11] *Archbold News*, 19/1/93 (Professor Griew). A similar view of the role of dishonesty was expressed earlier by Glanville Williams in his *Textbook* (2nd ed) 207–8.

spiracy to defraud is the statement by Lord Dilhorne with which all their lordships agreed in *Scot* v. *Metropolitan Police Commissioner*[12]

'. . . it is clearly the law that an agreement by two or more by dishonesty to deprive a person of something which is his or to which he is or would be or might be entitled and an agreement by two or more by dishonesty to injure some proprietary right of his, suffices to constitute the offence of conspiracy to defraud.'

A person is also defrauded if he is deceived into acting contrary to his duty. An agreement by deception to induce a public official to issue an export licence[13] or a national insurance number to a person not entitled to one[14] is a conspiracy to defraud the official. These examples are all concerned with public officials performing public duties. Lord Diplock, in *Scott*, said that the offence was limited to such cases.

In *Wai Yu-tsang* v. *R*, however, the Privy Council disapproved of Lord Diplock's dictum in *Scott*, pointing out that he alone took this point in that case. But no reference was made in *Wai* to *Withers*[15] where Lords Simon and Kilbrandon seem to have been of the same mind as Lord Diplock. However that may be, the Privy Council[16] considered that:

'the cases concerned with persons performing public duties are not to be regarded as a special category . . . but rather as exemplifying the general principle that conspiracies to defraud are not restricted to cases of intention to cause the victim economic loss. On the contrary they are to be understood in the broad sense described by Lord Radcliffe and Lord Denning in *Welham's* case.'[17]

Lord Denning said in *Welham*: 'If anyone may be prejudiced in any way by the fraud, that is enough;' and Lord Radcliffe said 'What it [the law] has looked for in considering the effect of cheating on another person and so in defining the criminal intent is the prejudice of that person; what Blackstone's Commentaries (4 Bl Com (18th ed) 247 called "to the prejudice of another man's right." '

This suggests that conspiracy to defraud is an agreement dishonestly to do any act prejudicial to another. The House in *Withers* rid the law of an offence of public mischief (an act prejudicial to the public) and conspiracy to effect a public mischief; but we seem to be left with something like an offence of conspiracy to effect a private mischief which is little, if any less objectionable.

Purpose, intention or mere recklessness

There are dicta that conspiracy to defraud requires a purpose to defraud: 'where the intended victim of a "conspiracy to defraud" is a private individual the purpose of the conspirators must be to cause the victim economic loss . . .'—per Lord Diplock in *Scott*, cited with approval by Lord Roskill in *Hollinshead*.[18] The *Scott* definition (above)—'an agreement . . . to deprive . . . an agreement . . . to injure . . .'—also suggests that deprivation or injury must be the objects of the conspiracy. *A-G's Reference (No 1 of 1982)*[19] (the whisky label case) is a decision to that effect.

Such decisions and dicta, however, are irreconcilable with other cases. In *Cooke*[20] British Rail stewards boarded a train equipped with their own food which they dishonestly intended to sell to passengers instead of that provided by their employers. The House of Lords had no difficulty in holding that they were guilty of conspiring to defraud BR. The whisky label case was not cited but it seems irreconcilable.

While it was not the object of the conspirators in those cases to cause loss to the alleged victim of the conspiracy it might fairly be said that they intended the loss in the sense that they must have known that it was an inevitable consequence of the achievement of their purpose. But it appears the law is more far-reaching; it is sufficient that the conspirators are reckless whether the harm be caused. In *Wai*[21] the court said that it is enough that—

"the conspirators have dishonestly agreed to bring about a state of affairs which they realise will or may deceive the victim into so acting, or failing to act, that he will suffer economic loss or his economic interests will be put at risk.'

[12] [1975] AC 819 at 1039. Referred to by Lord Goff as 'the narrow definition of conspiracy to defraud' in *Wai Yu-tsang* [1991] 4 All ER at 670, below, footnote 16.

[13] *Board of Trade* v. *Owen* [1957] AC 602, HL.

[14] *Moses and Ansbro* [1991] Crim LR 617.

[15] [1975] AC 842, a case decided by the same judicial committee of the House at the same time as *Scott*. The two cases should, it is submitted be read together.

[16] *Wai Yu-tsang* v. *R* [1991] 4 All ER 664 at 670, PC. (Chief accountant of a bank convicted of conspiracy to defraud the bank by dishonestly concealing in the accounts of the bank the dishonouring of cheques in the sum of $US124m. The defence was that this was done for the purpose of preventing a run on the bank and that D believed that he was acting in the best interests of the bank. It was held that the judge had rightly directed the jury that it was fraud for D to take a risk which he had no right to take of imperilling the economic or proprietary interests of another, even though D did not desire to bring about any loss. Lord Goff said that D may be dishonest although his motive is benign.

[17] [1961] AC 103.

[18] [1985] AC 975.

[19] [1983] QB 751.

[20] [1986] AC 909.

[21] The court rejected an explanation of *Allsop* (1976) 64 Cr. App. R. 29 that there was an intention to defraud in that case, thus holding that such an intention is not necessary. The courts have got into such a mess over the concept of recklessness that some of the judges are now terrified of using the word.

The words 'will or may' can only mean that it is sufficient that the conspirators are knowingly taking a risk that V will be deceived and will consequently act in such a way that his economic interests will be put at risk. To take a risk of creating a risk of loss is enough. This is in sharp contrast with the definition of statutory conspiracy in the Criminal Law Act 1977 under which it must be proved that that parties have agreed on a course of conduct which, if pursued, *will necessarily* amount to or involve the commission of an offence by one of the parties.

The partial definition in *Scott*, revised to take account these developments would have to read something like this:

> 'an agreement by two or more dishonestly to do an act which is intended or which they know creates a risk that a person might be deprived of something which is his or to which he is or would be or might be entitled; or which might injure some proprietary right of his.'

Theft and defrauding compared

An agreement to deprive must involve an agreement to do or procure some act by which the deprivation is to be effected, so the first half of the *Scott* proposition goes beyond theft only (i) in that it does not explicitly require that the deprivation be permanent; and (ii) in that it extends to property in which the victim has no present proprietary interest. It is sufficient that he is to be deprived of property to which he 'would or might be entitled.' The second half of the proposition is limited, like theft, to proprietary interests but requires only 'injury', a very vague term in this context, not permanent deprivation.

So if DD tell lies to T so as to induce him to cut V out of his will, they have apparently conspired to defraud V. An agreement to shoot the grouse flying over V's land is an agreement to defraud him because V will be entitled to the grouse (and, indeed, will have a proprietary interest in them) when they are killed on his land. Of greater practical importance is the case exemplified by a recent newspaper report[22] according to which the finance director of a large company boasted of its success in delaying payment to its suppliers for as long as 67 days and

> 'as a direct result . . . contributing £8/9m to the funding position at the end of the year.'

This seems to have all the elements of a conspiracy by the officers of the company to defraud the company's suppliers, with the possible exception of dishonesty. Failure to pay on the due day is a breach of contract so they were agreeing on unlawful conduct. Their view to gain is manifest. The creditors are deprived unlawfully, if only temporarily, of the price due to them, and they are deprived permanently of the interest which they could have earned on the money between the due date and the actual date of payment- -something to which a creditor 'would be or might be entitled.' The prejudice is obvious and, indeed, it is said that it is often late payment that drives small companies to insolvency.

A director could hardly allege that he has a 'claim of right' to do this because he must know that he is acting in breach of contract. But the fact that the director regards his achievement as something to boast about suggests that, even if a jury considered this to be dishonest according to the ordinary standards of reasonable and honest people, it would be very difficult to prove that he realised that reasonable and honest people regard what he did as dishonest.[23] It does not seem very different in principle (only much more damaging to the 'defrauded' persons and the public interest) from the belief in some sections of the community that shop-lifting from large companies is a legitimate sport.

A principal objection to the law of conspiracy to defraud then is that, like theft, almost everything depends on the meaning of dishonesty. The objection is greater because the other elements are even less than the minimal requirements of theft.

The same vice also attaches to proposals[24] for the creation of a general fraud offence to take the place of conspiracy to defraud. The Law Commission's tentative proposal[25] is as follows

> Any person who dishonestly causes another person to suffer [financial] prejudice, or a risk of prejudice, or who dishonestly makes a gain for himself or another commits an offence.'

There is a suggested exclusive definition of '[financial] prejudice,'[26] an alternative being 'loss'. Definitions of these terms are derived from s. 34(2) of the Theft Act 1968.

The SPTL Criminal Law Reform Sub-Committee criticised this definition on the ground that, without

[22] *The Independent on Sunday, Business*, 1–2 (articles by David Hellier and Patrick Hosking).

[23] According to Patrick Hosking, loc. cit., the 'culture of feet-dragging is . . . deeply embedded in companies' and 'The reality is that the brownie points go to the finance director who can find the most reasons for delaying payments to suppliers.'

[24] See particularly the careful analysis by G. R. Sullivan, 'Fraud and the Efficacy of the Criminal Law: A Proposal for a Wide Residual Offence' [1985] Crim LR 616. Mr Sullivan suggests procedural safeguards to ensure that the offence would not be used oppressively.

[25] Working Paper No 104, *Criminal Law, Conspiracy to Defraud*, para 12.4.

[26] Para. 12.12.

the element of dishonesty, the offence would be extraordinarily wide and would cover much commercial activity which would be generally regarded as legitimate. To take just one example, an act would be to a person's prejudice if it would result

'in his being deprived of an opportunity to earn remuneration or greater remuneration.'

Every employee who is dismissed or not promoted and every applicant for job who is struck off a short-list appears to be deprived of an opportunity to earn remuneration or greater remuneration. The only question would be whether the act was done dishonestly. The SPTL Sub-committee, commenting on the proposal, took exception to dishonesty being 'elevated to a central role in the offence', saying 'In our view dishonesty in the Theft Acts is better seen as a negative feature which controls liability that would otherwise arise in respect of prima facie lawful conduct.'

The problem running through the issues of the definition of theft, conspiracy to defraud and any general fraud offence which might be enacted, is to supply other elements in the actus reus which will confine the offence within reasonable limits, apart from the concept of dishonesty. It was all very well for their Lordships in *Welham* to enunciate a very broad definition of defraud, but they were doing so in relation to the offence of forgery which has a substantial actus reus. The defendant had to be proved to have made a false document. Dishonesty was not the essence of the crime but provided, as the SPTL said, a limiting factor.

Mr P. R. Glazebrook suggests[27] that there is a 'very simple' solution to the problem in theft

'If theft is (as it is) an offence involving dishonesty, legal logic requires that the conduct constituting its external elements be unlawful—either tortious, or a breach of trust, or, if the property belongs to a company, a fraud on its creditors or shareholders.'

The opinion that theft can be committed only by an act which is contrary to the civil law has had the formidable support of Glanville Williams from at least the early 1960s when the CLRC's Larceny subcommittee was debating the new definition of theft. It should require not merely an appropriation, but a *mis*appropriation. That view did not prevail in the CLRC but Professor Williams has argued[28] with his usual cogency that the Act should be so construed anyway. The courts have not taken this view, possibly because it has never been properly argued, though their well-known antipathy to the involvement of civil law issues suggests that extremely persuasive advocacy would have been required. It is worth looking at again because Mr Glazebrook's use of it leads to an ingenious way of taming the concept of dishonesty. Because 'appropriation' is now an unlawful act, his draft clause can provide:

'A person's appropriation of property belong to another *is to be regarded as dishonest unless*'

There follows a list of exceptions—where D believes he has the right to deprive, etc. This reduces dishonesty to the limiting role that academic opinion generally believes it should have. *Ghosh*[29] would become irrelevant and juries would no longer have to decide whether decent people would regard the conduct as dishonest and whether D knew that. Whether it is theft would be settled by the law, not the opinion of the jury. The attractions are obvious.

Glazebrook's method of incorporating the requirement of unlawfulness is to provide:

'*Any infringement of the rights that a person to whom the property belongs* has in respect of it amounts to an appropriation of it.'

This would include a breach of contract (which, if we are to have the rule at all, seems right) although that is not in the list of unlawful acts quoted above. An express requirement that the act be contrary to the civil law would be likely to create unnecessary alarm and despondency on the bench. On the other hand, merely to say 'misappropriates' or 'unlawfully appropriates' might not convey the message.

The effect of requiring the act to be unlawful in the civil law would be considerable. Acts done dishonestly but with the authority or consent of the owner would cease to be theft because there would be no trespass, conversion or breach of contract. The overruled case of *Fritschy*[30] would be restored. The dishonest shopper removing goods from the supermarket shelves would not commit an offence but the label-switcher (a trespasser) presumably would.[31] Tucker J's dishonest warehouseman (above), and the analogous company director, would have done merely preparatory acts.

The problem of conspiracy to defraud

Conspiracy to defraud is considered to be objectionable because (i) it is wrong in principle and absurd

[27] [1993] CLJ 191.
[28] [1977] Crim LR 127, 205 and 327. See also Arlidge and Parry on Fraud, 1.10, Sullivan [1985] Crim LR 616 at 626, 628.
[29] [1982] QB 1035.
[30] [1985] Crim LR 745.

[31] For this reason, the writer would prefer the actus reus to be the unlawful assumption of the rights (*all* the rights) of the owner. To hold that the label-switcher has already stolen the thing labelled seems to go too far.

that an agreement by two persons to do an act which is not an offence when done by one should amount to a crime; and (ii) its extremely vague and uncertain extent, violates the principle of legality—that no one should be punished for conduct which has not been declared in advance to be a crime.

On the other hand, the offence is considered to have legitimate and perhaps indispensable advantages including (i) it enables the prosecution of conduct which ought, in the public interest, to be criminal although it does not amount to an offence when committed by an individual; (ii) it better reflects the nature of the wrongdoing, especially where that consists in a series of offences committed over a long period; and (iii) it facilitates clear and simple presentation of the case to the jury.

Four options are put forward for consideration by the Law Commission in their Working Paper No. 104:

1. To retain the common law offence—i.e., to do nothing.
2. To abolish the common law offence and to create in its place a statutory offence of conspiracy to defraud. The offence would be based on the common law authorities but could of course be modified as thought appropriate.
3. To abolish the common law offence and to create new substantive offences to fill the gaps which would be left.
4. To abolish the common law offence and create in its place a general fraud offence (GFO).

It can be argued that we need do nothing because there is no evidence that conspiracy to defraud is used in an oppressive way or that it causes injustice—that the objections are theoretical and unimportant in practice. Even if this were right, however, the need to remove, as far as possible, the complexity and uncertainty of the law remains.

If Glazebrook is right in asserting that legal logic requires that an offence involving dishonesty should be capable of commission only by unlawful conduct, that principle must apply to any general fraud offence. Is this then a way forward? The Law Commission's tentative proposal would be modified to read:

> 'A person who, *by any unlawful act*, dishonestly causes another person to suffer [financial] prejudice, or a risk of prejudice, or who, *by any unlawful act*, dishonestly makes a gain for himself or another commits an offence,'

It would be consistent to provide that the unlawful act is to be regarded as done dishonestly unless it was done in the belief that he had the right to do it. This would at least remove the criticism that the offence would penalise much legitimate conduct, because, by definition, it would not. At the same time, it would impose a significant limit on the range of conspiracy to defraud. Cases involving deception would not be affected because the deception would presumably be an unlawful act. But this is less clear in a case of the type envisaged in the model indictment proposed in *Landy*[32]

> 'Causing and permitting the Bank to make excessive advances to insubstantial and speculative trading companies incorporated in Liechtenstein and Switzerland, such advances being inadequately guaranteed and without proper provision for the payment of interest.'

Such conduct does not obviously involve any tort such as deceit or conversion. It describes very imprudent conduct but that is all. In *Sinclair*[33] the court referred to 'the taking of a risk which there was no right to take'; but it is not apparent that the act was in breach of any rule of the civil law. If there was no 'right' to take the risk, this was only because it was a risk that no reasonable director would have taken. Is it the tort of negligence and, if so, should it be regarded as an unlawful act on that ground? Glazebrook includes among unlawful acts (though not specifically in his draft clause) 'a fraud on [a company's] creditors or its shareholders' but that hardly helps to solve the present problem—i.e., whether it *is* a fraud. If unlawfulness were to be an element of the offence, it would probably require a clause deeming the 'reckless' conduct of the directors to be unlawful.

A requirement of unlawfulness does not seem to be a complete solution to these problems. And the continuing breadth of the offence would remain an objection. If 'unlawful' includes a breach of contract, an employee taking the day off to go to the races might well be guilty of it, if he knows that he will cause his employer financial prejudice. That seems unacceptable. The search for a general fraud offence which does not extend potential criminal liability too far seems unlikely to succeed.

Statutory conspiracy to defraud?

The option of a statutory offence of conspiracy to defraud does not seem to have received much favour because it is said that it would be open to the same objections of principle as the common law offence, while forfeiting some of that offence's advantage of flexibility. The great virtue, as well as the great vice, of conspiracy to defraud is that 'defraud' is undefined. It is a virtue, certainly from the point of view

[32] [1981] 1 All ER 1172 at 1179.

[33] (1968) 52 Cr App R 618.

of the prosecution and perhaps also from the point of the public, that most reprehensible conduct can be brought within it. Once we define it, we are inevitably into arguments about the meaning of words which do not arise when there are no words of definition but only a rather vague idea.

But we cannot have everything. To obtain more certainty it is necessary to sacrifice some flexibility; and the case for more certainty is very strong. Of course it would be illogical to provide that it is an offence to conspire to do X, when it is not an offence actually to do X. Yet it is arguable that the requirement of conspiracy provides a desirable constraint on what would otherwise be too wide-ranging an offence. Few would want to make a criminal of the person who quite deliberately defers payment of his gas bill until he gets the threatening red reminder, even though he knows perfectly well that he is causing an unjustifiable loss to the Gas Board; but the company directors, referred to above, who decide as a matter of policy to defer payment of their suppliers for long periods, being well aware of the damage they are doing, seem to fall into a quite different category. Of course, it is not only the fact of agreement which makes the conduct so serious—an individual in a large way of business might do the same—but it is a significant fact. Where there is no agreement the matter is likely to be trivial and the line between negligence and intention will be hard to draw. Where there is agreement, it is clearly intentional and likely to be substantial.

There is another good reason for replacing the common law conspiracy with a statutory one; it will bring the offence within the constraints of the Criminal Law Act 1977 and treat it like other conspiracies. If those limitations are right for conspiracies generally, how can they not be right for conspiracy to defraud? The way to do this would seem to be to provide that, for the purposes of Part I of that Act only, it is an offence to—and then to define the general fraud offence.

Section 1 of the 1977 Act requires that the contemplated offence is to be committed 'by one or more of the parties to the agreement.' In *Hollinshead*[34] the Court of Appeal held that this was a restatement of a common law principle and so was applicable to conspiracy to defraud. The parties contemplated that the fraud on the Electricity Boards would be carried out by third parties, not yet identified, who would buy the black boxes manufactured by the defendants and use them to defraud the Boards. The House of Lords restored the convictions holding that the purpose of the defendants was to defraud the Boards. That decision seems impossible to reconcile with the facts; but, however that may be, it seems clear that, if the defrauding of the Boards was the GFO, it was not to be done by one of the parties to the conspiracy. The effect would be to reverse *Hollinshead*. That seems right. The natural meaning of conspiracy to defraud is that the conspirators have agreed that *they*, jointly, will defraud someone, not that they will provide another with the opportunity to do so.

Section 1 also requires agreement on a course of conduct which will necessarily amount to or involve the commission of a crime 'if the agreement is carried out in accordance with their intentions.' So an allegation of conspiracy to commit the GFO will, it is submitted,[35] require an intention on the part of all principal conspirators[36] that at least one of them will commit the GFO.

The revision of the Theft Acts

The drafting of the Theft Acts has been subjected to severe criticism and certainly some of it was very bad. The worst provisions were those, such as s. 6 and s. 16 of the 1968 Act which were introduced without sufficient consideration after the draft bill had left the hands of the CLRC. In fact, the CLRC produced a basically sound bill but one that called for more discrimination in its application than it received. The major problems which arose concerned the relationship between theft, contrary to s. 1 and obtaining property by deception, contrary to s. 15. None of these need have arisen if prosecutors had followed the advice to use s. 15, not s. 1, whenever property was obtained by a trick or deception of any kind. *Gomez* itself was a textbook case of obtaining by deception and if that offence had been charged there could have been no argument as to the propriety of the conviction. Poor prosecuting was compounded by poor judging. The judges' reluctance to allow a manifestly dishonest person to escape is understandable but it has bedevilled the law of stealing for over hundred and fifty years. In the law of larceny it was the concept of possession which was stretched and strained to ensure that the morally guilty did not escape. Under the 1968 Act it was the

[34] (1985) 80 Cr App R 285, CA, [1985] Crim LR 301, revsd., [1985] AC 975, HL, [1985] Crim LR 653; discussed Smith & Hogan, 280, 290.
[35] *Pace* Lord Bridge in *Anderson* [1986] AC 27. See Smith & Hogan, 272–274.
[36] It is otherwise with a person alleged to be an abettor of conspiracy. As with abettors generally, he must be shown to intend or know that he is assisting or encouraging the commission of the offence (i.e., the conspiracy); but need not intend the commission of the offence that the principals are conspiring to commit.

idea of appropriation. If a narrow interpretation would lead to conviction, the court would probably adopt it; if the narrow interpretation would lead to an acquittal, the court would prefer a broad interpretation.[37] This naturally leads to inconsistency, confusion, and uncertainty. Whatever reforms may be made of the law of theft, it is likely that, within a few years, we shall be in the same difficulties again unless we have better informed prosecuting and more consistent judging. So long as we have a law of stealing 'property belonging to another' some complexity is inevitable because the civil law defining what is property belonging to another is complex. We hear that a distinguished judge laments the need to explain to a jury, inter alia, the idea of stealing a 'thing in action'. One can only sympathise with the learned judge—it is difficult enough with law students—but presumably he would agree that the law would be grievously defective if it did not forbid the theft of things in action and other intangible property; and if a jury is to decide whether such property has been stolen, do they not have to have some idea of what it is?[38]

It may fairly be said that an employee who receives and retains a bribe in the course of his employer's business equally deserves, or does not deserve, to be condemned as a criminal whether the English civil courts follow *A-G for Hong Kong* v. *Reid* or re-assert the authority of *Lister* v. *Stubbs*[39]. But in the latter event the employee commits no offence whereas in the former he is guilty of theft if the particular jury is satisfied that he is dishonest. The moral quality of his act and his dangerousness to society are unaffected by the state of the Civil law. All this applies equally to *Clowes (No 2)*.[40] If, however, we take the view that the outcome in the civil law should be irrelevant, then we have, in effect, opted in favour of a general fraud offence because we have removed the one element which prevents theft (as interpreted in *Gomez*) from being substantially coincident with the fraud which satisfies the law of conspiracy.[41]

Whether or not the law of conspiracy to defraud can be reformed there is certainly now a strong case for the revision and simplification of the Theft Acts. Now that the scheme devised by the CLRC has been wrecked by *Gomez*, s. 15 of the 1968 At should be abolished.[42] There is no point in maintaining an elaborate offence which merely duplicates a simpler one. As for penalty, it is difficult to see why obtaining something by deception should be regarded as worse than simply taking it; historically the reverse was true. As for land, the case for excluding it from theft was always tenuous. It should be made capable of being stolen. The 1968 Act, following the recommendation of the CLRC, rolled up the three offences of larceny, embezzlement and fraudulent conversion into one offence of theft (to the great advantage of the criminal law). The CLRC's Larceny sub-committee at one time proposed to include obtaining by false pretences as well and changed its mind ('to the regret of some members')[43] partly because a sub-sub-committee reported that it would be difficult to frame an indictment for stealing by false pretences. *Gomez* suggests that, whatever the position then, there is now no difficulty. The CLRC (reasonably enough) did not foresee the difficulties which prosecutors and courts would have; but now we know.

It is very doubtful whether we need the present range of obtaining offences. Section 1 of the 1978 Act, obtaining services by deception, is valuable but maimed by the decision in *Halai*,[44] (holding that a mortgage advance is not services) from which it should be rescued. That could solve most, if not all, of the mortgage fraud cases. The three complex and overlapping offences in s. 2 of the 1978 Act could surely be simplified. The CLRC who proposed these offences were much concerned by the rejection by Parliament of clause 12(3) of the draft Theft Bill accompanying their Eighth Report on the grounds of its 'dragnet' nature and were perhaps over-cautious in producing a provision which would not meet the same fate. The definitions suffered greatly from drafting in committee. The offence of procuring the exe-

[37] Cf commentary on *Monaghan* [1979] Crim LR 673 at 675.

[38] Many of the difficulties that have arisen could have been avoided by better prosecuting. The common use of s. 15 of the 1968 Act where D has induced P to draw a cheque in his favour leads to endless complex problems; yet we have the offence of procuring the execution of a valuable security by deception, contrary to s. 20(2), which is tailor-made for this situation.

[39] See above, p. 50.

[40] Discussed above, p. 50.

[41] See 'Theft and defrauding, compared', above, p. 52.

[42] Particularly if the present breadth of theft is retained. That an act merely preparatory to the offence of obtaining a thing by deception is theft of the thing is a nonsense we should not retain.

[43] CLRC, Eighth Report (Cmnd. 2977) para. 38.

[44] [1983] Crim LR 624. We need some procedure for reconsidering 'rogue' decisions, such as this. The rule that the Court of Criminal Appeal is bound by its own decisions worked well enough when it was affirmed in (1950) 34 Cr App R 138. As a glance at that volume of the Criminal Appeal Reports shows, the Lord Chief Justice was sitting in almost every case and, if he was not there, Humphreys J was. The court knew what it was doing. But now when it sits in numerous divisions, some of which appear, with all respect, to have an unimpressive grasp of criminal law and evidence, almost anything may happen. Contradictory decisions have been known to emerge on the same day, making nonsense of the doctrine of precedent. Perhaps the Attorney-General should have power to refer cases to the court for reconsideration.

cution of a valuable security contrary to s. 20 of the 1968 At—an old and obscure provision but now much relied on—received scant consideration by the Committee and is overdue for revision. We could do worse than revert to something like the much simpler section that was replaced in 1861 by the predecessor of the present obscure provision.

6. Some Procedural Problems in Criminal Fraud Cases

JEREMY ROBERTS QC

Introduction

'AN indictment is nothing else but a plain, brief and certain narrative of an offence committed by any person.' So wrote Sir Matthew Hale in the seventeenth century. If only it were always that simple.

It should be the aim of all practitioners of the law to say everything that needs to be said (and no more) in a manner that is 'plain, brief and certain'. This is usually the most effective way of putting one's case. It is not always easy to achieve. We have all had our failures: and I expect I will fail hopelessly in this paper.

The paper is going to be concerned mainly with indictments and other formal documents which are (or may be) brought into existence by the lawyers for the purpose of court proceedings in criminal fraud cases. Perhaps we can conveniently refer to these documents compendiously as 'the court papers'.

In Part II of the paper I shall hope to make some constructive suggestions about the types of documents which, in an ideal system, the court papers should comprise; about what the form and content of those documents should be; and about the way in which they should be used.

First, however, it may be of some interest to take a brief look at the way in which the practice of our courts, as regards the drafting and use of indictments and other court papers, has developed over the past couple of hundred years or so (and in particular over the last 15 years). I will try to do this in Part I. There are usually some lessons to be learned from those who have gone before us in the law. We tend to think that the City frauds which have achieved some publicity in recent years, and the particular problems which they present for our system of trial by jury, are modern phenomena. It may sometimes be salutary to remember that similar problems have been around for at least the last 200 years.

Part I: The Development of our Existing System

1. Indictments in the First Half of the Nineteenth Century

1.1 In the first half of the nineteenth century indictments tended to be rather lengthy affairs. There were good reasons for this. The common law rule, as set out in successive editions of Archbold's Pleading and Evidence in Criminal Cases (then, as now, the criminal practitioner's bible), was that:

> 'all the ingredients of the offence with which the defendant is charged, the facts, circumstances and intent constituting it, must be set forth with certainty and precision'.

1.2 The purpose of the indictment was to make clear to the judge and jury, as well as to the defendant himself, precisely what was the case which he had to meet. This was important

(a) from the jury's point of view, so that they would know what were the essential elements of the charge, which would have to be proved before they could return a verdict of guilty;

(b) from the judge's point of view, so that he could rule evidence admissible or inadmissible according to whether or not it had some relevance to one of those elements; and

(c) from the point of view of the defendant and his lawyers (if he had any) so that they could prepare their cross-examination, evidence and arguments with a view to rebutting the prosecution's case.

1.3 If you were a prosecution lawyer drafting an indictment, it was generally a good idea to err on the side of putting in too much detail rather than too little. If you put in too much, any 'immaterial averments' (i.e. statements of fact which you did not strictly need to prove in order to establish your case) could be disregarded: the judge could tell the jury that they did not have to be proved.

1.4 If you put in too little, on the other hand, you were liable to find that your error was fatal to the success of your case: the omission of even the least important 'material averment' would be seized on by the defence as invalidating the indictment altogether.

1.5 At that time any omissions or errors in the indictment could not, as a general rule, be cured by amendment at the trial. This was because the procedure in those days was that the bill of indictment, having been drafted by the prosecution lawyers, was first placed before a grand jury. The grand jury were sworn to determine whether it was 'a true bill'—i.e. whether the prosecution evidence (which was all that they heard) afforded what we would nowadays call a prima facie case in support of the allegations set out in the bill.

1.6 If so, the bill became an actual indictment, on which the defendant was presented by the grand jury to stand his trial. Since the indictment therefore represented a finding by the grand jury upon their oaths, it could only be amended with their consent before they were discharged: so it was particularly important for the prosecution lawyers to get it right from the outset.

1.7 Quite a good example of an early nineteenth century fraud indictment is to be found in the celebrated case in which Lord Cochrane and others were convicted of having committed a stock market fraud in 1814: it is reported under the name *R* v. *De Berenger* in Volume 3 of Maule and Selwyn's reports at page 67.

1.8 One of the more interesting aspects of Lord Cochrane's case is the sentence passed on the convicted defendants. They received prison sentences and fines (in Lord Cochrane's case 12 months and £1,000 respectively) but they were also ordered to be 'set in the pillory opposite the Royal Exchange in the City of London for one hour'. They cannot have enjoyed that experience very much, and one is tempted to suggest that the re-introduction of such a form of penalty for some modern day fraudsters might have its advantages.

1.9 Parts of the indictment against Lord Cochrane, De Berenger and their co-conspirators are set out, in somewhat abbreviated form, in the report of the case.

1.10 It began by averring that at the material time

> 'there was and for a long time before, to wit, two years and upwards, had been an open and public war between our Lord the King and his allies, and the then ruler of France, to wit one Napoleon Bonaparte, and the people of France'.

(One of the points rather optimistically taken by the defence was that the prosecution had failed to prove this.)

1.11 Count 3 (the first count on which the defendants were convicted) then alleged that the defendants

> 'on the 19th day of February in the 54th year of the King, unlawfully contriving etc. by false reports rumours and contrivances to induce the subjects of the King to believe that a peace would soon be made between the King and his subjects and the people of France, and thereby to occasion without any just or true cause a great increase and rise of the public government funds and government securities of this kingdom, and to injure and aggrieve the subjects of the King who should on the 21st day of February purchase and buy any part or parts, and share or shares of and in the said public government funds etc., then and there, to wit on the 21st day of February unlawfully etc. did conspire etc. to make and propagate and cause to be made and propagated unto and among divers subjects etc. in the county of Kent etc. and also unto and among divers subjects etc. at London and places adjacent thereto, divers false reports and rumours that the said N. Bonaparte was killed, and that a peace would soon be made between the King and his subjects and the people of France. . . .'

and a good deal more to a similar effect.

1.12 If anyone is interested in reading an excellent account of an early nineteenth century fraud trial, one is to be found in 'Lord Cochrane's Trial before Lord Ellenborough', written in 1897 by a Mr Atlay. Mr Atlay had been commissioned to write this book by Lord Ellenborough's grandson, who was fed up with a succession of publications produced by members of Lord Cochrane's family, protesting Lord Cochrane's innocence and criticising Lord Ellenborough's conduct as the trial judge.

1.13 Mr Atlay's book also describes the eventful aftermath of the trial, including Lord Cochrane's escape from prison, and his subsequent appearance in the House of Commons (while still an escaper) as the Member of Parliament for Westminster.

2. *Nineteenth Century Reforms*

2.1 During the course of the nineteenth century a number of Acts of Parliament were passed with a view to preventing well-founded prosecutions from being defeated by technical objections to the validity of indictments. Perhaps the most important of these Acts was the Administration of Criminal Justice Improvement Act 1851 (14–15 Vic. c. 100).

2.2 The preamble to the 1851 Act began with these somewhat plaintive words:

> 'Whereas offenders frequently escape conviction on their trials by reason of the technical strictness of criminal proceedings in matters not material to the merits of the case . . .'

To remedy this state of affairs the Act introduced a number of 'improvements'. These included a fairly wide power to amend the indictment if it was found that its contents differed from the evidence given at the trial (section 1). They also included such curiosities as the provision in section 24 that an indictment was no longer to be held invalid 'for stating the offence to have been committed on an impossible day, or on a day that never happened'.

2.3 Statutory provisions of this kind may well have reduced the number of unmeritorious acquittals, but they did little to alter the way in which indictments were drafted in practice. A good example of a fraud indictment from the second half of the last century is to be found in *R* v. *Gurney* (1869), reported in Volume 11 of Cox's Criminal Cases at page 414. Gurney and others were charged with conspiring to defraud the public by the formation and promotion of a joint stock company—not an uncommon type of fraud at that time.

2.4 The indictment contained no fewer than 32 conspiracy counts. Count 1 is set out in full in the report, where it occupies the whole of 3 closely printed pages. Many of the other counts were apparently of similar length.

2.5 Count 1 began by setting out various background circumstances. Then it set out, verbatim, the terms of the prospectus issued by the defendants. (The 1851 Act had abolished the old common law rule that, where a written instrument was relied upon as part of the prosecution case, it had to be set out in full in the indictment. Old habits nevertheless obviously died hard—they usually do, where lawyers are concerned.)

2.6 The count then went on to identify every statement in the prospectus which was alleged to have been false, and to set out what were alleged to be the true facts relating to each of those statements.

2.7 Despite its length, this count did enable the various issues which it raised to be seen clearly, very much in the manner of a civil pleading. No doubt the other counts did the same. It was not for nothing that 'Pleading' (in the sense of setting out one's case in a formal written document filed with the court) was selected by Archbold in 1822 to be the subject named first in the title to his book. It has remained so throughout all subsequent editions: the current (1993–4) edition is entitled 'Criminal Pleading, Evidence and Practice'.

3. The Indictments Act 1915

3.1 In 1915 Parliament made a determined attempt to introduce into indictments the qualities of plainness and brevity spoken of by Sir Matthew Hale. Section 3(1) of the Indictments Act 1915 (still in force today) provided that:

'every indictment shall contain, and be sufficient if it contains, a statement of the specific offence or offences with which the accused person is charged, together with such particulars as may be necessary for giving reasonable information as to the nature of the charge.'

3.2 Schedule 1 to the Act set out various rules for the drafting of indictments. These rules introduced the modern practice whereby each count on the indictment comprises 2 parts:

(1) the 'Statement of Offence', identifying the type of offence alleged: followed by
(2) the 'Particulars of Offence' which, said the rules in Schedule 1, should be set out 'in ordinary language, in which the use of technical terms shall not be necessary'.

3.3 The rules also contained specimen forms of indictment for various types of offences, including larceny (now theft), obtaining by false pretences (now obtaining property by deception) and conspiracy to defraud.

3.4 The rules in Schedule 1 of the 1915 Act remained in force until 1971 when they were replaced by new rules which are largely to the same effect. The specimen forms have not been reproduced in the 1971 rules, though by and large they have continued to be followed where applicable. The 1971 rules, echoing section 3(1) of the Act, state merely that the Particulars of Offence shall contain 'such particulars as may be necessary for giving reasonable information as to the nature of the charge'.

3.5 The 1915 Act undoubtedly succeeded in its aim of introducing simplicity and brevity into indictments. One by-product of the Act was, however, that over the years prosecutors in fraud cases came to draft their indictments in terms which were as general as they could get away with: which they could claim gave 'reasonable information as to the nature of the charge' but which did not tie them down too closely when it came to presenting their case to the jury.

3.6 There were understandable reasons for this. As is pointed out by the authors of Arlidge and Parry on Fraud, most fraud cases depend to a large extent on the inferences to be drawn from documents and from such facts as the prosecution are able to establish by direct evidence. In a complex case, while the prosecution may be quite right in the broad inferences which they seek to draw, it is likely that some at least of their detailed inferences may prove to be incorrect. Thus sensible prosecutors will always want to leave themselves a reasonable amount of room for manoeuvre.

3.7 By the time I started to practise in this field in the late 1960s, it was certainly common form, if you were defending, to receive from the prosecution several thousand pages of statements and exhibits, accompanied by an indictment (or, before committal, a charge sheet) which really told you very little about how the prosecution were proposing to put their case. You had to try to work it out for yourself.

3.8 You could ask for further particulars but, if you did, you were likely to be met by the standard response that all would be made clear in prosecuting counsel's opening speech. This was generally regarded by judges as an acceptable position, although one might have thought that the prosecution's opening speech was a little late in the day for the defence to receive information which they badly needed if they were to prepare their own case effectively.

3.9 Furthermore it was not (and still generally is not) the practice for a shorthand note to be taken of prosecution counsel's opening speech; and it is far more difficult to pin someone down (or to demonstrate a shift in his position) by reference to what he said in an oral address to the jury than by reference to a formal written statement of his case.

3.10 Thus it will be seen that, although the objective of introducing brevity and simplicity into indictments was a laudable one, one consequence of the 1915 reforms was that by the late 1960s indictments in fraud cases were often failing to fulfil satisfactorily the various functions identified in paragraph 1.2 above.

3.11 The wide terms in which they were drafted did not help juries to see exactly what had to be proved before they could convict, or judges to see the relevance or non-relevance of particular pieces of evidence; and the defence were not given the assistance which they should have received to enable them to prepare their cross-examination, evidence and arguments.

4. 'Broad' and 'Narrow' Offences

4.1 The problems just identified were particularly acute where the offence charged was itself a broadly defined one like conspiracy to defraud or fraudulent trading. Broad offences of this kind have always been favourites of prosecutors when it comes to selecting charges.

4.2 If you are prosecuting a fraud case, you often have a range of possible charges available to you on the facts which appear from the papers. There may be one or more specific offences, perhaps under the Theft Act 1968 or the Companies Act 1985, which you could allege: the difficulty with these is that they tend to have a number of ingredients which are very precisely defined, and a failure to establish any of these will be fatal to your case.

4.3 Insider dealing offences under the Company Securities (Insider Dealing) Act 1985 have proved particularly difficult, for this reason, to prosecute successfully; so have those under section 15 of the Companies Act 1985, which prohibits companies from providing financial assistance for the acquisition of their own shares.

4.4 In contrast to these narrowly defined offences, broad offences such as the common law offence of conspiracy to defraud are much more flexible. Conspiracy to defraud has been so widely defined by the courts that it catches any two or more people who (a) agree to carry out any course of conduct which they know will or may operate to the disadvantage of someone else and (b) (in the subsequent opinion of a jury) are acting dishonestly. It is not necessary that the conspirators should intend anyone else to end up worse off as a result of their actions: it is sufficient if they know that what they are agreeing to do will create a risk (or an increased risk) that that may happen.

4.5 Most smart commercial moves involve a potential advantage to those who carry them out, and a possible disadvantage to someone else. It follows that those who agree to carry out such a move are at risk of a conviction for conspiracy to defraud if there is any danger that a jury might subsequently conclude that they were acting dishonestly (something which is not always easy to predict).

4.6 By the late 1960s it had become common form for prosecutors to allege, in indictments for conspiracy to defraud, that the defendants had conspired to defraud other people by various specified means 'and by divers other false and fraudulent devices'. This catch-all phrase gave the prosecution almost complete flexibility, and made it very difficult for the defence to object to the admissibility of any potentially prejudicial prosecution evidence.

4.7 This unsatisfactory state of affairs was brought to an end in the early 1980s, as will be described in 6.1–16 below. Before we come to that, it may be convenient to refer at this stage to another problem associated with the offence of conspiracy generally, and conspiracy to defraud in particular. This is the vexed problem of 'overt acts' which has caused a great deal of confusion and difficulty to practitioners over the years.

5. Overt Acts

5.1 The concept of an 'overt act' seems to have made its first appearance in English law as an ingredient of certain forms of treason. For example, it was from earliest times an offence for a person to compass or imagine or intend the death of the sovereign, and to declare or express his compassing or imagining or intending by some ' overt fait' or 'apertum factum'.

5.2 The reason for the requirement that some open act be proved was explained by Sir Edward Coke in his Institutes (Book III, Page 12). The offence was so heinous, and was so heavily and severely punished ('as none other the like'), that the defendant's treasonable intentions had to be proved 'not upon conjectural assumptions, or inferences, or straines of wit' but upon good and sufficient proof. Good and sufficient proof would exist if, but only if, the defendant's treasonable intentions had manifested themselves in some open act which could be observed and testified to by witnesses. (One may note, in passing, the touching faith in the proposition that oral evidence from witnesses is more reliable than circumstantial evidence.)

5.3 Thus in the law of treason an overt act was regarded as evidence, and indeed the only sufficient evidence, of the treasonable state of mind which required to be punished so heavily. Because some overt act was always required to be proved, it became in effect an ingredient of the offence itself.

5.4 Conspiracy as a distinct criminal offence emerged at a later stage in the development of our law than treason: though, of course, if two or more people met and agreed to kill the sovereign, their agreement might constitute the necessary overt act for the purposes of the offence of treason.

5.5 It seems that the first form of conspiracy to be recognized as an offence in its own right was conspiracy to secure a false conviction for felony. Subsequently the Star Chamber and the common law courts found it convenient to expand the law so as to recognize a variety of other indictable conspiracies—including conspiracy to defraud.

5.6 Just as the courts had looked for overt acts as proof of treason, so they began to look for overt acts as proof of conspiracy. To this day judges habitually point out to juries that persons minded to enter into criminal conspiracies do not usually do so in writing, or in the presence of respectable witnesses who can afterwards testify to the fact: the existence of the conspiracy normally has to be inferred from the actions of the conspirators in carrying it into effect (or attempting to do so).

5.7 It has never been part of the law of conspiracy, however, that overt acts are the only kind of evidence which will suffice to prove the conspiracy alleged; and proof of overt acts has never been necessary to found a conviction for conspiracy. It is trite law that (a) the offence is the agreement between the conspirators, not the carrying out of that agreement, and (b) it is therefore immaterial whether any steps are in fact taken to carry it out. Consequently an overt act, if there is one, is not an ingredient of the offence of conspiracy: it is merely evidence of it, like any other evidence.

5.8 The purpose of an indictment is to set out the facts relied upon as constituting the alleged offence, not the evidence by which those facts are to be proved. In this respect, as in others, an indictment is comparable to a civil pleading. It follows from this that the overt acts should not, properly speaking, be included in the indictment.

5.9 Nevertheless, by the nineteenth century it had become the general practice to include them. Though the practice diminished following the 1915 Act, it has continued intermittently to the present day. My own experience is that it causes difficulty and confusion, and is not to be encouraged. In particular, it confuses the jury about what actually has to be proved if the prosecution are to succeed.

5.10 The difficulties which practitioners have had with overt acts are not confined to matters of pleading. They extend to questions of admissibility of evidence. Few rules have caused so many problems in practice as the long established rule that

> 'the acts and declarations of any of the conspirators in furtherance of the common design may be given in evidence against any other conspirator'.

A note discussing these problems is attached as an appendix to this paper.

6. Changes Introduced in the 1980s

6.1 As described in 3.5–11 and 4.6 above, a rather unsatisfactory situation had arisen by the late 1960s. This continued throughout the 1970s, but was brought to an end by two separate developments which occurred in the early 1980s.

6.2 One of these was the judgment of the Court of Appeal in *R* v. *Landy* (1981) 72 Crim. App. Repts. 237. Harry Landy and others had been convicted of conspiracy to defraud depositors and creditors of the Israel British Bank (London) Ltd. The indictment had been drafted in what had become the usual form, including the familiar catch-all '. . . and by divers other false and fraudulent devices'.

6.3 The convictions were quashed because of defects in the summing up. But the Court of Appeal did not stop there. Poor Mr Allan Green, who had prosecuted the case and had drafted the indictment according to the then standard practice, was no doubt somewhat aggrieved to hear the Court of Appeal say in their judgment that it failed to give adequate particulars, and that the words '. . . and by divers other false and fraudulent devices' were a relic of the past and should never again appear in an indictment.

6.4 The Court of Appeal made their own suggestion as to how the indictment should have been drafted. They stressed that, in criticising Mr Green's indictment, they were not saying that particulars of conspiracies to defraud should be set out in the same kind of detail as would be required in a Statement of Claim in a civil action for damages. What was wanted was conciseness and clarity.

6.5 The Court of Appeal's draft set out, in the Particulars of Offence, five ways in which it was alleged the defendants had dishonestly agreed to put the interests of depositors and creditors at risk. The first, for example, was by

> 'causing and permitting the Bank to make excessive advances to insubstantial and speculative trading companies incorporated in Liechtenstein and Switzerland, such advances being inadequately secured, inadequately guaranteed and without proper provision for payment of interest'.

6.6 The Landy case may be taken as an illustration of the difficulty, in a complex fraud trial, of making an indictment fulfil all of the functions identified in 1.2 above. The Court of Appeal's draft was certainly an improvement on Mr Green's in terms of tying the prosecution down and putting some limits on the ambit of the case which they would be permitted to present at the trial. Ideally those limits needed to be more precisely defined. But that could not be done without a great deal more detail which would have made the indictment a much longer and more cumbersome document: as it was, the Court of Appeal's Particulars of Offence occupied 23 lines (260 words).

6.7 Help was at hand, however, in the shape of another development which occurred at around the same time as the Landy decision—namely the introduction of a practice whereby the prosecution supplied the court and the defence with a written summary of their case. Such summaries had originally been introduced in the late 1970s, for largely administrative purposes, as a result of agreements between the Director of Public Prosecutions and the Presiding Judges of some of the circuits. They were, however, found to have a valuable role, especially in fraud cases, in defining the way in which the prosecution case was to be put.

6.8 In November 1983 a 'Fraud Trials Committee', chaired by Lord Roskill, was set up 'to consider in what ways the conduct of criminal proceedings arising from fraud can be improved, and to consider what changes in existing law and procedure would be desirable to secure the just, expeditious and economical disposal of such proceedings'.

6.9 The Committee's report was published in December 1985. It contained a large number of recommendations. Many of these related to the pre-trial stage, and in particular the holding of preparatory hearings before the judge alone. Part of the system recommended by the Committee involved written 'case statements' by the prosecution and (if they so wished) the defence being prepared before the trial, and placed before the jury during the trial.

6.10 The Committee envisaged that the prosecution's case statement would be a document 'setting out the nub of the case against each defendant within the compass of a few pages'; and that the defence case statement would be a similar document in response.

6.11 Many of the Roskill recommendations were implemented in the Criminal Justice Acts 1987 and 1988. Under sections 7 and 9 of the 1987 Act the judge was given the power to order the prosecution (at or before the preparatory hearing) to file a case statement and to order the defence (at the preparatory hearing) to file a written statement in reply.

6.12 The Act is silent as to whether the prosecution's case statement should be placed before the jury: but section 10 provides that the defence case statement should not be disclosed at the trial unless

(a) the defendant consent [see s. 10(3)]; or
(b) he departs from his case statement, and the judge thinks it appropriate for comment to be made on the departure [see s. 10(1) and (2)].

6.13 It seems likely that Parliament envisaged that what would happen in practice would be what had been recommended by the Roskill Committee—namely that the jury would be given copies of the prosecution case statement and (if, but only if, the defence so wished) the defence case statement.

6.14 This view would seem to be supported by the terms of section 7(5). That section enables the judge to require the defendant not only

(a) to indicate the principal matters of fact or law on which he takes issue with the prosecution [see s. 7(5)(i) and (iii)], but also
(b) to notify 'any objections that he has to the [prosecution] case statement' [see s. 7(5)(ii)]

Of these provisions, (b) would seem to make sense only on the basis that it was envisaged that the prosecution case statement would go before the jury.

6.15 However, what has happened in practice has, in 2 respects, not followed the Roskill recommendations. In the first place, prosecution case statements have tended to be very much longer documents than the 'few pages' envisaged by the Committee: on occasions they have run into hundreds of pages. Sometimes, perhaps, they have been longer than necessary: but they have generally had the desirable effect of setting out very precisely the limits of the case which the prosecution are to present. This has been of great assistance to the defence in preparing their evidence and arguments, and to the judge in ruling on admissibility and other matters such as severance.

6.16 In the second place, neither prosecution nor defence case statements have as a general rule been placed before the jury. This has no doubt been in part because of the length and detail in which prosecution case statements have been drafted, as contrasted with the (properly) much shorter form of defence case statement. Other reasons were given by the Court of Appeal in *R* v. *Mayhew* (unreported, Nov. 18, 1991). Giving the judgment of the court, Lord Taylor CJ said:

'. . . we share the learned judge's general view that it would be undesirable for case statements to be put as a matter of course before juries as if they were projections of the indictment or particulars thereof . . . to provide the jury with pleadings and to raise pleadings arguments would tend to confusion and diversion from the central issues. Moreover, since case statements include propositions of law and contentious assertions as to the conclusions to be drawn, there would be a danger of juries being distracted by the printed statements in front of them from the oral arguments of counsel and, still worse, from the oral directions of the judge'.

6.17 Everyone would, I think, agree (a) that it is undesirable for the jury to be troubled by rival contentions of law which will have to be resolved by the judge, who will then direct the jury accordingly; and (b) that one does not want the jury to be distracted by technical pleading points such as sometimes arise in civil cases.

6.18 However, I doubt whether the Lord Chief Justice would dissent from the view that it might be very helpful to the jury to have the central issues in the case concisely identified in writing, together with the principal contentions of each side on each issue. This, one would have thought, might tend to concentrate attention where it should be concentrated, rather than to cause confusion and diversion from the issues.

6.19 Equally there would seem to be no harm (and indeed to be a positive benefit) in the jury having in front of them, in a concise written form, the contentious assertions of the parties as to the conclusions to be drawn from the facts and documents in the case. I will return to these topics in a moment, when making suggestions as to how the system might operate to best advantage in the future.

6.20 First, I will just complete this little review of the way in which the system has historically developed to date. Perhaps because juries do not generally have either the prosecution or the defence case statement, indictments in some fraud cases over the last few years have been drafted in a great deal of detail. A good example of this occurred in the 'Blue Arrow' trial which took place in 1991. (I have to declare a personal involvement in that case, in that I appeared for one of the defendants.)

6.21 Ten defendants were tried on an indictment containing a single count which alleged that they had conspired to defraud potential purchasers of shares in Blue Arrow plc. The trial lasted just over a year, at the end of which five of the defendants were convicted by the jury. Their convictions were later quashed by the Court of Appeal on the ground that there had been a substantial and incurable risk of a miscarriage of justice resulting from the sheer volume and complexity of the issues raised by the prosecution's case as presented: the trial had, in this sense, become 'unmanageable'.

6.22 Although the indictment had contained only a single count, that one count occupied 7 whole pages of print, and ran to 1254 words. It would be unfair to put all the blame for the unmanageability of the trial onto the length and complexity of the indictment: but I think that those responsible for the Blue Arrow prosecution would agree, in retrospect, that a much shorter and simpler indictment would have saved them a great deal of trouble. (In fact, by the end of the trial the judge had cut the indictment down to a fraction of its original length—but by then it was too late.)

6.23 One of the problems was that the terms of the indictment allowed the familiar confusion to arise over the distinction between the conspiracy itself and the overt acts alleged to have been done in the course of carrying it into effect.

6.24 In most conspiracy cases the nature and object of the alleged conspiracy can be stated quite shortly and concisely. Thus in the Blue Arrow case, according to the prosecution, what the defendants agreed to do was to bolster the Blue Arrow share price by making and maintaining 2 false pretences, viz

(a) that the number of shares taken up by shareholders (or their assignees) before the closing time of the Blue Arrow rights issue in 1987 was greater than it really was; and
(b) that, on the morning after the close of the rights issue, willing purchasers had been found for all the shares not already taken up by the shareholders or their assignees.

6.25 Equally, in many cases of conspiracy to defraud, various steps have to be taken, during the life of the conspiracy, to maintain whatever false pretences the conspirators are making, or otherwise to try to ensure the success of the operation. Many of these steps will not have been contemplated when the conspiracy was formed: they become necessary in the event of unexpected situations arising. Some of them may be taken by individual conspirators without the knowledge or agreement of their colleagues.

6.26 The prosecution alleged that that was what had happened in the Blue Arrow case. They were, of course, entitled to adduce evidence of the various steps taken by the alleged conspirators, as tending to establish (a) the existence and object of the conspiracy, and (b) the participation of the defendants in it. They did not need to set these steps out in the indictment, but they elected to do so (actually describing them as 'overt acts'). They would, as it turned out, have been far better off if they had simply detailed the alleged overt acts in their case statement, and left them out of the indictment altogether.

Part II: Suggestions as to Future Practice

7. The Indictment

7.1 Past experience has shown that, certainly in complex fraud cases, there are practical difficulties in expecting a single document (the indictment) to fulfil all of the functions identified in 1.2 above. Nor is there any reason nowadays why it should be expected to do so. The prosecution's written case statement is a much more convenient and appropriate vehicle for defining, for the benefit of the judge and the defence, the outer limits of the case which the prosecution are to present.

7.2 The indictment can therefore be left to fulfil its primary purpose of setting out the minimum ingredients of the alleged offence—those matters about which the jury must be satisfied if they are to convict. Even in the most complex case, it should be possible to set out those ingredients shortly and concisely.

7.3 Thus for example

(a) in a future 'Blue Arrow' case it should not be necessary to do more than to set out the essential elements of the alleged offence in similar terms to those employed in 6.24 above; and

(b) in a future 'Landy' case the indictment could be even more concise than the form proposed by the Court of Appeal—there should be no need for anything more elaborate than a simple statement that the defendants conspired together to defraud depositors and creditors of the bank by dishonestly causing the bank to enter into transactions which
   (i) did not accord with normal banking practice, and
   (ii) put the interests of depositors and creditors at risk.

7.4 The practice of setting out the 'Statement of Offence' followed by the 'Particulars of Offence' has worked well ever since it was introduced in 1915, and there seems little point in changing it.

7.5 One practice which could with advantage be changed in suitable cases, however, is that by which the Particulars of Offence (however long they are) are traditionally set out in the form of a single sentence. There is no logical reason why these particulars, any more than any other written text, should not be split up into several sentences of sensible length. Such a change would surely make for clarity and simplicity.

7.6 Indeed on occasions there might be some considerable benefit in setting out each ingredient of the alleged offence in a separate numbered point. The indictment would then provide a useful 'check list' for the jury when debating their verdicts.

8. The Prosecution's Case Statement

8.1 The rather long and detailed form of prosecution case statement which has become the norm since the Criminal Justice Act 1987 came into effect has proved to have real advantages. It provides a detailed framework for the evidence which the prosecution propose to adduce in support of their case: in a conspiracy case, for example, it will set out any overt acts alleged by the prosecution as well as any other evidence relied on by them to prove the existence and objects of the conspiracy, and to show who participated in it.

8.2 A prosecution case statement in this form obviously makes clear to the defence exactly how the prosecution propose to put their case: the defence can thus plan their own case accordingly.

8.3 There is no logical reason why the prosecution case statement should be regarded as setting with absolute finality the limits outside which the prosecution should not be allowed to travel in their evidence. The onus should, however, obviously be on the prosecution to justify an application to go beyond those limits; and the defence must always have the rights (a) to object on the ground of incurable prejudice and (b) to request an adjournment, where necessary, to deal with any fresh evidence.

8.4 One of the principal benefits of a reasonably detailed prosecution case statement is that it enables the judge to begin to form an impression of the likely length and complexity of the trial which will ensue if the prosecution are allowed to proceed in the manner which they propose. One of the judge's responsibilities is to control the proceedings so as to ensure, as far as he can, that the trial does not become unmanageable in the 'Blue Arrow' sense.

8.5 The judge has various powers at his disposal to achieve this objective. If he can see that there is a danger that the combined volume and complexity of the issues will prejudice the prospects of a fair trial and a fair result, he may be able to pre-empt such a situation by

(a) severing the trial of some defendants from that of others; and/or

(b) severing the trial of some counts from that of others; and/or

(c) refusing to allow the prosecution to present all the evidence which they wish to present: he can achieve this by indicating that he will stay the proceedings on the ground of 'abuse of process' (i.e. on the ground that the defendant cannot be assured a fair trial) if the prosecution do not agree to reduce the scope of their case.

8.6 Experience tends to show that severance of the indictment by defendants is a solution to be adopted only as a last resort. It has in the past been popular with some judges as a means of cutting down the length of trials: but it tends to produce two or more unbalanced trials which are quite likely to produce unsatisfactory results.

8.7 Where two or more people are alleged to have been criminally involved in the same transaction or series of transactions, it is as a general rule highly desirable that they should be tried together, so that the jury may have the opportunity of examining the roles of each of them, and hearing their explanations. If any of the key figures are missing from a trial, it is often only too easy for those who are being tried to put all the blame onto those who are conspicuous by their absence.

8.8 Thus it is a common experience that, if there are two separate trials arising out of the same transaction or series of transactions, with different defendants in the dock in each trial, the story which emerges in the first trial will be a completely different story from that which emerges in the second.

8.9 In particular, although it is sometimes suggested that fraud cases could be shortened and simplified by trying the principal characters separately from the minor ones, such a course is likely to be a recipe for disaster. The 'minions' will very often be acquitted on the basis that they were merely used as instruments by the real villains, whilst the real villains are acquitted on the basis that they did not know what the minions were doing. At least if they are all tried together the jury will have the opportunity of seeing them all, and hearing their accounts, and deciding where the truth lies.

8.10 Severance of the indictment by counts can sometimes be a successful means of avoiding an unmanageable trial. Indeed, if different counts on the same indictment allege offences which are in truth quite distinct from one another, it will generally be desirable that they should be tried separately: otherwise there is always the risk that the jury, having rejected the defence to one count, may be predisposed to reject the defence to the other.

8.11 However, there are some cases where two or more counts on an indictment are closely linked and where severance of the counts would not result in any significant reduction in the length or complexity of the evidence or issues. There have also been examples of cases where severing the counts has led to just the same unbalancing of the resulting trials as is liable to be produced by severing the defendants.

8.12 Thus often the most satisfactory and effective means of producing a trial which is of a manageable shape and size will be to insist on a reduction of the scope of the evidence to be presented by the prosecution. A detailed case statement should enable the judge to see what categories of evidence the prosecution are proposing to adduce, and which of those categories could be eliminated without doing unreasonable damage to the prosecution case.

9. The Defence Case Statement, and Agreed Statements of Facts

9.1 In our traditional system of criminal justice, a defendant has always been entitled as a general rule to play his cards close to his chest; to sit back and see what the prosecution can prove and what they cannot; and to keep his defence or defences to himself until he chooses to reveal them.

9.2 Sometimes they may be revealed in cross-examination of prosecution witnesses; sometimes in the course of the defendant's own evidence (if he chooses to go into the witness box); and sometimes (especially if he does not go into the witness box) not until his counsel's final speech, by which time it is too late for the prosecution to comment on them.

9.3 Existing and proposed statutory infringements of a suspect's 'right of silence' at the stage when the authorities are investigating his alleged misdeeds lie outside the scope of this paper. It is, however, worth observing in passing that quite often, when a defendant is charged with a substantial fraud offence, he will already have been required to disclose his hand in answering questions from such authorities as D.T.I. inspectors or the Serious Fraud Office. These authorities have statutory powers to require the provision of information and documents, even by persons suspected of criminal involvement in fraud.

9.4 Once the defendant has been charged and his case has been committed or transferred to the Crown Court for trial, he will find that there are other statutory provisions awaiting him which may also prevent him from playing his cards close to his chest in the traditional way. In any case in which a preparatory hearing is held under sections 7 and 9 of the Criminal Justice Act 1987, the judge has 2 distinct powers to require the defendant to state his position.

9.5 The first is the power under s. 9(5)(i) to order the defendant to file a defence case statement 'setting out in general terms the nature of his defence and indicating the principal matters on which he takes issue with the prosecution'. In according with what appears to have been the intention of Parliament, defence case statements have tended to be relatively short documents. They have rarely told the prosecution anything they did not know already, or could not have anticipated. Unlike prosecution case statements they are not required to, and do not in practice, give details of the evidence (if any) proposed to be called by the defence.

9.6 The second power, perhaps more valuable in practice if it is effectively used, is the power under s. 9(5)(iv) to order the defendant to respond point by point to a detailed notice served by the prosecution under s. 9(4)(c) seeking the admission of specified facts and documents. An order under s. 9(5)(iv) requires the defendant, where he does not admit any particular fact or document, to state his reason(s) for not admitting it; and s. 9(8) provides that, if it appears to a judge that the reasons given by the defendant are inadequate, he may require him to give further or better reasons.

9.7 Section 9(5)(iv) is particularly valuable in those cases (of which there are many) where there is a substantial 'factual framework' made up of large numbers of facts and figures which are unlikely to be disputed but which the prosecution need to establish as part of their case.

9.8 It is fair to say that for many years non-contentious facts of this nature have very often been agreed on a voluntary basis by defendants and their legal advisers. Generally speaking it is a good tactic, if you are defending, to be seen to be playing a constructive role in the proceedings, and to be assisting the jury to establish the facts. This involves accepting the non-contentious facts as well as bringing out those which are helpful to the defence. Juries are not fools, and are not slow at spotting defendants who are trying to confuse matters by refusing to agree anything.

9.9 The statutory powers under s. 9(5)(iv) and s. 9(8) provide useful tools to procure a response in those cases where cooperation might not otherwise be forthcoming. What if a defendant, despite orders under these sub-sections, persists in a wholly unreasonable refusal to admit anything, or to make more than a few token admissions? Such a case would, I think, be extremely rare: few defendants wish to antagonize the judge who is to preside over their trial.

9.10 The Act provides no sanction for use in such a situation. Technically the judge might be entitled to commit the defendant for contempt of court (or to threaten to do so), but this would not be guaranteed to produce the desired result. Indeed, it might only cause the defendant to see (and portray) himself as something of a martyr, and to become determined to wreck the trial process.

9.11 A more satisfactory and effective sanction might be simply to allow the jury to see the prosecution's invitation to agree facts, and the defendant's response. At the moment, the terms of s. 10 of the 1987 Act almost certainly prevent this. If s. 10 were amended appropriately, the prospect of the jury being influenced against him by his obviously unreasonable attitude might operate as a powerful incentive to the defendant to adopt a more constructive one.

9.12 Subject to an amendment of s. 10 to cover this last point, the 1987 Act seems to strike quite a good balance when it comes to the question of defence disclosure.

9.13 On the one hand, it would not be satisfactory to go back, in this unusual class of case, to the traditional principle that a defendant is entitled to play all his cards close to his chest. The need to ensure manageability of fraud trials must be paramount: and manageability requires some form of disclosure by the defence. One aspect of this point is the need to ensure, so far as possible, that time is not wasted unnecessarily during the trial by listening to a lot of evidence to establish points which turn out in the end to be non-contentious. Another is the need for the judge to form a view in advance as to whether a case of the shape and size proposed by the prosecution is likely to become unmanageable: he cannot do this without knowing which matters are really in issue, and which are not.

9.14 On the other hand, most practitioners would regard it as undesirable that the defence should be required to set out details of their evidence in their case statement as the prosecution are expected to do in theirs. It rightly remains a fundamental principle of our law that it is for the prosecution, who bring a criminal charge, to prove it: and it is only right that the defendant, whose liberty is at stake, should know exactly how the case against him is to be put, and what evidence the prosecution are proposing to adduce from which witnesses.

9.15 I would not therefore suggest any change to the existing practice as regard prosecution and defence case statements, save for a small amendment to s. 10 of the 1987 Act.

10. Summaries of the Parties' Cases for the Jury

10.1 It will be recalled that both the Roskill Committee in their 1985 report and Parliament in enacting the Criminal Justice 1987 appear to have envisaged that the prosecution case statement would be placed before the jury, as would the defence case statement if the defence so wished; but that this has not happened in practice.

10.2 The detailed prosecution case statement which the judge and the defence will have received is clearly not an appropriate document to put before the jury, as the Court of Appeal pointed out in *R* v. *Mayhew*. There is, however, a good case for giving the jury (during or at the end of prosecution counsel's opening speech) a much shorter document, summarising the main points in the prosecution case in the space of a few pages only; and, of course, for allowing the defence, if they wish, to give the jury a similar document summarising their case.

10.3 These documents will of course contain contentious assertions. Most summaries placed before juries are agreed summaries of non-contentious matters. But there is no reason in principle or logic why documents should be denied to the jury merely because they contain contentious material—provided, of course, that it is made clear to the jury what is contentious and what is not. There should not be any difficulty about that.

10.4 Juries at the moment are expected to perform their important task in rather a curious way. They are expected to sit, maybe for weeks or even months, as spectators while speeches are made, evidence is presented and the case is summed up by the judge. They are permitted to make notes, but are given little guidance about doing so. Then at the end of it all they are expected to be able to undertake a careful and accurate analysis of the facts and issues.

10.5 However well the case is explained in prosecution counsel's opening speech, however well the evidence and arguments are presented, and however lucidly the summing up dissects the issues and reminds the jury of the principal parts of the evidence, one may doubt whether (when they retire to consider their verdicts) the jurors are always able to remember, and to give proper effect to, all the various factors and considerations which are relevant to their verdicts.

10.6 One may venture to suggest that any professional assessor of facts would be pretty surprised to be told that he or she had to decide important and detailed issues in this way. Judges are accustomed to the assistance of pleadings and skeleton arguments, as well as detailed notes of oral submissions and evidence.

10.7 Why should juries be denied the advantage of having the issues in the case, and the principal matters relied on by each side on each issue, set out for them in a convenient and concise written form? Surely this would be an excellent way of ensuring that their attention was focussed on the various key points.

10.8 Nor would there seem to be any reason why they should be given such summaries only at the beginning of the case, before they have heard the evidence. Why should they not also be given similar documents summarising the main points relied on by counsel in their final speeches, when all the evidence has been completed?

10.9 I do not envisage that any of these summaries would need to occupy more than a very few pages. Before being put before the jury, they would have to be shown to the other side and approved by the judge.

10.10 Nor do I envisage that the summaries would take the place of, or be allowed to distract attention from, the oral submissions of counsel. These are, and would remain, the principal means of putting across each side of the case to the jury. The purpose of the summaries would be to provide a convenient and accurate reminder of counsel's principal submissions.

11. Written Summaries of Factual Material

11.1 In a fraud trial which lasts for a number of months, the jury will see and hear evidence of a vast number of different facts, figures and dates. Many of the relevant details are likely to have been set out in schedules, summaries or charts prepared and agreed before the start of the trial, and presented to the jury as agreed material. But many more will have emerged in the course of the evidence.

11.2 To remember all of these details would require a prodigious feat on the part of the jury, even with the benefit of the judge's summing up. A judge trying the case alone would have the benefit of notes and summaries prepared as the case progressed. Why should the jury be deprived of such assistance, and required to rely on their memory?

11.3 Obviously there will be parts of the evidence (especially the contentious parts) which are not susceptible to being summarised in writing. But other parts may very well be. Experience shows that, where one of the parties suggests the possibility of agreeing a fair summary of some area of the evidence, such a document can very often be agreed and given to the jury. Such a course can only serve to make the jury's task easier. A typical example would be a brief chronology of events which have been spoken to by various witnesses and which relate to a particular part of the case.

12. Written Directions of Law Presented by the Judge in His Summing-up

12.1 In recent years there has been a marked increase in the practice of judges reducing their directions of law to writing, and/or giving the jury a written list of the questions they will need to answer in order to reach their verdicts.

12.2 This practice is entirely beneficial, and to be encouraged. It is amazing how often, when the judge has given his directions orally, the jury subsequently come back with a question asking for clarification. Sometimes the question shows that they have not really grasped the essential point at all. This is not necessarily a reflection on the clarity of the judge's oral directions, or on the jury's concentration or intelligence: it is sometimes extremely difficult to take in, and subsequently to remember accurately, the precise effect of what you are told orally about something which may be quite unfamiliar to you.

Appendix: Declarations of Co-conspirators

1. In this note

'Archbold' means the current (1993–4) edition of Archbold's Criminal Pleading, Evidence and Practice;

'a conspiracy case' means a case in which a defendant is on trial for an offence of conspiracy (whether or not his alleged co-conspirators are being tried with him); and

'a joint venture case' means a case in which a defendant is on trial for a substantive offence alleged to have been committed by some other person or persons in pursuance of a conspiracy to which the defendant is alleged to have been a party (again, whether or not his alleged co-conspirators are being tried with him).

The Rule as Stated in the Textbooks

2. In Archbold there is a chapter on the offence of conspiracy. Within that chapter there is a section headed 'Proving the Conspiracy'. Within that section the following statement appears (at paragraph 33–48):

> 'the acts and declarations of any of the conspirators in furtherance of the common design may be given in evidence against any other conspirator.'

Similar formulations of this rule appear in the other leading text-books.

3. The rule itself appears, at first sight, straightforward. Yet its application has caused untold difficulties for practitioners over the years. Before we look at the main areas which have caused these difficulties, it may be helpful to dispose of 2 points which are fairly non-contentious.

4. They are stated as follows in para. 33–48 of Archbold, and in similar terms in the other books:

(A) The rule appears whenever 'the charge is one of a crime committed in pursuance of a conspiracy, whether the indictment contains a count for conspiracy or not' (in other words it applies to conspiracy cases and joint venture cases alike); and

(B) 'It makes no difference to the admissibility of the act or declaration against the defendant whether the co-conspirator be indicted or not, or tried or not'.

5. It would seem that both these propositions must clearly be correct. There is no logical distinction between a conspiracy case and a joint venture case which would justify applying different admissibility rules to them; and the admissibility of a piece of evidence against a particular defendant should surely not depend on the fortuitous distinction between a case where he is tried with others and a case where (perhaps because the others have absconded or pleaded guilty) he is tried on his own.

6. The 2 principal problems which the rule has caused in practice may be identified as follows:

(A) What kind of 'declarations' does it cover? In particular, does it operate so as to make admissible against an alleged conspirator statements which would otherwise be inadmissible under the hearsay rule?

(B) In paragraph 33–50 of Archbold, still in the section headed 'Proving the Conspiracy', it is stated that 'Before the evidence given of the acts or declarations of one co-conspirator may be said to be evidence against the other alleged conspirators, the existence of the conspiracy must be proved, and also the fact that the parties were members of the same conspiracy, and that the act in question was done in furtherance of the common design.'

Is this really so in all cases? If it is, it entirely negatives any value which the rule might have in proving the existence of criminal conspiracies. It is also, it might be thought, somewhat illogical: if you have already proved the conspiracy and the defendant's participation in it, you do not need to prove the acts or declarations of other conspirators—they are irrelevant to the defendant's guilt.

7. The purpose of this note is to suggest that solutions to these and other problems associated with the rule may be found by going back to first principles. The most basic principle of all in the law of evidence may be thought to be that which says that, unless it is excluded by some exclusionary rule such as the hearsay rule, a piece of evidence is always admissible if, but only if, it is logically relevant as tending to prove or disprove some fact or matter which is in issue in the proceedings in question.

8. In this connection it may be pertinent to observe at this stage that, although the rule under consideration applies equally to conspiracy and joint venture cases, the issues in a conspiracy case will be different from those in a joint venture case. In a con-

spiracy case all that has to be proved is that the defendant entered into the unlawful agreement alleged: in a joint venture case the prosecution must establish not only that the defendant was a party to an agreement or plan to commit the substantive offence alleged, but also that that offence was actually committed in pursuance of the plan to which he was a party.

'Hearsay Declarations' of Co-conspirators

9. Practitioners are not always as careful as they should be in identifying what is, and what is not, a hearsay declaration. In the context of a criminal trial a hearsay declaration may be defined as a statement of fact, made by some person other than (a) the defendant himself or (b) someone authorized by him to make the statement on his behalf, which is sought to be proved as evidence of the truth of the facts stated in it.

10. A hearsay declaration is thus to be distinguished from

(A) a declaration which is not a statement of fact at all (e.g. a request or instruction to someone to do something); or

(B) a statement of fact which is sought to be proved not as evidence of the truth of the facts stated in it but as evidence of the fact that that particular statement was in fact made by that particular person on that particular occasion.

11. Non-hearsay declarations by persons other than the defendant are very often inadmissible in criminal trials—not because of the hearsay rule but because they are simply irrelevant to any issue arising between the Crown and the defendant. Where they are relevant to such an issue, however, they are generally admissible. Non-hearsay declarations of (alleged) co-conspirators are discussed later in this note.

12. Hearsay declarations are of course normally rendered inadmissible by the hearsay rule. The hearsay rule proceeds on the basis that, apart from out of court statements made by or on behalf of the defendant which may be regarded as admissions against his interests, statements of fact are only sufficiently reliable to be acted upon by the jury if they are made in the witness box in front of the jury, where they are (a) made under oath or affirmation (b) made openly and in public and free from external pressures, and (c) subject to being tested in cross-examination by the opposing party.

13. The rule against hearsay evidence is deeply embedded in English law. In recent years it has to some extent come under attack as being unduly restrictive: in particular, as posing unnecessary and unreasonable obstacles to the proof of matters which are unlikely to be contentious but which, if they are to be strictly proved by evidence not caught by the hearsay rule, will require the laborious and sometimes impossible task of tracing and obtaining witness statements from a very large number of witnesses. Hence various statutory encroachments of the rule, notably by sections 23 and 24 of the Criminal Justice Act 1988.

14. One situation, however, in which no-one has seriously doubted the validity and importance of the hearsay rule is that in which some assertion or admission of fact has been made by one of 2 or more persons alleged to have been involved together in a criminal venture. Such assertions or admissions are rightly regarded as potentially unreliable as against anyone other than the maker of them, and therefore as being inadmissible against anyone else.

[An exception to this general proposition is to be found where a statement is made by an accomplice in the presence of the defendant, and the defendant either (a) expressly or impliedly adopts it or (b) fails to challenge it in circumstances where it is reasonable to suppose he would have done so if it was not true. In these situations, which arise very rarely in practice, it is the defendant's adoption or non-denial which is the real evidence against him.]

15. It is suggested that there is an exception to the hearsay rule in conspiracy and joint venture cases where it is sought to prove against A (one of the alleged conspirators) some statement of fact made by B (one of his alleged co-conspirators) 'in furtherance of the common design'. This immediately begs the question: when may a statement be said to be made in furtherance of the common design?

16. In its narrowest sense that expression would cover only a situation where the making of a particular statement of fact was part of the course of conduct which the alleged conspirators agreed to carry out—or, at the very least, where it must have been within their contemplation that one of them would make that particular statement while carrying out that course of conduct.

17. In such a situation, however, there is no need for a special exception to the hearsay rule. The statement can properly be regarded as having been made by B with A's authority, and is admissible on that basis without breaching the hearsay rule.

18. It must of course be the case that, in order to lay the foundation for admissibility on this basis, the prosecution must first prove (a) the existence of an agreement to carry out a particular course of conduct (b) that the defendant was a party to that agreement and (c) that the agreed course of conduct included or

contemplated the making of that particular statement. It is not likely to happen very often in practice that statements of fact are admitted in evidence on this basis to prove the truth of their contents. This is in part because of the difficulty likely to be encountered in laying the necessary foundation; and in part because the prosecution will usually be challenging (as opposed to relying on) the truthfulness of statements of fact made by those who are alleged to have been criminal conspirators.

19. So far we have looked at the narrowest sense of the expression 'in furtherance of the common design'. In a somewhat wider sense B might be said to have made a statement in furtherance of the common design if he happens to have made it on an occasion when he was doing something to further that design (even if there is no evidence that A was aware of, let alone that he had agreed to, the making of that statement by B).

20. There would appear to be no basis in principle or logic for making such a statement admissible against A. If the general rule is that assertions or admissions of fact by one (alleged) criminal are too unreliable to be admissible against his (alleged) accomplices, it is to say the least a curious proposition that a particular statement may become reliable and admissible merely because B happens to make it while he is actually engaged in a criminal enterprise in which he and A are alleged to have participated.

21. The suggestion that there is a rule making 'hearsay' declarations of co-conspirators admissible outside the narrow circumstances referred to in paragraph 16 above appears largely to be based on the old case of *R* v. *Blake and Tye* (1844) 6 QB 126 which is regularly cited in the text-books as the leading case on the topic.

22. It was alleged that Blake and Tye had conspired to defraud the Crown of the duty on certain imported goods, Tye being the importer's agent and Blake being a landing waiter at the Custom House. It was alleged that they understated the quantity of goods imported. Tye had entered what the Crown alleged was the true quantity in his day book, and charged his principal for the duty on the quantity recorded there.

23. Tye's day book entry was admitted in evidence against Blake, who was convicted and applied for a new trial. One of his grounds was that the day book entry (which was clearly a 'hearsay' statement by Tye as to the quantity of goods actually imported) was not admissible against him. This ground did not actually have to be decided by the Court of Queen's Bench, which allowed his application on another ground and did not require argument from his counsel on the day book point.

24. In these circumstances the court's obiter observations to the effect that the day book entry was admissible evidence against Blake are, one would have thought, of doubtful value. It is hard to justify the court's observations given that (a) the Crown conceded that the day book could not be evidence against Blake unless and until a conspiracy was proved and (b) one looks in vain in the report for any other admissible evidence of the conspiracy.

25. The Crown's case was that Blake and Tye had agreed to split the difference between the amount of duty charged by Tye to his principal (on the larger quantity of goods recorded in the day book) and the amount of duty paid over to the Revenue (on the smaller quantity declared). If there had been any admissible evidence of such an agreement (which there was not: the Crown had relied on one of Tye's cheque counterfoils, but the court correctly held this to be inadmissible against Blake), the day book entry could have been regarded as admissible against Blake on the narrow basis referred to in paragraphs 16–18 above: the recording of the correct quantity in the day book would have been part of the course of conduct agreed to or contemplated by Blake.

26. In the circumstances it may be concluded that *R* v. *Blake and Tye*, despite its antiquity, is not a satisfactory authority for the existence of an exception to the hearsay rule in conspiracy and joint venture cases; and that the suggested exception is not justified by principle or logic.

'Non-hearsay Declarations' of Co-conspirators

27. Just as in the case of hearsay declarations, so in the case of non-hearsay declarations there is no need for any special rule relating to conspiracy and joint venture cases. One can simply apply ordinary principles. Non-hearsay declarations by (alleged) co-conspirators, like similar declarations by anyone else, should be admissible if, but only if, they tend logically to prove or disprove some fact or matter which is in issue in the proceedings in question.

28. In a conspiracy case the principal issue will be whether the defendant entered into the alleged unlawful agreement with his alleged co-conspirators. The existence of the agreement, and the identities of the parties to it, generally have to be inferred from evidence of things said and done by the parties in carrying it into effect. The following example may serve to illustrate how the (non-hearsay) declarations not only of the defendant but also of his co-conspirators may be highly relevant evidence to prove the conspiracy.

29. Suppose that defendant A tells a well-known philanthropist (X) that A's daughter B is seriously ill and can only be saved by expensive medical treat-

ment offered by Dr C: could X assist with the cost? X visits B who gives a convincing display of serious symptoms, and tells him all about the marvellous Dr C and his treatment. X then visits C at an address in Harley Street, and C gives him a lot of information about the treatment and about B's prospects of recovery. X declines to come up with the money.

30. It is later proved that C was not a doctor, and there was nothing wrong with B. It is not difficult to infer that A, B and C conspired together to obtain money from X by deception. Proof of the acts and declarations of all three is clearly admissible against each of them (whether they are tried together or not) to prove the conspiracy.

31. In this type of situation there is no reason why it should be necessary to prove the existence of the conspiracy before the declarations of the others can be used as evidence against any particular defendant. The declarations of all three are logically probative of the existence of the conspiracy, and are sufficient to prove it even if there is no other evidence.

32. The facts of this example may be adjusted slightly to illustrate a joint venture case (as opposed to a conspiracy case). Suppose that A himself has no contact with X, but in his possession is found a piece of paper (proved to be in his handwriting) setting out the false story to be told by B and C to X. B and C do in fact see X and tell him the false story. X swallows the story, and pays out £100,000 for C's 'medical fees'. B and C plead guilty to obtaining the money from X by deception. A is tried alone on the same charge.

33. B's and C's statements to X are relevant and admissible evidence, taken in conjunction with the piece of paper in A's handwriting, to prove the conspiracy between the 3 of them (even if there is no other evidence of it). They are also relevant and admissible evidence on the other main issue in the case, namely whether the substantive offence of obtaining by deception was committed in pursuance of the conspiracy to which A was a party. Unless A has a very good explanation, he is likely to be convicted.

Conclusions

34. The following conclusions may perhaps be drawn from the above discussion:

(A) The proposition that 'the acts and declarations of any of the conspirators in furtherance of the common design may be given in evidence against any other conspirator' does not result from some special rule applicable only to conspiracy and joint venture cases, but from the application to such cases of familiar general principles.

(B) The hearsay rule applies to statements of fact made by co-conspirators just as it applies to such statements by other persons.

(C) As a general rule, therefore, a statement of fact by a co-conspirator cannot be used to prove, as against the defendant, the truth of the matters stated by the co-conspirator.

(D) Such a statement can only be used as such evidence if the prosecution first prove (a) the existence of an agreement to carry out a particular course of conduct (b) that the defendant was a party to that agreement and (c) that the making of the statement in question was part of the agreed course of conduct, or at the very least that the parties must have contemplated that such a statement would be made in carrying out the agreed course of conduct. In that event the statement can be regarded as having been made with the defendant's authority, and does not therefore infringe the hearsay rule.

(E) Non-hearsay declarations of co-conspirators are admissible if they are relevant to an issue between the Crown and the defendant. They may be so relevant if they tend to prove the existence of the conspiracy. There is no rule that the conspiracy must be proved before such declarations are admissible. On the contrary, it is common practice for the existence of the conspiracy to be inferred from the declarations of the various conspirators.

7. The Right to Silence in Cases of Serious Fraud

A. T. H. SMITH

I The Scope of this Paper

IF and when the proposals in clauses 34 to 37 of the Criminal Justice and Public Order Bill 1994 become law,[1] the so-called right to silence will be diminished—its critics say seriously undermined.[2] But the proposals are as nothing to what has already happened in the context of what might loosely be called 'serious fraud', where the legislature[3] and the judiciary[4] have, in combination, made a striking series of assaults on the principle,[5] with the result that the right (and the allied privilege against self-incrimination) have been diminished to vanishing point. The extent and desirability of these developments is the subject of this paper. How far they can survive challenge in the European Court of Human Rights in the light of the articulation of a right to silence in *Funke* v. *France*[6] (where it has been held that Article 6(1) of the European Convention on Fundamental Human Rights and Freedoms implies the right to silence as part of the right to a fair trial, and that French Customs and Excise law requiring the production of self-incriminating documents was in breach of the European Convention) is also a subject of contemporary concern,[7] and it is the second topic addressed in this paper.[8]

II English Law[9] outlined

In addition to ordinary police investigations leading to the normal criminal trial, at least three further processes may be used to investigate what has happened when a company has collapsed or when particular sorts of fraud are suspected. These investigations may well unearth the criminal culpability of those implicated in the collapse. In all three of these investigative processes, the subject commits a criminal offence if he fails to attend without reasonable excuse, fails to produce documents as required or fails to answer questions put to him at the resultant interview. The important question for criminal lawyers in all of this is whether the person subject to the questioning can assert that, if he answers the questions, he will be putting his neck in the noose, and wishes therefore to avail himself of the refuge afforded by the privilege against self-incrimination. That question has been the subject of a number of recent cases, and the short answer is that he cannot; the privilege has more or less disappeared in cases of serious fraud.

Three levels of immunity

It may be helpful at the outset to identify three theoretically different positions governing the obligation to comply with investigating authorities that can be discerned in the current law:

[1] The references are to the Bill as brought from the House of Lords and ordered to be printed 12th July, 1994.

[2] It should perhaps be mentioned that this mooted change in the law was introduced in the face of the recommendation of the Royal Commission on Criminal Justice, which expressly rejected change (1993) Cm 2263, Chapter Four. See R. Ferguson Q.C., Chairman of the Criminal Bar Association, *The Times* 17 May, 1994; JUSTICE, 'The Right to Silence Debate: the Northern Ireland Experience' (1994); A. A. Zuckerman, 'The Inevitable Demise of the Right to Silence' (1994) 144 new Law Jo. 1104.

[3] The legislative provisions are outlined in the following section.

[4] J. Jackson, 'The Right of Silence: Judicial Responses to Parliamentary Encroachment' (1994) 57 M.L.R. 270. See also G. McCormack, 'Self-Incrimination in the Corporate Context' (1993) J.B.L. 425; 'judicial affirmations of the importance of the privilege . . . are often coupled with a willingness to infer statutory abrogation of the right from a not often clear legislative context'; at p. 442.

[5] I have used the terminology of rights, principles and privileges somewhat promiscuously throughout this paper; there is very little agreement about the proper terminology, which would itself be the subject of study.

[6] Eur. Court of H.R. Judgment of 25 February 1993, Series A, Vol 256A. Also reported at (1993) 16 E.H.R.R. 297.

[7] Even as the paper was being revised in late September 1994, the European Commission of Human Rights delivered judgment in the case of *Saunders* v. *U.K.* (Application No 19187/91) holding by a majority of 14 votes to 1 that the 'use at the applicant's trial of incriminating evidence obtained from him under compulsory powers was oppressive and substantially impaired his ability to defend himself against the criminal charges facing him. He was therefore deprived of a fair hearing within the meaning of Article 6, para 1 of the Convention' (at para 76). It has not been possible to extend this paper to take full account of the implications of this finding, but they are plainly considerable.

[8] The paper is to some extent speculative, and (since it is to be the subject of discussion) deliberately provocative, in places.

[9] I have no detailed knowledge of the Scottish and Northern Irish positions, and have therefore omitted them from my consideration. For a general overview of the law regulating this area, see D. Kirk and A. A. J. Woodcock, *Serious Fraud: Investigation and Trial* (1992).

1. The classic position is that the defendant has a complete claim to immunity from self-incrimination; he can decline to co-operate with the authorities entirely without repercussions in the form of prosecutorial or (within limits) judicial comment.[10] His immunity extends to all stages of the proceedings.
2. The privilege goes completely, the interviewee must answer under pain of penalty and the answers may be used against the interviewee in subsequent legal proceedings; this seems to be the regime adopted by the Insolvency Act 1986 in respect of both personal insolvencies and corporate failures.
3. There is also an intermediate position, whereby various immunities are offered in return for the divulging of information. Generally, the immunity is that the information compulsorily disclosed cannot be used in a subsequent prosecution. Sometimes, too, legal professional or other privilege continues to apply. To adumbrate: the principal difficulty with partial immunities of this sort would seem to be that manifest wrongdoing goes unpunished, and this, it might be thought, brings the legal system into disrepute.

The three types of inquiry further explored

Three leading cases can serve as a focus for discussion of some of the issues involved; they are but the tip of an iceberg of litigation. In particular, there has been considerable litigation on the question of the extent to which the section 2 powers of the Serious Fraud Office can be used to compel the production to the S.F.O. of the answers obtained compulsorily under the other procedures,[11] or by liquidators to compel the production to them of material compulsorily obtained by the S.F.O. as part of its section 2 (or other) investigation.[12]

1. Inquiries under the Companies Act 1985

A company may be the subject of a D.T.I. Investigation under section 432(2) of the Companies Act 1985, using specially appointed Inspectors; in addition, pursuant to section 447, the Department may require the books and papers of a company. Under sections 177 and 178 of the Financial Services Act 1986, the D.T.I. may appoint inspectors to investigate suspected cases of insider dealing.

In *Re London United Investments*,[13] the Secretary of State had appointed inspectors under the Companies Act 1985, s. 432(2), to investigate the affairs of L.U.I. and in particular the circumstances in which some $US46 million deductions had been made from reinsurance premiums. The inspectors sent W a list of questions which W refused to answer, insisting on his common law privilege against self-incrimination. The inspectors applied to the Companies Court 'for an inquiry into the refusal' to answer questions, and the Court of Appeal held that no such privilege was available. Parliament had enacted the recent legislation intending that a person possessing relevant information would be under a duty to comply with the investigating authorities, and the privilege had been impliedly removed. A refusal to answer questions was, therefore, declared to be unjustified.

2. Section 2 Inquiries

A suspected fraudster may be the subject of a 'section 2 notice', issued by the Serious Fraud Office under the Criminal Justice Act 1987, requiring him to attend and answer questions about the 'affairs of the person under investigation'. This power emanates from the Roskill Report on the investigation and conduct of fraud trials,[14] which recommended the establishment of a new system for the investigation and prosecution of serious fraud. The outcome was the establishment of a Serious Fraud Office, which has been endowed with considerable powers.[15] In particular, section 2 of the Criminal Justice Act 1987 provides as follows:

'2(1) The powers of the Director under this section shall be exercisable, but only for the purposes of an investigation under section 1 above, in any case in which it appears to him that there is good reason to do so for the purpose of investigating the affairs of any person'.
(2) The Director may by notice in writing require the person whose affairs are to be investigated ("the person under investigation)" or any other person whom he has reason to believe has relevant information to attend before the Director at a specified time and place and answer any questions or otherwise furnish information with respect to any matter relevant to the investigation.'

In addition to this power, the Director may require the production of documents (subsection (3)) from which copies may be taken and of which he may require an explanation. If he believes that a person has failed to produce the documents, he may obtain

[10] For the most recent decision describing the judge's powers of comment, see *Martinez-Tobon* [1994] 1 W.L.R. 388.

[11] See in particular the litigation reported as *Re Arrows Ltd (No 4)* [1993] Ch. 452; *Re Headington Investment Ltd ibid.* and *Re Bishopsgate Investment Management Ltd ibid.* Discussed by P. Paulden, 'Corporate Fraud: Civil Disclosures in Criminal Proceedings' (1994) 57 M.L.R. 280. The cases have now been heard in the House of Lords; *Hamilton and Another* v. *Naviede and the Director of the Serious Fraud Office* [1994] 3 W.L.R. 656.

[12] *Morris* v. *Director of the S.F.O.* [1993] Ch. 372.

[13] [1992] Ch. 578, 2 All E.R. 842.

[14] *Fraud Trials Committee Report* (1985).

[15] See Kirk and Woodcock, above, n. 9.

a search warrant. Legal professional privilege obtains (subsection 9) and banker's confidence must be respected although this can be overridden on the say-so of the Director (subsection 10). Falsifying or destroying (etc) documents known to be required by the S.F.O. is a particularly serious offence, carrying up to 7 years' imprisonment.[16] The only relief for the person subject to the investigation is that the answers given cannot, as a general rule, be used for purposes other than the investigation,[17] and in particular they cannot be use in subsequent criminal proceedings except

'(a) on a prosecution for an offence under subsection 14 (false statements); or
(b) on a prosecution for some other offence where in giving evidence he makes a statement inconsistent with it'.

It may well be important to distinguish between the power to demand answers to questions under s. 2, and the power to call for the production of documents, whose use is not protected from subsequent criminal prosecutions.

In *R* v. *Director of Serious Fraud Office, ex p. Smith*,[18] the Serious Fraud Office had given notice of its intention to use its section 2 powers of question even after the defendant had been charged. On an application for judicial review of the section 2 notice, the Divisional Court ruled that this was improper, being in effect in breach of the PACE Code of Practice for the Detention, Treatment and Questioning of Suspects, (Code C, para 16(5)), which forbids questioning after charge unless the questions are necessary for preventing or minimising harm or loss to the public. Taking an altogether more robust approach, the House of Lords held that the powers of question under section 2 did not come to an end with charge, and the person under question need not be cautioned in the traditional terms, so that the privilege against self-incrimination had no application in such circumstances. Parliament, so it was said, had clearly intended to establish an inquisitorial regime in relation to serious or complex fraud. This would be frustrated if the subject of the questioning were entitled not to answer.

What is really novel about *Smith* is the decision that questioning could be continued even after charge, when by definition there must have been enough evidence for the prosecutor to believe that he had a chance of conviction. Counsel for the applicant had posed some difficult and not entirely hypothetical questions: at what point (if any) must the questioning stop? When court proceedings have actually begun? After that, even? Their Lordships gave no satisfactory answers to these questions, dismissing the possibilities canvassed by counsel as 'unreal'. The Director of the Serious Fraud Office would never seek to use her powers as late in the proceedings as counsel's questions envisaged, but if s/he did, s/he could be constrained by judicial review or the discretion of a trial judge to prevent unfairness to an accused. Counsel's *reductio ad absurdum* was no ground for reading in to the Act a limitation that was not expressly there. Viewed purely as an exercise in statutory interpretation, this does not wholly satisfy. Parliament has not addressed the question of the privilege against self-incrimination in the context, but presumably, it legislated against a well-known common law background. It is not a matter of 'reading in' words to the statute, any more than the courts need to read in the principles of natural justice when they hold that the exercise of statutory discretion is subject to those principles.

As it is, the judgment in *Smith* leaves us with the uncomfortably difficult question: what principles are there to guide the courts in the exercise of this discretion when Parliament has, apparently, established an inquisitorial regime and by implication decided that there is no unfairness in asking a person questions answers to which might incriminate him? Are there, for example, identifiable public purposes similar to those specified in para 16(5) of the PACE Code (minimising harm or loss to the public) that might apply in the context of serious and complex fraud? Are they to be found, perhaps, at least in part in the complicated and inaccessible jurisprudence of the European Convention?

3. *Insolvencies*

If insolvency proceedings are begun, the potential bankrupt may be the subject of questioning by a court appointed 'office holder', in effect the company liquidator or Official Receiver. The impact of this regime became apparent in *Bishopsgate Investment Management (in provisional liquidation)* v.

[16] Section 2(16)(17).

[17] They could not be made available, for example, for the purposes of civil litigation; *Marcel* v. *Commissioner of Police of the Metropolis* [1992] Ch. 225.

[18] [1993] A.C. 1, [1992] 3 W.L.R. 66. For trenchant criticism, see Archbold (1993) para. 15–354 where it is argued that Parliament could not have meant what the House of Lords said that it meant, and that the provisions of the Act were supposed to apply to suspects as well as to persons charged. Citing *Hansard*, H.L. vol 487, col 578. Since *Pepper* v. *Hart* [1993] A.C. 593, it is clear that the remarks are relevant to the construction of the statue. Since Article 6(1) affords protection to suspects as well as to persons formally charged, this aspect of th decisions is arguably open to challenge in the European Court, in the light of the *Funke* v. *France*, Eur. Court of H.R. Judgment of 25 February 1993, Series A, Vol 256A. decision, as to which see below, n. 56.

Maxwell,[19] where the question was whether or not the liquidators of a company conducting a compulsory examination under sections 235 and 236 of the Insolvency Act 1986 could insist on having answers to their questions about the collapse of Bishopsgate.[20] In an unreported judgment (*Barlow Clowes Gilt Managers ltd)*,[21] Ferris J. had come to the conclusion that the privilege was available, but Vinelott J. in *In re Jeffrey S. Levitt Ltd*[22] thought otherwise. The Court of Appeal in *Bishopsgate* agreed with Vinelott J. and held that, on their true construction, sections 235 and 236 of the 1986 Insolvency Act were enacted specifically to enable the office-holders of a company to perform their functions in an effective and expeditious manner by giving them greatly extended investigative powers and by expressly placing insolvents under a duty to assist the office-holders. Accordingly, a person being examined under the sections was not entitled to rely on the privilege against self-incrimination in refusing to answer questions put to him by the office-holders of the company under investigation since to allow otherwise would be to defeat the purpose of the sections. The court drew upon upon the fact that it would be illogical to allow company directors to remain silent when individual insolvents were plainly not allowed to remain silent on a private examination under section 366.

It has long been the case that the bankrupt in the course of his compulsory examination can be required under pain of penalty to give answers, which are admissible against him in a subsequent prosecution; *Scott*;[23] *Re Atherton*.[24] Few appreciated that, with the changes effected by the Insolvency Act 1985 (now the Insolvency Act 1986), the same sort of regime was to be applied to the directors of failed companies. The effect of the *Bishopsgate* decision is to confirm that this is indeed what has happened. A knock-on effect of this is illustrated in *Kansal*,[25] where it was held that answers compulsorily extracted in the insolvency process can be used against the defendant on a prosecution for both Theft Act and non-Theft Act offences, neither being protected by the partial immunity conferred by section 31 of the Theft Act 1968.[26]

An historical point should, perhaps, be made. When the leading cases were decided in the middle of the nineteenth century, imprisonment for debt was still a feature of our legal system.[27] The purpose of the Bankruptcy proceedings was to enable the debtor to clear himself from debt and at the same time escape the rigours of the debtors prison. As a quid pro quo for this, it was not unreasonable for the law to require complete candour from the bankrupt about his affairs. Nor was it unreasonably oppressive to use evidence of criminal wrongdoing compulsorily extracted from him. To allow the dishonest debtor to escape imprisonment on both counts would, indeed, be overindulgent. Perhaps the same reasoning can be carried over into the corporate insolvency arena. The company director is seeking the benefits of the corporate structure, and it is not unreasonable to refuse to allow him to hide behind this veil when the company fails, especially when it may have done so as a result of his dishonesty.

4. *Miscellaneous Inquiries*

In addition to the inquiries which have been slightly further explored in this paper, the investigation is also available to prosecution and detection agencies under the Banking Act 1987, ss. 41–44,[28] The Insurance Companies Act 1982, s. 44, and the Financial Services Act 1987, ss. 94, 105, 177–178.[29] Such pro-

[19] [1993] Ch. 1. Discussed by B. Bix and A. Tomins, 'The sounds of silence: a duty to incriminate oneself?' [1992] P.L. 363.

[20] It might be said that the question whether the liquidators can insist on answers to questions from persons other than the prospective insolvent has also generated a considerable amount of litigation, and that the privilege against self incrimination forms an important strand in that litigation. See generally M. Stallworthy, 'Inquiries into Company Dealings under Section 236 of the Insolvency Act 1986: Balancing Conflicting Interests' [1993] 54 J.I.B.L. 139.

[21] 31 July, 1990.

[22] [1992] Ch. 475.

[23] (1856) Dears & B. 47, 169 E.R. 909.

[24] [1912] 2 K.B. 251.

[25] [1992] 3 All E.R. 844.

[26] Section 31(1) provides that 'A person shall not be excused, by reason that to do so might incriminate that person or the wife or husband of that person of an offence under the Act

(a) from answering any question put to that person in proceedings for the recovery or administration of any property, for the execution of any trust or for an account of any property or dealings with property; or

(b) from complying with any order made in any such proceedings;

but no statement or admission made by a person in answering a question put or complying with an order made as aforesaid shall, in proceedings for an offence under this Act, be admissible in evidence against that person or (unless they were married after the making of the statement or admission) against the wife or husband of that person).'

[27] Imprisonment for debt, it will be recalled, was abolished by the Debtors Act 1869.

[28] In *Bank of England* v. *Reilly* [1992] Ch. 475, the Court of Appeal held that a person must answer questions put to him under s. 42 of the Banking Act even if the answers might incriminate him.

[29] Other provisions, although not in the serious fraud area include the Representation of the People Act 1983, s. 141(2); Explosive Substances Act 1883, s. 6(2); Official Secrets Act 1920, section 6; Drug Trafficking Offences Act 1986, s. 24(1); Financial Services Act 1986, s. 105(10); Children Act 1989, s. 98; Merchant Shipping Act 1894, s. 728, 1979 s. 27(1)(i); s. 27(7).

visions are, in other words, a systemic part of the English system.[30]

The policy behind abrogating the principle

It is clear that the privilege against self-incrimination, and the associated privileges protecting privacy are almost completely obliterated by the legislation of the kind just considered. What policy considerations might have prompted Parliament to make such inroads? The principal argument is that if the interviewee were to be permitted to maintain his silence, the legislation would not achieve its purpose.

The point was well put by Scott J. in the *L.U.I.*[31] decision:

'. . . perhaps the most important of all, I am of the opinion that if the privilege against self-incrimination remained, the statutory purpose of many, if not most, of the section 432 investigations by inspectors would be frustrated. It is common to find inspectors appointed under section 432 where fraudulent or dishonest conduct in relation to a company's affairs appears to have taken place. Parliament must be taken to have been aware of this at least in 1985, when the current Act was enacted and probably in 1948 as well. The circumstances justifying the appointment of inspectors often involve suspicion that persons in management have been involved in suspected misfeasances. These are the persons who will be questioned by the inspectors in their endeavours to find out what has happened. If the witnesses can simply refuse to answer, pleading the privilege against self-incrimination, the inquiries will, I think, in many cases be wholly frustrated.

It is a regrettable feature of commercial and corporate fraud in these modern times that facilities are available for sophisticated fraudsters to prevent the trail leading to the unravelling of the fraud from being followed up. The secrecy provisions of some countries' corporate and banking laws operate to this effect. Nominee shareholdings in offshore companies do so as well. There is often no alternative if frauds and dishonest stratagems are to be laid bare but to demand answers from those who are in a position to give them. This, in my opinion, is at least part of the statutory policy behind Part XIV of the Companies Act 1985.'[32]

These are, when held up to the light, fairly crudely utilitarian reasons suggesting that the end justifies the means used to achieve them, irrespective of considerations of principle that might interpose. Considerations of privacy and procedural due process are swept aside by the need to make a legislative framework operate.

Cole J. in the *Spedly* decision[33] puts the point as follows:

'In my view, the public interest requires that those receiving moneys of the public, or administering companies in which the public invest, should be obliged to explain transactions and conduct related to such moneys and business transactions. I see no public interest in such persons being able to escape either civil or criminal responsibility, if such exists, because parties injured by the conduct of such persons, or prosecuting authorities on behalf of such persons, is known only to such persons. The law, at present, protects the interests of the civil and criminal wrong-doers. It should protect the interests of the investing public.'

According to this view, then, it is all a matter of policy and the perceived importance of stamping out the incidence of serious fraud. But the question can be asked whether the achievement of such objectives is more important than the need to ensure that murderers, rapists and robbers receive their just desserts.[34] That is, Parliament can be assumed to be in favour of reducing the incidence of all serious crime. What is it about fraud, in particular, that justifies sweeping aside the protections that are routinely afforded, in the right to silence, to persons accused of other and in many ways even more serious offences? The difference is, perhaps, that evidence of fraud is more diffuse, indirect and difficult to obtain. As the Royal Commission on Criminal Justice put the point, 'These powers have operated in the interests of justice without unfairness, we believe, to those being questioned, who are persons in responsible positions with ready access to legal advice, charged with sophisticated offences which might otherwise go not merely unpunished but undetected.'[35]

In *Bishopsgate*, the court stressed the public purposes of the examination (whether it was a public or a private examination) and was insistent upon the public interest element in insolvency proceedings. Dillon L.J. cites with approval the reference by Lord

[30] The best analysis of this question of which I am aware is J. D. Heydon, 'Statutory Restrictions on the Privilege against Self-Incrimination' (1971) 87 L.Q.R. 214.

[31] Unreported judgment. The appeal is reported at [1992] Ch. 578.

[32] [1992] B.C.L.C. at page 113–4.

[33] *Spedley Securities Ltd (in liquidation)* v. *Bond Brewing Investments Pty Ltd and Another* (1991) 9 A.C.L.C. 522.

[34] See the remarks of the practitioner (it was David Kirk) quoted below, at n. 43.

[35] *Report*, Chapter Four, para 30. In a footnote the Commission makes reference to the various powers possessed by D.T.I. Inspectors and those operating the Financial Services Act 1986, the Insolvency Act 1986, the Building Societies Act 1986, the Banking Act 1987 and the Friendly Societies Act 1992, noting also that the answers may be used in later criminal proceedings. The Commission made no recommendations in the area. Whether those powers can survive the decisions in *Funke* is considered below p. 83. The decision of the European Commission in *Saunders* (above n. 7) must make their survival in present form highly problematic, especially in that the evidence obtained by compulsion is usable in a subsequent prosecution.

Hanworth M.R. in *Re Paget*,[36] to 'a side of the bankruptcy law which we are constantly affirming in the Court, where it has been necessary over and over again to point out that in matters of bankruptcy it is not merely the creditors who have their rights, but it is also the public themselves who have interests to be safeguarded.'

The implication of the observation is that, so important is the public interest in being protected from fraud that the privilege must give way to it. This introduces a familiar theme in English rights jurisprudence, which is that rights are a matter of balancing conflicting interests, often the interests of an individual against the rights of 'society'. Whether or not this approach is compatible with a European approach to rights, which tends to see at least some rights as non derogable (the right not to be tortured, for instance), and others as having a special weight remains for discussion.[37]

A paradox

Insofar as the purposes of the D.T.I. inquiry under the Companies Act might include general questions about the mismanagement of the company and the whereabouts of any money that has gone missing and which should be made available to creditors, it could be argued that the lack of a privilege against self-incrimination will actually hinder the accomplishment of these objectives. In *Pike*[38] Wright J. expressed the view that 'it might be right to alter the law in this respect for two reasons. First, there is a certain unfairness in using against a man a compulsory admission by him; and, secondly, if a man knows that it can be used against him there is some danger that he will not make full admissions in his statement,' and the same might equally be said of the insolvency inquiry. By contrast, the whole purpose of the section 2 inquiry is that of establishing criminal liability, if any. Yet, curiously, the statements thus obtained cannot be used in a subsequent prosecution, or at least can only be used in limited circumstances.[39] The difference between the two inquiries might not be as sharp as this dichotomy suggests, since the answers might reveal the existence of bank accounts or other incriminating evidence that can be employed in the course of the prosecution. We appear to have no 'fruit of the tree' jurisprudence of the kind developed in America[40] that would preclude the prosecutor from using evidence unearthed in this way.

Even so, it looks odd, to say the least, that D.T.I. answers are admissible, when the genesis of the enquiry might be (for example) that shareholders are not given enough information, but the answers are not admissible when extracted as part of a fraud investigation. Of course, history and Parliamentary compromise are to blame for this situation. Although there have been representations for section 2 powers to be widened,[41] so that the answer is available in a straightforward way in any prosecution that might result from the section 2 enquiry, these suggestions did not find favour with the Royal Commission on Criminal Justice, which took the view that the limited immunity conferred by section 2 was not making the section unworkable.[42]

Some issues of principle

Whenever the 'right to silence' and the associated privilege against self-incrimination are threatened with abolition or amendment, there is vociferous opposition to change. The Eleventh Report of the Criminal Law Revision Committee was a notable casualty of this reaction; the privilege was an inherent part of our adversarial process and must not be tampered with. In cases that might involve serious fraud, however, the privilege has been eroded to the point of extinction; we have in effect established an inquisitorial regime, and done so with remarkably little public discussion.

Those who represent businessmen in trouble are dismayed by this development; one prominent practitioner in the serious fraud field, for example, writing in *The Times*[43] put the objection thus:

> 'Society strives to be scrupulously fair to murderers and rapists, protecting their rights in a variety of ways. By contrast, for the fraudster, all these safeguards have been partly or wholly swept away, and nobody has raised so much as a whisper of protest.'

Cross on Evidence makes much the same point about the various statutes that take away the privilege against self-incrimination, if in slightly more temperate tones:

> 'The number and effect of these abrogations of the privilege should give pause for thought on the part of anyone who

[36] [1927] 2 Ch. 85, at p. 92.

[37] See below, p. 82 ff.

[38] [1902] 1 K.B. 553.

[39] Criminal Justice Act 1987, s. 2(8).

[40] For an account of this, see Pitter, (1968) 56 Cal. L. Rev. 579.

[41] The then Director of the Serious Fraud Office, Mrs Barbara Mills Q.C. was reported in *The Times*, 12 January 1991 as saying that 'It might be worth considering putting our powers of interview on the same footing as those of the D.T.I. It is inconsistent that we can use transcripts of interviews with potential defendants which the D.T.I. have taken, while we are prohibited from using those we take under section 2.'

[42] *Report* (1993), p. 56, para 29.

[43] (December 3rd. 1990).

regards the privilege as a fundamental principle of English law'.[44]

Even if the case against the abrogation of the principle cannot be made by a crude contrast of the relative treatments of the rapist and the company director, the juxtaposition of the two different types of suspects certainly highlights the fact that they are quite differently treated within the criminal justice system, in a way that calls for justification. Are the differences quite as anomalous as they might at first sight seem to be? Is it true that the protections available to the one have been stripped from the other without any rhyme or reason, or can those differences be articulated and persuasively explained?

What are the safeguards?

One challenge that arises from the passage cited from *The Times* concerns the nature of safeguards for the interviewee. Safeguards against what?[45] If the principal concern is with the reliability of the information extracted, there cannot in all honesty be too much to fear.[46] In the D.T.I. enquiries, there is the safeguard of the seniority of inspectors, usually a Q.C. and an accountant. But whilst this may be true of the major investigations, so far as the section 447 powers are concerned, there is no independent scrutiny of the powers being exercised. The questions and answers are recorded, and in some cases, the proceedings are on oath.[47] Interviewees are generally allowed to have legal advisers present. What the advisers can do, since they cannot counsel silence is another matter. They can, presumably, ask that questions should not be framed in a way that is question-begging or misleading or oppressive. There is no real likelihood of the verballing against which much of the ordinary procedure as outlined in PACE and the relevant Code is the protective shield, at least within the police station.[48] Even so, they may well be giving advice somewhat in the dark, since it has been held that the rules of natural justice do not apply to questioning by D.T.I. inspectors, so that the subject of the questioning need not know of what he is suspected: *Re Pergamon Press Ltd.*[49]

In insolvency, there is (potentially) court supervision. The discretion of the judge to which the House of Lords refers in *Smith*[49a] may be of limited value as a safeguard. Given that Parliament has, apparently, established an inquisitorial regime, how can the discretion be exercised in a way that protects the suspect against questioning?

Some implications of terminating or curtailing the privilege against self-incrimination

For the interviewee who has behaved dishonestly, the options in the absence of a privilege against self incrimination such as the legislation under consideration establishes are these:

1. The subject of the questioning can remain silent—and be convicted for that—one of the defendants in *Seelig*[50] (where it was held that there was no need for the PACE caution when questioning under the Companies Act s. 434) claimed that this might have been his preferred course of action had he been aware that this was an available course of action.[51]
2. The guilty interviewee can tell lies—in which case he runs a risk of being convicted of perjury. But by definition the authorities do not have sufficient alternative evidence of his guilt, and he may well consider that there is a game of cat and mouse worth playing.
3. He could tell the truth and risk conviction for any wrongdoing that he thereby exposes and co-incidentally risk losing any property that he may have salted away.

Perhaps the most important practical implication of this range of unpalatable choices is, however, that the decision to question under a regime such as this is, therefore, potentially the most important decision of all.[52] The dishonest (or possibly even incompetent) director or insolvent is like a fish in a barrel

[44] 7th Ed (1990) at p. 427.

[45] See H. Mainprice, 'Quis Custodiet' (1993) 143 New Law Jo. 22 October; G. Staple, (1993) 143 New Law Jo. 1560, 5 Nov.

[46] This is subject to what is said below about the temptation to tell lies if the subject of the question believes that he has too much to lose by telling the truth.

[47] See the *Investigation Handbook* D.T.I. (1990) describing the procedures to be followed.

[48] Outside the station, questioning remains largely unregulated by the use of technical devices; see [1993] Crim. L.R. 806.

[49] [1971] Ch. 388.

[49a] Above n. 18.

[50] [1991] 4 All E.R. 439, 1 W.L.R. 148.

[51] Instead, he decided to act as his own counsel, thereby exhausting himself to the point where he was driven to consider doing 'something irrevocable', and the trial judge relieved the jury from having to arrive at verdict.

[52] This is perhaps implicit in the grounds of appeal stated in the *Saunders* decision: European Commission of Human Rights, *Saunders* v. *United Kingdom*, 7 December 1993, Application No 19187/91. 'The applicant complains of the use at his trial of incriminating statements obtained from him by D.T.I. Inspectors in exercise of their statutory powers of compulsion. He submits in addition that the prosecuting authorities deliberately delayed the commencement of the police investigation in order that statements incriminating the applicant could be gathered for use in subsequent criminal proceedings. He complains that as a result he was deprived of a fair hearing within the meaning of Article 6 para. 1 of the Convention.' The Commission has now held, by a majority of 14 to 1, that English law is in breach of Article 6.

waiting to be shot. Also implicated at this stage is that the timing of the questioning becomes important. Perhaps there is nothing wrong with these developments, but potentially they have the dangers just described.

III The European Convention

Parliamentary Sovereignty ensures that nothing done by Parliament is legally questionable, and if Parliament has decided to abolish the privilege against self-incrimination, that must (subject to the dictates of European Community law)[53] be an end of it so far as the courts are concerned. But that is not necessarily the end of the matter. One of the points of taking rights seriously is that they may need to be protected against the undermining of *inter alia* the tyranny of democracy and elective dictatorship.[54] Parliament may well have acted in breach of its international obligations in the legislation under discussion. Article 14(3)(g) of the International Covenant on Civil and Political Rights explicitly guarantees a person the right 'not to be compelled to testify against himself or to confess guilt.'[55] Parliament's recent handiwork appears to require the serious fraud suspect to do just that, and the wisdom of its doing so remains open to question and debate.

Although there is nothing specific on the privilege in the European Convention on Human Rights and Freedoms, the Court of Human Rights has held in *Funke* v. *France*[56] that Article 6 does indeed enshrine a right to silence. The relevant parts of the Article provide that:

'1. In the determination of his civil rights and obligations or of any criminal charge against him everyone is entitled to a fair and public hearing within a reasonable time by an independent and impartial tribunal established by law. . . .
2. Everyone charged with a criminal offence shall be presumed innocent until proved guilty according to law.'

Funke had been suspected by the French Customs authorities of a breach or breaches of French Exchange Control regulations. A demand was made by the Customs authorities for the disclosure of documents, and when he failed to comply with these demands, the applicant (as he eventually became) was convicted and fined by the Strasbourg police court. The fine was a daily one (*asteinte*), which was imposed until such time as he complied with the order to produce his overseas bank accounts. Although the applicant died before the proceedings could be resolved, his widow persisted, and the European Court (by eight votes to one) held (a) that the applicant's conviction secured by the customs authorities in order to obtain certain documents which they believed existed was an attempt to compel the applicant himself to provide the evidence of other offences he had allegedly committed and (b) anyone 'charged with a criminal offence' within the autonomous meaning of this expression in Article 6 has the right to remain silent and not to incriminate himself. The applicant's conviction was an infringement of this right which the special features of French customs law did not justify. Accordingly, there was a breach of Article 6.

It must be said at once that the exact scope of the decision in *Funke* is obscure, which precipitates a corresponding (even greater) obscurity as to the effect that the decision will have upon English law and practice. No basis for the right is provided by the Court, and the Court is implying the right into the Convention. When it has done this on previous occasions, the Court has also implied limitations into the area,[57] and it remains to be seen what exceptions may be permissible. But on one reading of it, the decision appears to hold that the right to a fair trial, as protected by Article 6(1) includes for an accused or for a suspect the right to remain silent and not to assist those investigating or prosecuting him by providing evidence of offences he has allegedly committed. Conversely, neither the investigator nor the prosecutor is entitled to require an accused or a suspect to provide such evidence, since he cannot be obliged to incriminate himself. The ruling appears to apply whether the person has been formally charged or is still merely a suspect; this is implicit in the holding that the expression 'charged with a criminal offence' in Article 6 has 'an autonomous meaning'. The Court unanimously rejected the French government's preliminary objection that *Funke* was not within the autonomous meaning of the Article, because he had not yet been charged with the exchange control offences. The assertion that the Article has an autonomous meaning indicates that the questions whether or not a person has been

[53] The *Factortame* litigation shows that not even Acts of Parliament are immune from judicial review now. *R* v. *Secretary of State for transport, ex parte Factortame Ltd* [1990] 2 A.C. 85; [1991] A.C. 603 and [1992] Q.B. 680.

[54] This analysis is to be found in diverse sources such as Ewing and Gearty's *Freedom Under Thatcher* (1990) and Lord Hailsham's *The Dilemma of Democracy* (1978), Ch. XX. Its most recent expounder is Sir Thomas Bingham, M.R. in 'The European Convention on Human Rights: Time to Incorporate' (1993) 109 L.Q.R. 390.

[55] There is no right of individual petition under this Treaty, and in consequence it does not confer rights in quite the same way as does the European Convention.

[56] Eur. Court of H.R. Judgment of 25 February 1993, Series A, Vol 256A.

[57] Access to the courts was implied to be a part of the Convention in the *Golder* case; Eur. Court H.R., Series A, Vol. 18, Judgment of 21 February 1975, Articles 6 and 8.

'charged with a criminal offence' are determined by Convention jurisprudence, and not by domestic law. Thus a person may count as 'charged' under Convention jurisprudence, even though he has not actually been notified of the intention to charge him. The protection of Article 6 may, in other words, be extended backwards on point of time.[58]

The impact of Funke

What follows is a sketch of the sorts of objections that might be taken to the legislation governing investigations and inquiries in the light of the *Funke* decision.

Companies Act inquiries

Compelling the production of incriminating documents by the suspect himself which can then be used against the suspect in subsequent prosecutions, as is permitted by English law, would seem to be highly vulnerable to challenge. If the core of the right to silence means anything, it must mean that a person cannot be compelled (under pain of judicial punishment)[59] to produce material that actually incriminates him, and is subsequently used for this purpose. Whether the evidence is oral or material should make no difference. Compelling persons other than the suspect should not cause any difficulties. The question whether or not a company or bank might have the right to silence under the Convention becomes important here, but the better view would seem to be that it does not.

Section 2 inquiries

It seems probable that although the questioning of suspects is within the protection afforded by Article 6(1), it can be justified by reference to section 2(8), which precludes the use of answers in subsequent prosecutions. But quaere the production of documents as required by section 2(3), which are not protected from use in subsequent prosecutions, and any further information or evidence that is discovered as a result of information given in question and answer sessions.[60] These would seem to be within the protection of the rules as enunciated in *Funke*, and it is somewhat difficult to see how they could be justified when, as Lord Mustill put it in *Smith*, 'the whole purpose of this Act is to extract material that will lead to a conviction'. There must be a question whether the safeguards envisaged by the House in that case such as the exercise of a discretion to exclude by the trial judge would count as sufficiently precise and tightly drawn to satisfy the requirements of justification under the Convention. Where the section 2(3) powers are used to obtain compulsorily statements that have been obtained from the suspect in other compulsory context,[61] this too would seem to be vulnerable under the Convention.

Insolvency inquiries

It may be in connection with these proceedings that English law is at its most vulnerable to challenge in the European Courts, since this affords absolutely no immunity should a prosecution be brought. Again, this would seem to fall squarely within the protection afforded by Article 6.

Ways of distinguishing Funke

As already indicated, the precise scope of the decision in *Funke* is obscure, and it may be a considerable time before the jurisprudence of the Court (and the Commission, for so long as it continues to exercise jurisdiction in these matters) becomes clarified. The lag time in applications to the Court is considerable—nine years in the *Funke* case itself, for example. It may well be said that this injects intolerable uncertainty into the criminal process, and some ways should be found of ascertaining more precisely the scope of the current law.

It is perhaps arguable that *Funke* was not on its facts a case about serious fraud, but a relatively minor fraud (if fraud at all). Individual countries are entitled to compromise with the principle against self-incrimination in certain situations (prevention of terrorism, protecting children etc), so that what Parliament has done in these cases is perfectly permissible.

Funke was not actually prosecuted for the offences that were disclosed by the documents that he had initially refused to produce but for the failure to produce them. It might be argued that this is a different thing, and that the court is merely saying that the contempt-type procedure that is being invoked offends Article 6, especially when the authorities could not even prove that the documents actually existed. The authorities could have pursued other avenues of investigation.

[58] This is a complaint made by *Saunders*, above n. 7 who argues that the should have been within the protection of the Convention well before he was officially charged.

[59] Improper compulsion will obviously include the use of force or torture, but also covers judicial pressure.

[60] *In Istel Ltd* v. *Tully* [1993] A.C. 45, the House of Lords held that the courts were entitled to provide substitute protection in place of the privilege against self-incrimination, where the claim for the privilege would have the effect of defeating a civil action, provided that the protection against prosecution offered by the court was an adequate safeguard.

[61] See the litigation referred to in n. 11 above.

The Status of the European Convention

Questions (increasingly indignant questions, perhaps) may be raised about the legal status of the European Convention. What obligations does it place the British Government in the event of an adverse finding? The short answer is that the Convention is not directly applicable in the domestic law of the United Kingdom.[62] That said, however, it provides an increasingly significant yardstick against which that law is measured internationally. Where English rules do not conform to the requirements of the Convention, there is an obligation in international law[63] that the municipal law should be changed to reflect this objection.[64] In addition to this, however, the Convention has a status that is almost *sui generis.*

First, the courts are under a self-imposed obligation to give effect to the Convention (as with any other treaty) when construing Acts of Parliament[65] since it will be presumed that Parliament is aware of and does not intend to legislate at variance with international obligations. But the courts cannot insist that ministers *must* take account of the Convention, on pains of holding the resulting determination *Wednesbury* unreasonable.[66] Ministers are free to refer to or ignore the Convention at their own discretion. So far as settling the scope of the common law is concerned, by parity of reasoning, it can be said that the principle is that the courts may take the Convention in to account, but are not in any sense obliged to do so.[67] Since there is, however, an individual right of petition to Strasbourg in the event that English law is found not to comply with the terms of the Convention, it may be suggested that there is a greater jurisprudential obligation than there would be if the courts were to decline to follow other persuasive authority, such as that afforded by the superior Commonwealth courts. The disappointed individual cannot appeal to the Supreme Court of Israel[68] or the High Court of Australia, but he can appeal directly to Strasbourg from a ruling of the English Courts. The jurisdiction of the European Court has 'come to resemble more that of a domestic supreme court than an international tribunal',[69] and it can be argued that its judgments, and the source material by which that court is bound, are entitled to a greater weight than other sources in the English Common Law.

Another possible entrance point for the Convention is through the exercise of judicial discretion. The significance of this point was highlighted in *Middlebrook Mushrooms Ltd.* v. *Transport and General Workers Union,*[70] where an employer sought an injunction to restrain a trade union from organising a picket to boycott one of its shops, the court said that

> 'Though counsel for the defendants did not place any specific reliance on article 10 of the European Convention of Human Rights and Fundamental Freedoms (1953) Cmd 8969) it is relevant to bear in mind that in all cases which involve a proposed restriction on the right of free speech the court is concerned, when exercising its discretion, to consider whether the suggested restraint is necessary.'

The injunction being a discretionary remedy, the fact that its exercise might inhibit a guaranteed right was, in other words, a factor to be taken in to account by the court. To what extent, then should the judge in exercising the discretion that he undoubtedly has to exclude evidence in fairness to the defendant, as referred to in, for example, the *Smith* decision[71] be a factor that the judge ought to take in to account?

The argument against permitting the courts to take specific and explicit account of the Convention, as a matter of legal obligation, is that being a treaty, it is a creature of the exercise of the prerogative power, and it should not be possible for the executive to change the common law in such a wholesale way.[72] Even so, it can be argued from the existence of the right of individual petition,[73] most unusual in international treaties, that the courts in the country are under a slightly greater obligation to acknowledge and give effect to the Convention and its jurisprudence.

[62] The leading statement of the position of the Convention in English law now is *R* v. *Secretary of State, ex parte Brind* [1991] A.C. 696. See C. Warbrick, 'Rights, The European Convention on Human Rights and English Law' [1994] 19 European Law Rev. 34.

[63] As to which, see I. D. Brownlie, *Principles of Public International Law* (1990) 4th ed 36.

[64] In *The Sunday Times Case* (1979) E.C.H.R. Series A, vol. 30, for example, three members of the European Court ruled that the United Kingdom's law of contempt was insufficiently certain in its scope to be acceptable as a restriction 'prescribed by law'.

[65] *R* v. *Secretary of State Ex Parte Brind* [1991] A.C. 696. The courts speak only of resolving an ambiguity, but ambiguity is *only one of the vices* to which language is prone, and there is no reason in principle why other linguistic and semantic indeterminacies should not be resolved by reference to the Convention.

[66] *R* v. *Home Secretary Ex Parte Brind* [1991] A.C. 696.

[67] *Derbyshire county Council* v. *Times Newspapers Ltd* [1993] A.C. 534.

[68] The analogy is suggested by the analysis of Sir John Laws in his article 'Is the High Court the Guardian of Fundamental Constitutional Rights?' [1993] Public Law p. 59.

[69] See C. Gearty, 'The European Court of Human Rights and the Protection of Civil Liberties' [1993] C.L.J. 89 at p. 93.

[70] [1993] I.C.R. 612.

[71] Above n. 18.

[72] The argument is forcefully put by Sir John Laws, *op cit.* at n. 65.

[73] The present government has affirmed the unconditional nature of the right of petition; it will no longer be necessary to ratify the existence of the right at five-yearly intervals.

The scope of and reasons for the right to silence

The expression 'the right of silence' is a phrase used to describe an amalgam of rights enjoyed by an accused person under English law; in addition to being non-compellable as a witness and not punishable for failure to answer questions under interrogation the accused can remain silent in the face of accusation whether before or at trial without such silence being evidence of his guilt or corroborating the case against him.[74] It is linked historically and procedurally with the accusatorial nature of the trial system and the rule that the burden of proof lies on the prosecution. It is also linked with the maxim 'nemo debe see ipsum accusare'—nobody should be compelled to provide evidence against himself, or in modern terms, influenced to take part in compiling the case against himself.

In what might be compendiously referred to as 'non-fraud' types of inquiry, the Police and Criminal Evidence Act 1984 now regulates the whole machinery and structure concerning the detention, questioning, searching or and obtaining intimate bodily samples from suspects. The right of silence in so far as it relates to investigations carried out by the police—although occasionally placed under threat and called in to question—under the terms of PACE remains intact.[75]

At the risk of caricature through brevity, it seems fair to say that what emerges from all the literature on the subject is that the reasons underlying the right to silence in these non-fraud cases are largely concerned with the position of the individual who might be confused, inarticulate, in very unfamiliar surroundings etc, in such a way that the evidence becomes unreliable. Just as lack of reliability is now the essential test for the admissibility or exclusion of a confession,[76] what underlies the concern with the preservation of the right to silence is the possibility that the answer extracted under compulsion of the criminal sanction might also be unreliable.

> 'At the most basic level, uninhibited police interrogation poses a serious risk to the physical and mental integrity of the suspect and to the probative value of the confessions obtained from the suspect. Questioning in the police station is often conducted under conditions of pressure and tension. Suspects under investigation are likely to experience considerable strain even when they are innocent, while those who have something to hide or fear may be doubly susceptible to confusion or suggestibility. If one adds to this the not unnatural tendency of the investigator to manipulate the suspect's responses and interpret them in a way that confirms his own suspicion, one realises that the scope for unreliability of confessions is great.'[77]

These sorts of considerations are allowed to prevail, even though most interviews are now at least tape-recorded, and many of them are video recorded.

Arguably, fears expressed about the reliability of information extracted by the police in a cell or on the way thereto are of little or no relevance to fraud inquiries conducted by inspector or office holders especially appointed for the purpose. Complete records of the interviews are kept and are readily available to the interviewee and his legal advisers.[78] Their significance is at all events greatly diminished where the suspect has with him his solicitor,[79] the risk of physical compulsion is completely absent, and any confusion will be apparent to the adviser as well as to the questioners and a subsequent court.

So far as the production of 'real' evidence in the form of books and documents is concerned, again, the fears of unreliability are less well grounded. To an extent, this is already reflected in existing legislation, where the privilege against self-incrimination is either relaxed or completely absent. In the area of road traffic, for example, we have overcome our diffidence regarding the penalties for failure to provide

[74] But see the provisions of the Criminal Justice and Public Order Bill 1994 adverted to in n. 1.

[75] See A. A. S. Zuckerman, 'Trial by Unfair Means—The Report of the Working Group on the Right of Silence' [1989] Crim. L.R. 855; S. Greer, 'The Right of Silence: A Review of the Current Debate'; (1990) 53 M.L.R. 709. See also A. A. S. Zuckerman, 'The Right Against Self-Incrimination: An Obstacle to the Supervision of Interrogation' (1986) 102 L.Q.R. 43. For a spirited attack on the right,m see The Hon. Mr Justice E. W. Thomas, 'The So-Called Right to Silence' [1991] 14 N.Z.U.L.R. 299. See also D. J. Galligan, 'The Right to Silence Reconsidered' (1988) 41 C.L.P. 69. Cf. B. Robertson, 'The Right to Silence Ill-Considered' (1991) 21 V.U.W.L.R. 139.

[76] Section 76 of PACE reads: '(1) In any proceedings a confession made by an accused person may be given in evidence against him in so far as it is relevant to any matter in issue in the proceedings and is not excluded by the court in pursuance of this section.

(2) If, in any proceedings where the prosecution proposes to give in evidence a confession made by an accused person, it is represented to the court that the confession was or may have been obtained—

(a) by oppression of the person who made it; or

(b) in consequence of anything said or done which was likely, in the circumstances existing at the time, to render unreliable any confession which might be made by him in consequence thereof,

the court shall not allow the confession to be given in evidence against him except in so far as the prosecution proves to the court beyond reasonable doubt that the confession (notwithstanding that it may be true) was not obtained as aforesaid'.

[77] Zuckerman, [1989] Crim. L.R. at 857.

[78] See generally *Investigation Handbook* (1990) H.M.S.O. for the procedures that are to be adopted.

[79] Who cannot, however, either advise the suspect not to answer the questions, or give advice as to the proper way in which responses should be framed. The role of the legal adviser in insolvency and D.T.I. investigations is something that might be the subject of separate consideration. See the article in the Law Soc. Gazette (1991) 27 February.

the very evidence which will convict the motorist such as a specimen of breath, urine or blood.[80] The significance of real evidence is, perhaps, that it is extremely difficult to tamper with it or alter it, or at any rate argue with its significance. If a person has been found with a gun in his hand, or a quantity of alcohol in his bloodstream, that is an incontrovertible fact. A statement is much more likely to be opinionative, and the subject of distorting forces such as poor memory, the ambiguities of language etc, about whose significance there can be considerable later dispute.

This analysis suggests that reliability of the evidence is an important factor in deciding whether or not it is unfair to use it.

The notion that there is a privilege against self-incrimination is deeply ingrained as part of our beliefs about the criminal justice system.[81] There is something very un-English about requiring a person to convict himself, or to help to do so, and the Law Reports are full of spacious phrases about the right as being 'most sacred'[82] and 'a general rule established with great justice and tenderness'.[83] Quite how and why it etched itself so deeply in to the system is less clear, and it has long had it antagonists. The very idea that there was something unfair about requiring a person to convict himself out of his own mouth was characterised as the sporting theory of criminal justice, which was rightly derided by Bentham;[84] the criminal justice process should not be seen as some sort of game in which the quarry is given a sporting chance.

A slightly different formulation of the same point is that the privilege against self-incrimination is an aspect of the requirement that the state must prove a person's guilt. The state has resources available to it, and it is appropriate that it should be required to use these, rather than to rely on the confession of a suspect.

Another reason for preserving the privilege is that the system should not come to rely on confessions of guilt. Sir James Fitzjames Stephen put the point graphically when he spoke of the investigator who becomes lazy and sits in the shade rubbing pepper in the poor devil's eyes which is far pleasanter (for the investigator) than toiling all day in the hot sun.[85] The ability to rely on confessions, in other words, reduces the incentive to look for other and independent evidence of wrongdoing.

None of the reasons that have been offered so far indicate that there is any sort of fundamental human right underlying the two principles under discussion. There is nothing like the right to life or even the right to freedom of speech that seems to be at stake. There may be, however, other factors that must be considered.[86] It can be argued that the policy considerations lying behind the maxims about not assisting the prosecution to compile the case against oneself include in part a respect for the right to privacy.[87] Respect for this value is to be found (in a slightly different context) in the language of Millett J. in the *Barlow Clowes Gilt Managers* case,[88] where it was held that information supplied voluntarily and in confidence to liquidators cannot be used to assist directors of companies in defending criminal charges. Millett J. says:

> 'the courts have never assumed or been granted the power to compel the production of all such information regardless of its nature and source. That would amount to an intolerable invasion of privacy. . . .
>
> in a criminal case, the defendant is under no obligation to assist the prosecution. With certain limited exceptions, he is entitled to the so-called "right of silence" '.

'Parliament has determined the extent to which the individual's right to privacy may be invaded in the interests of criminal justice.'[89] That is, if privacy is the basic human 'right' that underlies the principles

[80] For a discussion, see Susan M. Easton, 'Bodily Samples and the Privilege Against Self-Incrimination' [1991] Crim. L.R. 18.

[81] See John H. Langbein, 'The Historical Origins of the Privilege Against Self-Incrimination at Common Law' (1994) 92 Mich. L.R. 1047.

[82] *Ex parte Cossens* (1820) 1 Buck 531, 540 per Lord Eldon.

[83] *Harrison* v. *Southcote* (1751) 2 Ves Sen 389 at 394 per Lord Hardwick. The significance of the privilege was recently affirmed by Lord Griffiths in *Lam Chi-Ming* [1991] 2 A.C. 212.

[84] 'The use of a fox is to be hunted; the use of a criminal is to be tried', *Rationale of Judicial Evidence* (ed. Bowring, *Works* VII), Bk IX, Pt 4, chap. 3, p. 455. That is, there is not much fun to be had if the fox has no chance of escape. Bentham was highly critical of the privilege against self-incrimination saying that: 'if all the criminals of every class had assembled and framed a system after their wishes, is not this rule the very first they would have established for their own security? Innocence never takes advantage of it; innocence claims the right of speaking, as guilt invokes the privilege of silence': ed. M. Dumont, *Treatise on Evidence* (1825), p. 241.

[85] 1 *History of the Criminal Law* (1883) 442, n. 1.

[86] It is true, as Professor Galligan has pointed out, that in permitting the exclusion of evidence obtained through oppression, the legislature might be recognising other values and protecting other rights, but it is very difficult to say with any precision what those rights and interests actually are; 'The Right to Silence Reconsidered' (1988) 41 Curr. L.P. 69.

[87] See Lord Mustill in *Smith* [1993] A.C. 1, at p. 31: 'all states recognise this assertion of personal liberty and privacy'. The European Convention also affords a right to respect for private and family life, a person's home and 'his correspondence'. In the *Funke* case (1993) 16 E.H.R.R. 297, the Court also decided that French law fell foul of this Article.

[88] [1992] Ch. 208.

[89] And see *Marcel* v. *M.P.C.* [1992] Ch. 225; see especially at 240C–E (Browne-Wilkinson V.C.). Making available compulsorily seized documents—the general principle is that this is an unwarranted invasion of privacy, and when Parliament says that this may be done, it is highly exceptional.

under consideration, it is, like other rights, not an absolute or even, it might be said, a particularly strong one.[90] Where other interests conflict with it, we are prepared to give greater weight to those interests in preference.

IV Some Conclusions and Some Questions

I have posed a number of questions throughout the paper that seem to me to call for discussion and resolution,[91] and see no need to repeat them. They range from the technical to the jurisprudential. It is clear that the European Convention on Human Rights and Fundamental Freedoms is having a considerable impact upon the legal system of Britain. The *Funke* decision has considerable repercussions for our own jurisprudence; the courts are not simply free to ignore it. There is, though, a case for saying that the courts should not be asked by Parliament to make good the deficiencies of the law, and that special consideration should now be given to the various statutes referred to in this paper, with a view to examining their compatibility with the Convention

What precisely is the scope of the right 'to remain silent and not to contribute to incriminating himself'? As the section of this paper headed 'A paradox'[92] amply shows, the present law is not the result of some carefully devised legislative scheme, but a topsy-like system that has emerged through a fitful collaboration between Parliament and the judiciary. How far does European jurisprudence permit the signatories to the Convention to compromise with the right to silence in the pursuit of other social ends such as the prevention of serious fraud?

There are a great many topics that could have been covered as part of this paper. Whether, for example, we should follow the Australian example, and hold that companies should not have the right to silence?[93] What does the Convention require or permit in this respect? The officers of the company would be, in effect, claiming the privilege on another's behalf. The question arose, but was not settled, in *In Re Westinghouse Union Contract.*[94]

Another issue that might have been tackled is the problem created by the privilege in civil proceedings, in which context it has been described as 'an archaic and unjustifiable survival from the past'.[95] Might the possibility of self-incrimination ever count as a 'reasonable excuse' for failure to answer questions under the section 2 questioning. Might it be sensible to extend the section 2 compromise immunity in other areas of investigation, especially in the light of the *Funke* decision?

A more general question concerns the role of the courts and the judges as protectors of rights in this context. The present Master of the Rolls, Sir Thomas Bingham, in a recent address,[96] reminded his audience of the agreed statement issued at the end of an international conference on human rights over which the Lord Chancellor had presided:

> ' "In democratic societies fundamental human rights and freedoms are more than paper aspirations. They form part of the law. And it is the special province of judges to see to it that the law's undertakings are realised in the daily life of the people" '.

How well does this square with the decisions of the courts in this context that the right to silence and the privilege in this context have been 'impliedly abrogated'? The rhetoric seems to be quite strikingly at variance with the determination of the judges to make the legislation against serious fraud work, even in the absence of a clearly stated abrogation of the principle by Parliament itself. Lord Mustill in *Smith*,[97] having offered an illuminating and sophisticated analysis of the various claims that are being made under the 'privilege against self-incrimination rubric' put the point as follows:

> 'in these circumstances I think it clear, given the diversity of immunities and policies underlying them, that it is not enough to ask simply whether Parliament can have intended to abolish a long-standing right of silence. Rather an essential starting point must be to identify what variety of this right is being invoked, and what are the reasons for believing that the right in question ought at all costs to be maintained'.

Rights are not treated by the British Courts as imperatives, let alone as absolutes, but as expressions of

[90] Privacy is not, of course, protected *eo nomine* by English law: *Malone* v. *M.P.C.* [1979] Ch. 344. Malone subsequently succeeded in the European Court of Human Rights, Eur. Ct HR, Series A, No. 82, Judgment of 2 August 1984, 5 E.H.H.R. 385. It is a concept of complexity. See D. Feldman, *Civil Liberties and Human Rights in England and Wales* (1993) ch. 8.

[91] See, on the implications of the decision in *Smith*, above, text at n. 18: what is it about the difference between serious fraud and other crimes, that prompts us to dispense with the principle quite so readily? How should the judge regard the European Convention in the exercise of his judicial discretion to exclude the answers to questioning.

[92] Above, p. 80.

[93] *Environment Protection Authority* v. *Caltex Refining Co Pty Ltd* (1993) A.L.J.R. 127; for comment, see C. Tapper (1994) 110 L.Q.R. 350.

[94] [1978] A.C. 547.

[95] By Lord Templeman in *Istel Ltd.* v. *Tully* [1993] A.C. 45, at 53. See also the Lord Chancellor's Department consultation paper, *The Privilege Against Self-Incrimination in Civil Proceedings* (July 1992).

[96] 'The European Convention on Human Rights: Time to Incorporate' (1993) 109 L.Q.R. 390.

[97] [1993] A.C. 1.

value and policy, which may be compromised in pursuit of other social aims and policies. When the suppression of serious fraud is the objective, the experience is that the right counts for virtually nothing. Whether the European jurisprudence will permit that stance to prevail remains to be seen.

8. Self-incrimination and the European Convention on Human Rights

COLIN WARBRICK

A major consideration of Tony Smith's paper for the All Souls meeting was the compatibility of the various statutory forms of investigation of company affairs and the use of testimony and documents obtained in the course of them in criminal trials with the international human rights obligations of the United Kingdom.[1] My commentary on his paper took the form of a more detailed investigation of the provisions and case-law to which he had drawn attention. This paper is an expanded version of those comments. I am very conscious of my limited knowledge, particularly of the company laws involved, in addressing these matters. As will become apparent, I think that much may turn on the details of individual cases which reach the institutions of the European Convention on Human Rights in Strasbourg. While the position may be somewhat different with respect to the International Covenant on Civil and Political Rights, in general, it might be said, generalisations will not take us very far but generalisations are all that I can offer about what I will call the 'investigatory powers'.

The prescience of Tony Smith's reference to the Convention is demonstrated by the references made to the *Funke* case[2] in *Arrows (No. 4)* by Lord Browne-Wilkinson, where he said:

> The principle [against self-incrimination] has been carried over into the jurisprudence of all common law countries, including the United States. It is one of the basic rights protected by the European Convention on Human Rights. In *Funke, Cremieux and Miahilhe*, Article 6 of the Convention was held to render unlawful a demand to produce self-incriminating documents.[3]

Especially if it be the case that *Arrows (No. 4)* represents a change in attitude that the courts take to these investigatory powers,[4] it would appear that the influence of the Convention has made itself felt in English law. This leads to two questions: what does the Convention require of States? and has Lord Browne-Wilkinson reacted accurately in this case? International lawyers in general and human rights lawyers in particular will be pleased that the courts are willing to take account of the international obligations of the State. To the extent that it is constitutionally feasible for them to do so, as organs of the State, the courts have an obligation to comply with international law. To do that, judges need to know what it is that international law requires of them. In the present context, this is not easy to find out.

The procedures of the European Convention[5]

The European Convention differs from other human rights treaties to which the United Kingdom is a party because the government has accepted the right of individual application,[6] which allows persons who feel their human rights have been violated to resort directly to the international machinery of the Convention, machinery which, if the application is successful, may lead to a binding judgment of the European Court of Human Rights that the United Kingdom is in breach of its duties under the Convention.[7] There have been several cases where this has happened.[8] In all of them, the government has taken steps to remedy the grievance, reluctantly and minimally sometimes, but always to the satisfaction of the Committee of Ministers of the Council of Europe which is responsible for the supervision of States' compliance with judgments against them under the Convention.[9] Since some importance is attached to the investigatory powers in dealing with large-scale fraud, it is clearly of some consequence to the authorities that these powers be found to be in accordance with Convention. Because of the possibility of a challenge to them being brought by an individual, the prospect is a real rather than a theoretical one, that the government will have to defend the powers before the Convention institutions.[10]

Before an individual application may be entertained by the Commission, certain conditions of 'admissibility' must be satisfied. Among the most

[1] A. T. H. Smith, The Right to Silence in Cases of Serious Fraud, pp. 15–21, revised version, about pp. 000.

[2] *Funke* v. *France* ECtHR A/256A (1993), 16 EHRR 297 (1993).

[3] *Re Arrows (No. 4), Hamilton* v. *Naviede* [1994] 3 All ER 814, 821. Reference was made also to *Orkem* v. *EC Commission* 374/87 [1991] 4 CMLR 502.

[4] See G. R. Sullivan, above p. 000.

[5] For an accessible account, see S. Livingstone and T. Owen, Prison Law: Text and Materials (1993) pp. 78–92.

[6] European Convention on Human Rights (ECHR), Article 25.

[7] ECHR Articles 46, 53.

[8] F. Hampson, The United Kingdom before the European Court of Human Rights, 9 YEL 121, 136–156 (1989).

[9] R. Churchill and J. Young, Compliance with Judgments of the European Court of Human Rights and Decisions of the Committee of Ministers: the Experience of the United Kingdom, 1975–1987, 53 BYIL 283 (199).

[10] *Saunders* v. *UK* App. No. 19187/91, Report of 10 May 1994: the complaint concerns the admission in evidence at a subsequent criminal trial of information obtained by inspectors under s. 432 and s. 442, Companies Act 1985.

important are that the applicant has exhausted domestic remedies[11] and that he show himself to be a 'victim'[12] of the Convention violation. The domestic remedy requirement has been interpreted strictly by the Commission. If claims about the Convention violations can be settled in the national legal system, there are several advantages that they be so and the Commission has been keen to ensure that individuals test remedial routes that offer some hope of avoiding cases going to Strasbourg.[13] Identifying effective domestic remedies in English law is particularly difficult, because the Convention has not been implemented into domestic law nor is there a national bill of rights which would allow the substance of many Convention claims to be raised before a national tribunal. On the face of it, since there is no remedy in English law against legislation alleged to contravene, the Convention, there are no domestic remedies to challenge the statutory powers we are presently considering. However, Lord Browne-Wilkinson's judgment in *Arrows (No. 4)* does open the possibility that a criminal court may exclude evidence obtained as a result of one of these investigatory procedures on the ground that to admit it would be to deprive the defendant of a fair trial.[14] To the extent that the test overlaps with the Convention test about the acceptability of this kind of evidence, a matter to be considered below, an applicant would be advised to raise the issue before the trial court. In practice, this ought not to be a burdensome obligation for, following *Arrows (No. 4)*, objection to the admissibility of the compelled evidence will surely be almost a routine practice for defendants. If the decision of the trial court goes against the defendant, the domestic remedies rule requires that he exhaust whatever lines of appeal are open to him, unless they are obviously futile.

Article 25 of the Convention requires that the applicant be a 'victim' of a violation of the Convention, that is to say, a person directly damaged by the alleged violation.[15] The Commission will reject claims which it regards as raising purely abstract issues about the compatibility of national laws with the Convention (with the exception, hardly likely to be relevant here, of inter-State cases). Nor does the Commission recognise an *actio popularis* which would allow someone not directly affected to bring a claim that another person is being damaged by a breach of the Convention. Applicants are entitled to be represented in bringing their applications but they must be their own cases. This emphasis on the individual as victim concentrates attention on the details of his case. The Court makes it clear that it is disposing only of the case before it.[16] There is no formal doctrine of precedent for the Court,[17] a feature of some importance, given that it sits with increasing frequency in chambers of nine judges, relatively small samples of a Court which now has thirty-two judges.[18] Focusing on the particular case has another advantage for the Court. Unusually for an international tribunal, the Court has committed itself to a progressive approach to interpretation, allowing that changing political, social and technological factors may influence the interpretation of the Convention.[19] By avoiding, as it usually does, any wide-ranging theoretical excursuses, the Court does not handicap itself if it later feels the need to embark on a new line of interpretation to take into account extrinsic developments. The drawback to all this is that the jurisprudence sometimes looks no more than a set of single instances.[20] It is possible to suggest a line of argument to put to the Court: it is less easy to predict whether it will be accepted. Furthermore, the risk of becoming embroiled in the factual details of a particular case, which may be contested between the government and the applicant, does not fit altogether happily with the rather underdeveloped evidential processes of the institutions.[21]

These somewhat critical remarks about the capacities of the European Court are less in point if the language of the Convention or the jurisprudence of the Court establishes a clear 'bright-line', where what the Convention requires is not greatly influenced by the specific features of a particular application. Such cases are rare.[22] In the present context it should be noted that the text of the Convention has no express

[11] ECHR, Article 26.

[12] ECHR, Article 25.

[13] For a brief account, see D. Gomien, Short Guide to the European Convention on Human Rights (1991) pp. 134–136.

[14] Above, n. 3, pp. 831–32.

[15] The 'victim' may be 'any person, non-governmental organisation [which includes companies] or group of individuals', ECHR, Article 25.

[16] This has been markedly so in cases deciding whether the applicant has had a fair criminal trial, e.g. *Barbera et al* v. *Spain* E Ct HR A/146 (1988).

[17] C. Warbrick, Annual Survey, The European Convention on Human Rights 10 YEL 535, 587–593 (1990).

[18] ECHR, Article 38: the number of judges is the same as the number of members of the Council of Europe and so will go on increasing as the membership does.

[19] *Ireland* v. *UK* A/25 (1978) para. 154; *Tyler* v. *UK* A/26 (1978) para. 31.

[20] This has been the case with 'civil rights and obligations' in Article 6(1): for a recent example, see *Schuler-Zgraggen* v. *Switzerland* A/263 (1993) paras. 45–46.

[22] See K. Rogge, Fact-Finding, in R. Macdonald, et al., The European System for the Protection of Human Rights (1993) pp. 677–701.

[22] Note the divisions among the judges about whether a 'bright-line' had been established in *Beldjoudi* v. *France* A/234A (1992).

language which guarantees either the right to silence or the privilege against self-incrimination.[23] I shall use the 'right' against self-incrimination to denote a mandatory and essentially absolute right of the individual, a Dworkinian 'trump'. By the 'privilege' against self-incrimination. I indicate a strong interest of the individual, to be taken into account in establishing the content of other rights, such a the right not to be mistreated and the right to a fair trial, where the privilege may be qualified to take into account other interests.[24] We shall have to consider whether the interest against not incriminating one's self is in either of these senses, protected impliedly by the Convention. Before doing so, one, final preliminary remark about the juristic style of the Court's judgments is in order. Not only is it rare for the Court to pronounce itself on the theoretical underpinnings of its judgments but some of its judgments are quite terse, with little explanation of why the Convention requires the outcome upon which the judges have decided. There are probably a variety of reasons for this, including the different national traditions of judgment writing. However, another reason is likely to be that it is sometimes easier for the judges to reach agreement on the result of a case than on the reasons for it. The somewhat peremptory and unqualified tone of a judgment should not obscure the possibility that it disguises different justifications for the result, differences which can be crucial when the Court is faced with slightly different circumstances. This possibility should be borne in mind when reading the *Funke* case, to which I now turn.

Funke v. *France*[25]

Funke's house was searched by customs officers acting on information from the tax authorities. As a result of what they found, the customs men suspected that Funke has been carrying on overseas financial transactions in contravention of strict foreign exchange laws. They asked him to produce statements for bank accounts which they believed he maintained abroad. Although he had originally agreed to do this, Funke later refused to cooperate and the authorities commenced proceedings to fine him for not doing so and to impose upon him a daily fine until the documents were produced. The Courts did impose both a general and daily fine on Funke, decisions later confirmed by appeals courts which, *inter alia*, considered and dismissed arguments that the seizure of the documents contravened Article 8 (respect for home and family life) and that the proceedings to produce bank statements violated Article 6 (the right to fair trial) of the European Convention (to which the French courts may make direct reference). Before these proceedings were complete, the customs anticipated commencing proceedings against Funke to obtain orders that he forfeit undeclared foreign funds and pay a fine. To this end, the authorities obtained interim measures of attachment against Funke's property. The determination of these proceedings was prolonged and, in the course of them, Funke died. The Commission allowed the continuation of the application by his widow.

Funke alleged that the customs proceedings against him for the purpose of obtaining documents which might be used in the subsequent criminal proceedings against him violated his right to a fair trial under Article 6(1) and his right to be presumed innocent under Article 6(2). The claims had to be made in these ways because, as indicated already, the Convention contains no express guarantee against self-incrimination. The Commission rejected the government's argument that Article 6 was not applicable because Funke was not 'a person charged' (Article 6(2)) with an offence, nor had any 'criminal charge' against him been 'determined' (Article 6(1)). The Commission held that suspicion had focused on Funke sufficiently for interim measures to be ordered against him and that the nature and consequence of the customs offences in French law made them 'criminal charges' in the Convention sense.[26]

Funke claimed that the coercive proceedings against him to obtain the documents about his foreign bank accounts would result in them being used in his subsequent prosecution for violating the foreign exchange laws. This 'violated the general principle that everyone has the right not to give evidence against himself'.[27] The government observed that 'the principle that a person facing criminal charges cannot be obliged to prove his guilt is not set forth in any part of the Convention and cannot be inferred from the case law of the Convention institutions.'[28] While the Commission had already rejected the government's claim that customs offences were not really criminal, it did concede that there was a 'special character' to inquiries designed to protect

[23] Compare the International Covenant on Civil and Political Rights, below p. 000.

[24] I do not pretend that this corresponds to any regular use of the words. Cf. Smith, above, n. 1, p. 1, n. 5. For a wider consideration of the place of rights in criminal procedure, see G. Maher, Human Rights and the Criminal Process, in T. Campbell et al., Human Rights: From Rhetoric to Reality (1986) pp. 197–222.

[25] Above, n. 2.

[26] *Funke* v. *France*, App. No. 10828/84, Report, 8 Oct. 1991, paras. 49–51.

[27] *Ibid.*, para. 57.

[28] *Ibid.*, para. 58.

the State's economic policies.[29] It was necessary here, as generally throughout the Convention, to strike a balance between the interests of the community and the rights of individuals protected by the Convention. Resort to the balancing process is a clear indication that the Commission did not think that there was any free-standing and unqualified right against self-incrimination as a necessary implication of the right to a fair trial. Instead, it noted that States did require that individuals affected by fiscal legislation should supply documentary evidence about transactions relevant to inquiries that the authorities were undertaking. The object of such obligations was to ensure the efficacy of the fiscal regime and not to facilitate the prosecution of offenders. On this basis, though by seven votes to five,[30] the Commission held that the requirement that Funke surrender his bank accounts, subject to coercive penalties did not violate his right to a fair trial.[31] Although the Commission goes no further, once it had taken this position, arguably it was premature to decide whether Funke had had a fair trial on the principal customs charge because that trial never took place. It cannot be ruled out that in the particular circumstances of such a trial, reliance on evidence gained in the way it was sought to be obtained here might be unfair to the defendant and, while there was no principled bar to the French authorities behaving in the way that they had, the use to which they put information in a subsequent criminal trial could be subject to review. The Commission disposed quickly of the presumption of innocence claim. The mere fact that the documents in issue might be used later in evidence against him did not render Funke's conviction on the charge of failing to produce them a violation of the presumption of innocence. He had been charged and convicted of failing to produce them by a proper procedure.

The judgment of the Court took a quite different approach. The substantive part of its judgment is so short that it is reproduced in full:

> The Court notes that the customs secured Mr Funke's conviction in order to obtain certain documents which they believed must exist, although they were not certain of the fact. Being unable or unwilling to produce them by some other means, they attempted to compel the applicant himself to provide evidence of offences he had allegedly committed. The special features of customs law . . . cannot justify such an infringement of the right of anyone 'charged with a criminal offence' within the autonomous meaning of this expression in Article 6, to remain silent and not to incriminate himself.[32]

On the fact of it, this is the affirmation of an independent right against self-incrimination as a necessary ingredient of a fair trial. The right will be available to all defendants in all criminal trials. It does not depend upon the nature of the evidence nor upon the way in which it was obtained.[33] It would seem to follow, although it was not necessary for the Court to address this point, that if self-incriminatory material is obtained, then a defendant would have the right to have such evidence excluded from any subsequent criminal trial. If this be the purport of *Funke*, then it causes obvious difficulties for the use of evidence obtained in the special investigatory procedures with which we are concerned. Before considering these and other practice of the institutions, it is worth looking a little more closely at the kinds of circumstances in which the problem arises.

First, as the Commission accepts, there are situations familiar to all legal systems where the State imposes an obligation on individuals to keep records and where it criminalises a failure to do so or to produce the records when requested.[34] Most typically, this is so for the records of income and expenditure for tax purposes and it is the case also for company records. Conviction for refusal to produce records on request does not infringe the principle against self-incrimination. It is the very essence of the offence. Where the records are kept in order that the State can obtain the performance of obligations imposed on individuals or to check whether they have performed their obligations faithfully, the revelation of records may show that a person should have made certain payments or performed certain services that he has not done. Requiring him to do this when such will be the consequence of producing the records does not impinge upon his right against self-incrimination because the proceedings are not criminal but regulatory.[35] Presentation of inaccurate or incomplete records may expose an individual to penalties beyond the mere performance of the regulatory obligations. Here the proceedings may be criminal and

[29] *Ibid.*, para. 63.

[30] Among the dissents, note the affirmation that the interest against self-incrimination is a 'fundamental right', Soyer, para. 14.

[31] Above, n. 26, paras. 64–65.

[32] Above n. 2, para. 44. Funke argued also that the coercive request for the documents was in breach of Article 6(2), which protects the presumption of innocence. The Court found no need to decide this question. If the effect of *Funke* is narrowed by subsequent cases, the Article 6(2) point will almost certainly be resurrected, see Commission in *Saunders*, above n. 10, para. 72.

[33] This is the way *Funke* was understood by the Commission in *Saunders*, above n. 10, paras. 69–72.

[34] Above n.l 26, para. 65.

[35] And consequently fall outside Articles 6(1) altogether.

the documents may be crucial evidence against the defendant. This is the situation in *Funke* and, of course, the European Court said that the use of the documents in the subsequent criminal trial would violate the Convention. However, the authorities surely have the right to obtain the documents for the purpose of regulatory proceedings—in this case to see what Funke owed the State. It is the use of the documents, rather than their collection, which may be the injury and to this extent, at least, *Funke* seems excessive for the honest taxpayer could not resist the discovery of his records and the possibility of an increased impost after the assessment by the authorities, whereas the suspected dishonest taxpayer could and thus his fiscal responsibilities could not be properly calculated. The Court in *Funke* assumed that the demands made of Funke were for criminal rather than fiscal purposes and that they would have been used in the proceedings against him. Given this, it seems that *Funke* is of compelling effect where, as, say in s. 2(3) of the Criminal Justice Act 1987, the very purpose of the request for documents is for criminal prosecution and it is specifically contemplated that evidence so obtained and, indeed in some limited circumstances, oral statements made by a defendant under compulsion, may be used in subsequent criminal proceedings. The power to obtain documents under s. 2(3) goes further than documents which a defendant is required to keep but it includes them. If this be the proper interpretation of *Funke*, then compelled requested by the SFO for documentary information, including the transcripts of DTI investigations, of an incriminating nature for the purpose of investigating serious fraud, where there is the prospect that it may be introduced in evidence will be contrary to the Convention. This will be so regardless of any procedural safeguards introduced at the evidence-gathering stage and of any discretion in the trial judge to exclude evidence, the admission of which would lead to an unfair trial. Given the importance of the investigatory procedures and, indeed, as Tony Smith's paper mentions, there have been calls for their extension,[36] the significance of *Funke* can hardly be underestimated. This, or something like it, appears to be the understanding of *Funke* of Lord Browne-Wilkinson in *Arrows (no. 4)* and may have contributed to the apparent change in emphasis in this judgment compared to earlier ones on the admissibility of evidence obtained through the investigatory procedures.[37] It is a position shared by the majority (14–1) of the Commission in *Saunders*.[38] Saunders alleged that the failure of the trial judge to exclude from his trial evidence obtained as a result of his questioning by inspectors appointed under s. 432 of the Companies Act 1985 violated his right to a fair criminal trial. While the Commission 'accepts that the right [to silence] may not be unqualified'[39] and that,

> 'Whether a particular applicant has been subject to compulsion to incriminate himself and whether the use made of the incriminating material has rendered criminal proceedings unfair will depend on an assessment of the circumstances of each as a whole,'[40]

the remainder of its language does not leave much scope for limitations to be implied into he right (whether of silence or not to incriminate oneself)[41] nor for a trial to be fair where previously compelled testimony is a 'not insignificant'[42] part of the case against the defendant. Nonetheless, given what is at stake, it remains for the British government to try to distinguish *Funke* when *Saunders* is argued before the Court.

Can *Funke* be distinguished?[43]

First, one reiterates the word of warning already given about the notion of precedent in the European Court. It would be a mistake to regard *Funke* as binding in the same way that the judgment of a superior court would be regarded in England, the more so since it is the judgment of a chamber of the Court and the judgment itself is notably devoid of explanation for a conclusion which may have such far-reaching effects.

The single, dispositive paragraph of the judgment includes the words 'The special features of customs law . . . cannot justify such an interference with the right [not to incriminate one's self]. . .'.[44] These words are open to two possible interpretations. The first is that they are gratuitous—referring to an argument of the French government which the Court thought of no consequence to the outcome of the case. If that be the case, then the British government can gain no help from them. Alternatively, the character of the offence may be relevant but the Court did not think it to be so on the facts of *Funke*. Even if this be the case, the offences with which we are

36 Above n. 1, p. 11.
37 Above n. 4.
38 Above n. 10.
39 *Ibid.*, para. 70.
40 Para. 73.
41 Paras. 71 and 72.
42 Para. 75.

43 The Commission Report in *Saunders* and hence the government's arguments seeking to distinguish *Funke* only became public after this paper had been completed. Those arguments and the Commission's responses are referred to in the notes to the following section which has not been revised since *Saunders* was published.
44 Above n. 32.

concerned seem even less distinctive than the customs offences involved in *Funke*. Fraud and theft are ordinary crimes and there does not appear to be anything about the regulatory nature of the companies offences which distinguishes them from the French customs laws in any relevant way. While one should not rule out the prospect of the Court conceding that certain kinds of criminal conduct are 'special' in the sense that the State has a greater leeway in dealing with them than the ordinary crime—terrorist offences are perhaps the most likely candidate, though even here one would be cautious[45]—unless 'big company fraud' was widely regarded by the Convention States as warranting a relaxed regime of protection for its effective prosecution, the Court is unlikely to concede that there should be a departure from the standards of Article 6.

If this be the case, then we must try another tack. Whatever the nature of the interest against self-incrimination recognised by the Court in *Funke*, the right or privilege is implied. In the terms in which it is expressed in the judgment, it is an unqualified right and it is not surprising that the judgment has been read as though it were an express and expressly unqualified right. However, the Court has acknowledged that implied rights are subject to implied limitations. The principle is well-established by *Golder*[46] and *Ashingdane*.[47] Permissible limitations must:

1. not destroy the substance of the right;
2. serve a legitimate aim;
3. be proportionate to securing the legitimate aim.[48]

It is, then, necessary to try to determine the substance of the right not to incriminate one's self. There are two approaches. The first considers the right against self-incrimination as an aspect of a wide right to personal integrity, the protection of which might have consequences for the way in which any criminal trial is to be conducted.[49] If this were the Convention understanding of the right, it is surprising that it be not spelled out expressly. As will be seen, where there are express rights which might be taken to embrace a privilege against self-incrimination in the Convention, the rights to respect for private life[50] and the right to freedom of expression,[51] these are qualified rights and it is by no means clear that such protection as they might afford to an individual would not yield to some public interest like the prevention of crime.[52] This suggests that the essence of the protection against self-incrimination is related to the concept of the fair trial. Why might it be said that there can be no fair trial if the accused has been forced to incriminate himself? In particular, why might it be so said that *any* self-incrimination *must* mean no fair trial? Here there appears to be a close similarity between the justification of the privilege against self-incrimination and the right to silence. Anglo-American cases constantly refer to the origin of both rights: information obtained by torture should not be admissible against a defendant.[53] It was conceded by Lord Browne-Wilkinson in *Arrows (No. 4)* that this was not a consideration germane to modern companies investigations.[54] Besides, the Convention provides protection in the event of evidence extracted under torture as an implied right under Article 3 of the Convention. What is more, recent scholarship has case doubt on traditional claims that the origins of the protection are to be found entirely in the distaste for the goings on of the High Commission.[55] Nonetheless, the protection against oppressive questioning by the interrogator is a recurring theme in the justification of a right or privilege against self-incrimination.[56] If the risk is high, making the privilege a right may be necessary to protect effectively the individual. Otherwise, the privilege is seen as an aspect of fair trial, where safeguards against misleading questioning or unreliability of evidence may compensate the individual sufficiently while allowing otherwise useful evidence into a criminal trial.[57]

If, instead of regarding the interest against self-

[45] In *Brogan* v. *UK* A/145B (1988), the Court refused to allow a period of pre-trial detention without judicial supervision in a terrorist case longer than that which it allowed for ordinary crime. Commission in *Saunders*, above n. 10, para. 71.

[46] *Golder* v. *UK* A/18 (1975).

[47] *Ashingdane* v. *UK* A/93 (1985).

[48] *Ibid.*, para. 57.

[49] This is the way it is regarded in US law (Constitution, 5th Amendment) and much energy is spent on considering the limits of the right: for an extended discussion, see L. Herman, The unexplored relationship between the Privilege against Compulsory Self-Incrimination and the Involuntary Confession Rule, Parts I and II 53 Ohio State L.J. 101, 497 (1992).

[50] See below, p. 000.

[51] See below, p. 000.

[52] Where the interference with one of these rights is clearly based on law and said to be for the prevention of crime, the European Court has hardly ever found that it was not justified.

[53] L. Levy, Origins of the Fifth Amendment (1968).

[54] Above n. 3, p. 820.

[55] J. Langbein, The Historical Origins of the Privilege against Self-Incrimination 92 Mich LR 1047 (1994).

[56] Commission in *Saunders*, above n. 10, para. 72—'an important element in safeguarding an accused from oppression and coercion during criminal proceedings'.

[57] Despite the strong language in some English judgments about the fundamental character of the interest against self-incrimination, Parliament has been quite ready to interfere with it if it thought the public interest justified it, Smith, above n. 1, pp. 8–9. See also, A. Dongan, The Right not to Incriminate Oneself, in E. Paul et al. (eds), Human Rights (1984) pp. 137–148, distinguishing between legal rights with a moral foundation and moral rights, regarding the interest against self-incrimination to be the former and, therefore, not to be insisted upon in every circumstance.

incrimination as some absolute, bedrock right, it is examined as a factor, doubtless an important factor, in deciding whether the defendant has had a fair trial, then, in accordance with the *Golder-Ashingdane* precepts, we can then look to see why it should be qualified in cases of large scale company fraud. The answer given by the authorities is that inquisitorial investigation with compelled testimony and duties to produce documents is the *only* way to police effectively the operations of companies and the financial markets and that information gained by these processes should be available as evidence in the protection of those charged with very serious crimes. The prosecution of crime is the legitimate aim of the interference; the necessity of it is the demonstration of its proportionality,[58] combined with those other procedural protections, such as the giving of notice and allowing persons to be interrogated in the presence of their lawyers[59] to guard against any abusive recourse to the power, a guarantee which would not be there if it were simply another prosecutorial power available to the police.[60] Under the Convention, the fairness of criminal trial is assessed taking into account pre-trial procedure, even before the defendant has been charged.[61] It is enough that suspicion has fallen on the defendant and that there is a risk that he will be prosecuted.[62] The relevant period will clearly cover inquiries made by the SFO in reliance s. 2 Criminal Justice Act 1987 and, since it is established that the SFO can call for proceedings of or documents produced in other investigatory proceedings, they will be included too unless there is a specific provision which excludes the information from a subsequent criminal trial. There is one other consideration which bears here which does not affect crime in general, however difficult it may be to prosecute. Most of the defendants will be company controllers who have specific obligations as to how they conduct their business arising from company and insolvency law. Furthermore, it is the corporate structure which both facilitates the crimes and enables the evidence of the wrong doing to be concealed. This is not to suggest that there is some kind of implied waiver of their rights by company controllers as a condition of enjoying the advantages of incorporation: the Convention's strict requirements for waiver make such a claim implausible.[63] Rather, that a State which makes the calculation that the effective regulation or company activities and the prosecution of crimes committed in reliance on or facilitated by incorporation may make it a feature of its company law that some inroads may be made on the principle against self-incrimination.[64] To the extent that an individual complains about the effect of these provisions, his Convention remedy will be contingent on him showing that he has not had a fair trial. In practice, that will mean showing that the manner of obtaining the evidence or the use to which it was put in the trial has unfairly prejudiced him. This is the suggestion of Tony Smith in his paper[65] and, if one reads it correctly, of Lord Browne-Wilkinson in *Arrows (No. 4)*.[66] One makes the assumption[67] that Lord Browne-Wilkinson did not intend that the mere fact that the evidence had been obtained in breach of the privilege against self-incrimination would lead to its exclusion under the Police and Criminal Evidence Act 1984, s. 78: that would be to restore self-incrimination in its strong, absolute sense, considered above. If this is what the English courts are to do, whatever decisions they make in favour of admissibility are unlikely to be reviewed in Strasbourg. The Court has left the very widest margin of appreciation to the States to establish their own rules of evidence and for national courts to apply them.[68] What one needs now are a few decisions of trial judges indicating how they will apply the judgment in *Arrows (No. 4)*.

The British government will continue to press these and similar points when *Saunders* is argued before the Court, despite the apparently conclusory language of *Funke*. If it were to lose in *Saunders*, it must hope that the Court will decide that it was the particular circumstances of the case which were the explanation for the violation of the Convention and not that recourse to the fruits of investigatory

[58] Funke alleged that the evidence sought to be obtained from him by compulsory process could have been obtained by the authorities by application to the appropriate foreign sources, above n. 2, para. 51. The Court noted, para. 44, that the authorities 'Being unable or unwilling to procure [the documents] by other means' sought to compel Funke to produce them'.

[59] Because Funke was informed of the proceedings against him and was not detained in custody, there was no obstacle to him consulting his lawyers.

[60] Government's arguments in *Saunders*, above n. 10, paras. 64–65.

[61] *Barbera*, above n. 16.

[62] For consideration of this in relation to Funke, see above n. 26, para.s 52–55. In his dissenting opinion in *Saunders*, above n. 10, Professor Schermers, like the trial judge, drew the line *for the purposes of the privilege against self-incrimination* at the time when the defendant was charged. After that, he could not be compelled to provide evidence.

[63] *De Weer* v. *Belgium* A/35 (1980).

[64] See Professor Schermers dissenting in *Saunders*, above n. 10. Also, though in a different context, *Fayed* v. *UK* A/294B (1994) para. 69.

[65] Above n. 1, p. 22, referring to s. 76 Police and Criminal Evidence Act 1984.

[66] Above n. 3, pp. 831–32, referring to s. 78 Police and Criminal Evidence Act 1984.

[67] Though this assumption is optimistic in the light of the Commission's Report in Saunders, above n. 10.

[68] *Schenck* v. *Switzerland* A/140 (1988).

procedures for all criminal trial purposes had been condemned.

Self-incrimination and other provisions of the Convention

On the other hand, this speculation might, from the government's perspective, prove rather optimistic. Other provisions of the Convention may provide incidental protection of the privilege against self-incrimination. Where the coercion involves the seizure of material evidence, Article 8 may apply to ensure 'respect for the private and family life, home and correspondence' of an individual. Because of the willingness of the institutions to condone as 'necessary in a democratic society' measures for the investigation of crime which interfere with these interests under Article 8(2), so long as such measures have a legal basis in the national law, then the protection available to an individual may not be so extensive.[69] Rather surprisingly, the Commission's report in *K* v. *Austria*[70] suggests a more substantial basis might be found in Article 10, which protects the right to freedom of expression. The applicant had been charged with possession of a small quantity of heroin. He was then required to give evidence in the trial of drug dealers, having been told that a refusal to answer questions might expose him to prosecution. When he refused to testify, he was fined. Proceedings against K were discontinued but an attempt to have the order originally made against him quashed failed. The Commission first found that the proceedings against K for refusing to testify were not 'criminal' in the sense of Article 6 and, accordingly, no issue of fair trial arose.[71] On the Article 10 claim, K's argument was that he had been made to speak when he did not want to, and, since Article 10 protected both the positive and negative aspects of expression, his Convention right had been interfered with. The Commission confirmed this, a result surprising only insofar as the argument is seldom made under Article 10, although it has been of some importance in Article 11.[72] Somewhat more unexpected was the Commission's conclusion that the sanctions against K were not necessary within Article 10(2). The Commission spoke in strong terms:

> . . . the principle of protection against self-incrimination is, like the principle of the presumption of innocence, one of the most fundamental aspects of the right to a fair trial.[73]

When he was required to testify in the trial of the dealers, K was facing the prospect of his own trial. The Commission was not convinced that it was necessary to override K's privilege in this case, although it said expressly that it was not deciding whether, in all cases where there was a risk of self-incrimination, the duty to testify was abrogated.[74] Nonetheless, one of the items in the friendly settlement reached between K and the Austrian government was the proposal to amend Austrian law so that,

> Persons who are suspected of committing an offence, in respect of which they are under investigation, or whose statements may expose them to the risk of prosecution, shall be exempted from the obligation to give evidence.[75]

This is a strong version of the right not to incriminate one's self despite the use of 'privilege' in the report and, if this is what the Convention requires, we are back with the unqualified interpretation of *Funke*.

If *Funke* cannot be avoided, what are the alternatives?

If it be the case than *Funke* leaves no room for the effective use of the statutory investigatory powers in connection with criminal proceedings, then a search for alternatives must be made. Given that the argument for the powers is that they are essential for the effective prosecution of big corporate fraud, there will be few options commensurate with the existing model of criminal procedure. Rather surprisingly, the European Court has endorsed prolonged detention and intensive interrogation as an approach to major crime as being compatible with the Convention. In this case, *W* v. *Switzerland*,[76] the issue arose under Article 5(3), which deals with pre-trial detention. W was prosecuted for a series of substantial company frauds. He was detained for a period of four years and three days, a period which came to an end with his conviction. The Commission was overwhelmingly of the view that there had been a violation of Article 5(3).[77] The Court emphasised that the determination whether a period of detention was proper was not to be fixed in relation to any particular length of time but was to be assessed in the light of all the circumstances of the case. It is always necessary that reasonable suspicion that the defendant

[69] An Article 8 claim was raised in *Funke*, above n. 2, paras. 47–59, where the Court found a violation because of a lack of procedural controls over search powers exercised by customs. To the same effect, *Cremieux* v. *France* A/256B (1993); *Miailhe* v. *France* A/256C (1993). The issue was distinct from the self-incrimination point.

[70] *K* v. *Austria* App. No. 16002/90, Report, 13 Oct. 1992.

[71] *Ibid.*, paras. 32–40.

[72] Which is concerned with freedom of association.

[73] Above n. 62, para. 49.

[74] *Ibid.*, para. 52.

[75] *K.* v. *Austria* A/255B (friendly settlement) para. 14.

[76] *W.* v. *Switzerland* A/254 (1993).

[77] *W* v. *Switzerland* App. No. 14379/88, Report 10 Sept. 1991, paras. 145–148.

was involved in criminal conduct should persist throughout his detention. Beyond that, the State was entitled to take into account three principal criteria to determine whether continued detention were justified. They were: the danger of absconding; the danger of collusion; and the prevention of further offences. The assessment of these factors was primarily for the national authorities. When persons were subject to pre-trial detention, the State had a special responsibility to ensure that the proceedings were conducted expeditiously. In this case, the European Court endorsed the findings of the Swiss courts that there were good reasons for continuing to detain W and that the length of the proceedings had been in large measures due to the conduct of the defendant, in particular his unwillingness to cooperate in this investigation. Accordingly, there had been no breach of Article 5(3).[78] There was a fulminating dissent by Judge Pettiti in which he emphasised the value of Article 5(3) as a protection where the authorities used prolonged detention,

'in order to put pressure on accused persons and induce them to make admissions or denunciations, which tends to abolish the right to silence.'[79]

Even if W's refusal to cooperate made the investigation more difficult and delayed bringing the case to trial, it could not justify this long period of detention.

It does appear surprising that the majority in *Funke* attached such importance to the right against self-incrimination that it was willing to accept that the imposition of relatively small fines for refusing to cooperate with the authorities constituted a violation of the right and yet the majority in *W* was willing to countenance such extended detention with the same objective. The applicant, it is true, did not raise the Article 6 point but the Court was clearly not unaware of its relevance. If extended detention is to be the answer, there would need to be changes in English bail law and in the exercise of judicial discretion to allow detention to be continued. It seems to me to be a less attractive option than regarding self-incrimination as a qualifiable privilege and a further reason why *Funke* should not be read to its widest meaning.

However, if *Funke* cannot be constrained and *W* is unacceptable, not many options remain. Reliance on regulatory mechanisms[80] as a device to avoid the limitations of Article 6 encounters two problems. The first is that regulatory sanctions do not carry the stigma attached to criminal penalties and the gravity of the damage done by large scale fraud is both enormous in its size and grievous to individuals so that regulatory sanctions, however stringent, may appear not to meet the seriousness of the wrong. Second, it is far from clear that the European Court would regard a regulatory regime equipped with serious sanctions as falling outside Article 6. 'Criminal charge' for the purposes of Article 6 is, in the Convention language, an 'autonomous' concept, that is to say, the institutions will look at the substance of the matter and not (or not just) at its classification by the national legal order.[81] One of the features the Court takes into account to determine whether an offence is 'really' criminal is the severity of any punishment. In *Bendenoun*,[82] the Court categorised as 'criminal' proceedings against a taxpayer to impose for non-payment of tax surcharges against him in excess of the tax which he had not paid. Wholly compensatory orders might keep the offences out of the 'criminal' category. Sanctions which go to the suspension or exclusion of individuals from professional or company practice sometimes involve the determination of 'civil rights' within Article 6(1)[83] and, if there were no risk of subsequent criminal proceedings, the right against self-incrimination would not apply. Where, in relation to either kind of process, there were a prospect of a future of a criminal trial, the strict interpretation of *Funke* demands that the individual be given an immunity against prosecution if he is made to testify in the non-criminal proceedings.

Conclusion

Enough has been said to demonstrate why it matters to the British government to establish that *Funke* guarantees only a qualifiable privilege against self-incrimination as an element in the right to a fair trial. English judges should be aware that the exact meaning of *Funke* remains to be established and that, since the case had some influence on Lord Browne-Wilkinson's judgment in *Arrows (No. 4)*, they might still have some leeway in applying s. 78 Police and

[78] Above, n. 68, paras. 39–42.

[79] *Ibid.* J. Murdoch, Safeguarding the Liberty of the Person:Recent Strasbourg Jurisprudence, 42 ICLQ 494, 517 (1993) says that *W* is 'exceptional' and may be the 'low-water mark' of what the Court will tolerate by way of pre-trial detention.

[80] Note *Thompson Newspapers* 67 DLR (4) 141 where the Canadian Supreme Court avoided the self-incrimination rules of the Canadian Charter by classifying restrictive practices proceedings as regulatory rather than criminal.

[81] *Osturk* v. *Germany* A/73 (1984); minor road-traffic offences 'administrative' in German Law; Court said 'criminal' for Article 6(1).

[82] *Bendenoun* v. *France* A/284 (1994). See S. Frommel, The European Court of Human Rights and the right of the accused to remain silent: can it be invoked by taxpayers? (1993/II) Intertax 520, seeking to apply *Funke* to tax investigations.

[83] *Le Compte et al.* v. *Belgium* A/43 (1981).

Criminal Evidence Act 1984 to the fruits of investigatory proceedings. However, even if the government's view of *Funke* prevails, this may not be the end of its troubles. The United Kingdom is a party to the International Covenant on Civil and Political Rights, Article 14(3) of which reads:

In the determination of any criminal charge against him, everyone shall be entitled to the following minimum guarantees, in full equality: . . . (g) Not to be compelled to testify against himself or to confess guilt.

The United Kingdom, has not accepted the Optional Protocol to the Covenant which allows individual communications to the Human Rights Committee. It is however, obliged to make quinquennial reports to the Committee on the application of the Covenant and to submit to questioning by the Committee on its Report. It is easy to anticipate that because of the interest in the general question of the limitation of the right to silence in criminal proceedings[84] that the government will have to be prepared to answer questions about the investigatory procedures considered here. The specific textual enunciation of the principle in Article 14(3)(g) will make it harder to justify them, especially given the non-discrimination rider.*

[84] In a case involving judicial comment at trial on the silence of a defendant during police interrogation and at the trial, the Commission has recently held that that was no violation of Article 6(1), *Murray* v. *UK*, App. No. 18731/91, Report, 27 June 1994.

* I am grateful to officials of the Council of Europe and the Legal Advisers Department of the Foreign and Commonwealth Office for the prompt supply of Convention documents.

9. The Particularity of Serious Fraud

G. R. SULLIVAN

THE dominant theme of the papers and seminar discussion was the extent to which we should treat serious or complex fraud as a discrete phenomenon within the criminal law requiring provisions of procedural and substantive law peculiar to itself. Or should we, as asserted by a prominent practitioner with much experience of fraud investigations, refuse to countenance any measure in respect of fraudsters which we would not be equally prepared to use against, say, murderers or rapists.[1] Taking the latter view, we would revert to more restrained and limited conceptions of procedural and substantive law, uprooting much statutory and judge-made law in the process. By contrast, a stress on a more effective response to fraud would argue for retention of present fraud-related provisions and even further developments in that vein.[2]

To an extent, this divergence may reflect differing assessments of the enforcement difficulties that serious fraud gives rise to. One could point to the fact that the Fraud Investigation Group of the Crown Prosecution Service enjoys a similar 'success' rate to the Serious Fraud Office[3] despite the lack of investigative and procedural measures exclusively available to the latter agency. Against that, prior to the establishment of the Serious Fraud Office, with its particular powers, prosecutions against certain cases of large scale City fraud were not brought because of the size and complexity of the cases.[4] A reversion to such quiescence is, surely, a thing of last resort.

However, certain measures currently employed seemingly fall below minimum standards imposed by the United Kingdom's treaty obligations arising under the European Convention on Human Rights. Notably under threat are those many provisions which override or undermine the privilege against self-incrimination. The loss of such investigative muscle could lead to a significant diminution of effectiveness in fraud investigation. That in turn may lead to a greater emphasis on administrative/regulatory responses to fraudulent conduct. Significant 'decriminalisation' of serious fraud however is unattractive. The ultimate sanction of imprisonment is likely to have greater deterrent impact on serious fraudsters as a class by comparison with more visceral and impulsive offenders.

These intractable issues will now be treated in the terms in which they arose in the papers and the ensuing seminar. The path to be followed will be that of a serious fraud case itself: investigation; preparatory hearing; trial.

The Investigation of Serious or Complex Fraud

As Tony Smith's paper relates,[5] the courts have given full effect to those investigative powers vested in Department of Trade and Industry inspectors, liquidators, banking regulators etc. A line of decisions[6] have ruled that provisions reposing powers of compulsory questioning and which render admissible coerced answers in subsequent criminal proceedings override the common law privilege against self-incrimination. Furthermore, they have allowed the Serious Fraud Office access to incriminating answers obtained under these inquisitorial powers for use as evidence in criminal trials notwithstanding that the SFO's own powers of investigation expressly exclude the direct use at any subsequent trial of any incriminating answers made to SFO investigators.[7] A recent House of Lord's decision, *Re Arrows Ltd* (No. 4)[8] fits with this body of case-law in terms of its specific ruling which was that the SFO was to be permitted access to incriminating answers obtained by the Companies Court under powers invested under section 236 of the Insolvency Act 1986. Moreover, the Companies Court was denied any jurisdiction to impose terms and conditions on the access. Nonetheless, there is a marked difference in the tone and

[1] David Kirk writing in *The Times* (December 3rd 1990). Mr Kirk was present at the seminar and repeated this view.

[2] Suggestions to this effect can be found in *The Royal Commission on Criminal Justice* (CM2263, 1993) and in the Treasury review (*Review of the Handling of Serious Fraud*, 1994) of the working of the Serious Fraud Office and the Fraud Investigation Group of the Crown Prosecution Service. These will be discussed *infra*.

[3] Since the inception of the Serious Fraud office its conviction rate has averaged 65% and in the same period the conviction rate of the Fraud Investigation Group has averaged 75%: *Review of the Handling of Serious Fraud* para. 4.57. There is an overlap in the case load of the two bodies in terms of complexity and size of case but the average value of the fraud is much higher for the SFO than FIG (£m 87; £m 8: *ibid.* para. 5.2). Moreover, annexe 6 of the Report contains a summary of selected FIG cases where the investigation foundered for the lack of investigative powers exclusively available to the SFO.

[4] Kirk and Woodcock, *Serious Fraud: Investigation and Trial* (1992) at p. 2.

[5] A. T. H. Smith, 'The Right to Silence in Cases of Serious Fraud' in *Pressing Problems in the Law* (ed. Birks, 1995) at 000–000.

[6] Discussed, *Loc. cit* at 000–000.

[7] Criminal Justice Act 1987 section 2(8).

[8] [1994] 3 All E.R. 814.

orientation of this judgment compared with earlier judgments in this sequence of cases.

Those earlier judgments give primacy to effectiveness in combatting fraud. By contrast, the House of Lords in *Re Arrows Ltd* (No. 4) gives equal billing to the rights of suspects and defendants. The privilege against self-incrimination is described by Lord Browne-Wilkinson in his judgment as 'one of the basic freedoms secured by English law'[9] and as 'one of the basic rights protected by the European Convention on Human Rights'.[10] At any criminal trial where self-incriminatory answers compulsorily obtained are to be tendered as evidence the trial judge, according to Lord Browne-Wilkinson, should consider the discretion vested by section 78 of the Police and Criminal Evidence Act 1984 to exclude evidence on the grounds of fairness to the accused. He indicated that one factor properly to be taken into account in exercising that discretion is the 'unexplained anomaly' that the Director of the SFO can make direct use, because of his statutory power to obtain documents,[11] of incriminating answers obtained by means of compulsion by other investigators but cannot directly use any incriminating answers obtained by his own investigators. It is by no means unlikely that, post *Re Arrows Ltd (No. 4)*, the Director will be restricted to using compelled incriminatory answers from whatever source as an investigatory tool and will not be permitted to use such material as admissible evidence. This outcome is all the more likely in the light of the decision of the European Court of Human Rights in *Funke* v. *France*[12] that self incrimination violates the fair trial guarantee in Article 6 of the European Convention and the recent decision to the same effect by a 14:1 majority of the European Commission of Human Rights in *Saunders* v. *United Kingdom*.[13] Lord Browne-Wilkinson gave salience to Convention obligations and explicitly referred to *Funke*.

How far the discretion to exclude evidence will be taken in future will be a function of judicial perception of the values and policies protected by the privilege against self-incrimination. Discussion at the seminar did not produce any agreement as to the nature and rationale of this privilege.[14] At its most expansive, it can be characterised as an intrinsic, first order right analogous to the right not to be tortured or subjected to cruel and unusual punishment. The rhetoric supporting such a conception would present the choice between giving a truthful, incriminating answer or risking punishment for maintaining silence as involving unconscionable psychological pressure, excessive diminution of dignity, unwarranted intrusion of privacy. Such an absolutist stand point arguably lies behind Article 14(g) of the United Nations Covenant on Civil and Politics Rights[15] which grants a right against self-incrimination in unqualified terms. The cryptic judgment of the European Court of Human Rights in *Funke* v. *France*,[16] can be read to the same effect. Explicitly, it merely informs that the requirements of French customs law do not justify overriding the right against self-incrimination, a right implicit in the Article 6 guarantee of a fair trial. The protection, however, is notably firm. There had been no attempt to adduce incriminating answers at a criminal trial. The applicant had been fined for a failure to produce documents. That the documents could be adduced at a subsequent trial was enough to invoke the protection.

Even on the broadest view of the privilege against self-incrimination, it is uncertain to what extent it precludes recourse to coerced self-incrimination as an investigatory tool under schemes, such as the Criminal Justice Act 1987, which repose powers of compulsory inquisition in officials but disallow the use of coerced answers as evidence in any subsequent trial. Such a limitation will not placate those commentators who locate the privilege in the prosecution's burden of proof, who claim that any obligation on the defendant to further the case against himself is incompatible with the prosecution's duty to establish its case. Arguably, however, this confuses facilitation of the discharge of the burden of proof with derogation from that burden. The substantive requirement—proof beyond any reasonable doubt—remains intact under the 1987 Act scheme.[17]

Compromise schemes such as the Criminal Justice Act 1987 may prove attractive for those who regard the privilege against self-incrimination as a value in its own right but a value which must be balanced against countervailing values and police. *A fortioti*, such is the position for those who are unconvinced that non self-incrimination has any intrinsic value,

[9] [1994] 3 All E.R. 814, at 830g.
[10] *Ibid.*, at 821a.
[11] Criminal Justice Act 1987 section 2(3).
[12] (1993) 16 EHRR 297.
[13] Application No. 19187/91.
[14] For explorations of this question see Stuntz, 'Self-Incrimination and Excuse (1988) 88 Col. L. Rev. 227; Delinko 'Is there a Rationale for the Privilege against Self-Incrimination?' (1986) 33 U.C.L.A.L. Rev. 1063; Donagan, 'The Right Not to Incriminate Oneself' in *Human Rights* (eds Paul, Miller and Paul, 1984), pp. 137–148.
[15] 'In the determination of any criminal charge against him, everyone shall be entitled . . . not to be compelled to testify against himself.'
[16] Loc. cit., note 12.
[17] Any provision which places the formal burden of proof on the defence is vulnerable to an article 6 challenge: *Salabiaku* v. *France* A/14a/1988; and see too *AG of Hong Kong* v. *Lee Kwong Kut* [1993] 3 All E.R. 939.

but accept that in the context of police questioning the privilege may provide a measure of protection against unacceptable modes of interrogation. Common to both non-absolutist positions is to acknowledge that compulsory questioning in serious fraud cases is not carried out in police cells and that serious fraud presents particular investigative difficulties.[18]

That latter point was directly contested by *David Kirk, who as alluded to earlier, took the view that the SFO should be denied any exceptional powers of investigation which are unavailable in respect of other serious crimes. Making the point that investigative difficulties were not confined to fraud, he instanced a case of a body found at a roadside, probably the victim of a hit and run motorist, but where proof of what happened is frustrated by the absence of witnesses. By comparison cases of suspected serious fraud may seem less intractable. The cast-list of suspects is often known at the outset, whatever production difficulties loom ahead. But the contrast is one-dimensional. In homicides, violent robberies etc., the fact that a serious crime has occurred will be obvious whatever the problems, sometimes insoluble, of linking particular individuals to incidents. Contrast the case of company X plc. In June its share price is riding high and it is regarded as a sound investment. By October, the share price has collapsed, the quotation suspended and its creditors put on hold. The affair may exemplify the unpredictability of commerce or mismanagement or serious fraud or any combination thereof. If there is fraud, the company's published accounts and public documentation will tell a false or incomplete story. There will be other, secret accounts and things left unrecorded. Without powers of compulsory questioning and documentary requisition it may never be known whether criminal conduct was a factor in the company's demise.[19]

This is more than surmise. In the recent Treasury review of the operations of the SFO and the Fraud Investigation Group of the Crown Prosecution Service, an appendix to the report[20] gives details of FIG investigations (which are conducted without access to SFO powers) frustrated by an inability to unearth the salient facts. The report recommends a considerable extension of powers of compulsory questioning.[21] If such powers are to be radically cut back, other means may have to be considered. As Colin Warbrick relates,[22] the European Court of Human Rights has accepted that the intricacies of an investigation into serious fraud may justify custodial questioning of an individual suspect for a period of over 4 years.[23] It is questionable whether the introduction of such measures in the United Kingdom, in lieu of present investigative powers, would constitute any enhancement of the rights of suspects.[23a]

The Preparatory Hearing

The preparatory hearing, introduced by the Criminal Justice Act 1987,[24] is the most conspicuous feature differentiating serious fraud trials from other criminal proceedings. The view of practitioners at the seminar was that these hearings had failed to limit and clarify the issues to be contested at trial. Although a statutory obligation is imposed on the defence to set out 'in general terms' the nature of the defence,[25] compliance typically takes the form of a wholly uninformative general traverse of the prosecution case.[26] This reinforces a natural tendency on the part of the prosecution to play safe by advancing on a broad front. Fraud trials remain exceedingly long and are, as *Henry L.J. put it, to be regarded as part of the punishment.

It was agreed that the response of defence counsel was wholly to be expected in an adversarial system. Why should defence counsel, other than tactically, do any more to help the prosecution shape its case than the strict minimum legally required? It can be said that to require any forensic assistance from the defence is to shift the burden of proof. In reply, one may again advise against confusing the easing of he discharge of the burden with dispensation from that burden. Nonetheless, there is an essential difference between criminal and civil proceedings; in the former the relationship of the State to the defendant is hostile. Accordingly, it may be said, no duties of

* Denotes a contribution to seminar discussion.

[18] Both factors were influential with *The Royal Commission on Criminal Justice* (CM 2263) which recommended the extension of SFO investigative powers to FIG and permitting constables attached to these bodies to use them in non-police station settings: paras. 68–74.

[19] The ECHR has recently ruled in *Fayed* v. *UK* (28.1993/423/502) that compulsory self-incriminating questions are legitimate for the purposes of regulatory fact finding.

[20] *Review of the Handling of Serious Fraud* (1994) appendix 6.

[21] In accord with the earlier proposal of the Royal Commission, *loc. cit.*, note 18.

[22] 'Self-Incrimination and the European Convention on Human Rights' in *Pressing Problems of the Law* (ed. Birks, 1994) at 000–000.

[23] *W* v. *Switzerland* A/254/1993.

[23a] Concerns about lengthy pre-trial detention have prompted a major re-examination of French criminal procedure: Trouille, 'A Look at French Criminal Procedure' [1994] Crim L.R. 735.

[24] Sections 7–11.

[25] Criminal Justice Act 1987, section 9(5).

[26] E.g. Roger Seelig's response in Guiness II: a denial of all the facts as the prosecution interpreted them and a general assertion of honesty.

co-operation and compliance arise on the part of an accused subject. Yet the limited notion of citizenship on which this view ultimately rests can be challenged by contractarian or communitarian theories of the State provided we can postulate a criminal justice system of sufficient integrity and utility to command respect.

At present, the defence can adopt a policy of non-co-operation with impunity. As Jeremy Roberts points out, there is little if anything by way of sanction for a refusal to inform as to the lines of defence or to agree facts.[27] He suggests that the law should be changed so as to allow the judge to reveal to the jury the defence's response to any invitation on the part of the prosecution to agree facts. In *Henry L.J.'s view, this would not be enough. He favoured an obligation on defence counsel to provide details of the projected defence together with an indication of the nature of the evidence supporting the defence. Crucial to the effectiveness of any such change in the law would be the sanction for non-compliance. Should it ever go beyond adverse comment by the judge to the jury? Auld J. has suggested, extrajudicially, that the defence should be precluded from relying on any evidence that it has failed to notify in advance.[28] In terms of compliance, the suggestion has much force.

In this matter, concerns of efficacy and manageability sharply conflict with principle. Can it ever be right to imprison a person in the knowledge that his defence has gone unheard? Take the case of D, a clerk in a fraudulent investment company. His role in the fraud was limited to taking cash and bearer bonds out of the country to deposit in overseas accounts. He calculates that the prosecution has insufficient evidence against him and he asserts that he was unaware of the fraudulent nature of the company that employed him. At trial it becomes obvious to him that his calculation was wrong. He now says that his involvement was coerced by threats of serious violence.

This would appear exactly the kind of case that Auld J. had in mind. If D had been a witness for himself, in relation to the first story he would have committed perjury. If D has any evidence at all for his second story, the burden of disproof will fall to the prosecution, perhaps requiring extensive new lines of inquiry months into the trial. But if there is evidence sufficient to raise a defence of duress the case for investigating the matter thoroughly is surely very strong.[29]

The Trial

(a) Size and complexity of issues to be tried

Whatever is done, successfully or otherwise, to make preparatory hearings more effective, fraudulent machinations of any scope and duration will continue to generate exceedingly lengthy trials. Blue Arrow and Guiness were massive; we now have *Kellard and others*,[30] the case which has, in the words of the Court of Appeal, the 'ignoble distinction' of being the longest criminal jury trial in English legal history. The first of the preparatory hearings was in February 1989 and the trial closed at the end of January 1992. Moreover *Kellard* was a case of 'straightforward' business deception unencumbered by any City complexities. The Court of Appeal, as ever, urged restraint in the calling of evidence on the part of future prosecutors and called for a spirit of co-operation in the agreeing and elimination of contested issues on the part of the defence.

Whatever change, if any, in the adversarial mind set comes to pass, the key element of dishonesty in the major fraud offences (theft; deception; fraudulent trading; conspiracy to defraud) will continue to protract trials. As *Jeremy Roberts explained, the broad value judgment involved has an expansionary effect on what may constitute relevant evidence. There is ample scope for yet another coat of black paint. As the ultimate issue is one of jury evaluation,[31] the prosecution evidence has to be very strong before the defence will throw in its hand.

The length and complexity of fraud trials will keep live the issue whether jury trial is a suitable forum for such cases. The unsuccessful appeal in *Kellard* yielded a firm ruling that the length of the trial does not of itself constitute a reason why the jury verdict should be regarded as unsafe or unsatisfactory.[32] The Court of Appeal buttressed that conclusion by expressing its confidence in the grasp of the jury in the instant case. Inevitably that confidence must have been conjectural, given the lack of knowledge of the jury's deliberations. It seemed largely based on the court's good opinion of prosecution counsel's command of his case and in his clarity of presentation. *Henry L.J. and *Jeremy Roberts, when reflecting on juries, spoke of them allowing a case 'to wash over

[27] 'Some Procedural Problems in Criminal Fraud Cases' in *Pressing Problems in the Law* (ed. Birks, 1995) at 000–000.

[28] At p. 60 in *The Gradual Convergence: Foreign Ideas, Foreign Influences* (ed. Markensinis, 1994).

[29] Zuckerman, writing of the statutory requirement to give advance notice of an alibi, states that it would be, 'a rare case for the court to prohibit an accused adducing alibi evidence on the grounds of non-compliance with the notice requirement: *The Principles of Criminal Evidence* (1989) at p. 85.

[30] [1994] The Times, law report August 5th.

[31] *Ghosh* [1982] Q.B. 1053.

[32] And see too *Attorney Generals Reference (No. 1 of 1990)* [1992] 3 W.L.R. 9.

them' and of the assistance they derived from their 'sense of smell'. The latter, of course, can be an unpredictable property. There is much force in *Peter Glazebrook's suggestion that a defendant should have the option to waive jury trial. Moreover, as *Henry LJ observed, an explicit, detailed judgment may offer better prospects for defence appeals.

As the jury is to remain for the foreseeable future,[33] thought should be given to measures enhancing confidence in jury decision making. Reservations were expressed about the quality of those jurors who were available for trials of 12 months or more. *Stephen Silber suggested that there should be some degree of scrutiny as to the capacity of the persons empanelled to understand the issues likely to arise. *Henry L.J. drew a striking contrast between the passivity of many jurors and the involvement of a judge presiding over a civil trial. Typically he would take copious notes, seek immediate clarification of any misunderstanding or confusion as to the evidence and have the back-up of a full transcript. *Henry L.J. endorsed Jeremy Roberts's suggestion for more written assistance for juries and expressed the view that juries should be provided with as much documentary assistance as they would find useful.

The more documentation fraud juries are given the greater the contrast there will be with juries trying more conventional crime. They are far removed from their paradigm task of resolving conflicts of oral testimony relating to a discrete incident. There is more of a resemblance to a lay commission of inquiry into the conduct of a set of individuals over what may be a lengthy period of time. Nonetheless, the case for retention of the jury is strong. As *Peter Birks emphasised, the jury constitutes an important practical and symbolic link between the general public and the imposition of state punishment. Yet such is the nature of the task in lengthy fraud trials, the thought arises whether juries should be provided with some form of professional assistance such as a clerk to the jury. There is the analogy with the magistrate's clerk. Such an innovation, were it ever to commend itself, would have to be crafted in a manner which ensured that such an official did not in any way usurp the role of the jury or the judge. But it might be useful for a jury to have constantly to hand someone who can help clarify issues of fact and law[34] whenever the chairperson considers such clarification to be useful.

(b) The substantive law

The size and manageability of fraud trials is to some extent a function of the offences charged. As Jeremy Roberts proposes, an indictment ideally should be short and informative, focusing the issues to be contested.[35] That aim will be facilitated if the offences to be charged have a substantial, tightly defined actus reus. Indictments confined to such offences as false accounting, unlawful financial assistance by a company in relation to the acquisition of its shares, procuring the execution of a valuable security etc., entail that the evidence at the trial is shaped and limited by the specifics of such offences.

It is very rare, however, in cases of substantial fraud, for the charges to be so confined. Offences of the kind referred to above are frequently peripheral or incidental to the main elements of the fraud. The core wrongdoing in such cases is best, indeed may only be captured, by invoking offences of deception theft and, notoriously, conspiracy to defraud. The last two offences in particular are exceptionally broad as Sir John Smith's paper relates.[36] The actus reus of theft is any act that assumes one or more rights in property belonging to another and need not involve any element of adverse taking or usurpation.[37] Conspiracy to defraud, in its broadest formulation, is an agreement to act in a manner which may prejudice another's rights or expectations or cause him to act in a manner contrary to his duty.[38] A key element in both offences is dishonesty, which, as touched on earlier, has an expansionary effect on the scope of relevant evidence.

Apart from the tendency of these offences to protract trials, a further and more basic objection is that they afford too little in the way of guidance as to what can or cannot be done. In this vein of criticism, *Peter Glazebrook described the continuance of conspiracy to defraud as 'intolerable'. If we take the maxim 'nulla poena sine lege' to mean that any offence should afford concrete guidance as to the specifics of transgression, conspiracy to defraud and, indeed, theft in its current form cannot be allowed to continue. The former would go entirely and theft

[33] *The Royal Commission on Criminial Procedure* (CM 2263, 1993) examined the role of the jury in the context of serious fraud trials (paras. 76–81) and did not recommend abolition or waiver. There are no current legislative proposals for abolishing or limiting jury trial in serious fraud cases. The matter however continues to raise public discussion e.g. Rees-Mogg, 'Through a glass darkly' [1994] The Times, September 22nd, 1994.

[34] A letter to The Times (September 26 1994) from a Dr. D. G. D. Wise refers to a case where a jury after two days discussion sought assistance from the judge on the meaning of 'intent to defraud', the essential issue in the case and dealt with at length in the summing up.

[35] *Loc. cit.*; note 26 at 000.

[36] 'Fraud and the Criminal Law' in *Pressing Problems of the Law* (ed. Birks 1995) at 000–000.

[37] *Gomez* [1993] A.C. 442.

[38] *Wai Yu-tsang* [1991] 4 All E.R. 664.

would be remaindered to adverse assumptions of the entirety of another's proprietary interest and would be insulated from expansionary civil law developments in the things that may constitute property.[39]

Undeniably, such a step would inhibit an effective response to some serious frauds. After the House of Lords disembowelled conspiracy to defraud in *Ayres*,[40] a series of cases demonstrated that significant forms of fraudulent conduct could not be reached without recourse to the offence.[41] Accordingly, it was restored in all its amplitude by Parliament,[42] pending final resolution of its future in the light of Law Commission proposals.[43] *Sir George Staple confirmed the current utility of the offence. Sir John Smith regards the scope of the offence to be both a blessing and a curse and, while setting his face against any general fraud offence which may be committed by an individual, he opts, reluctantly perhaps, for conspiracy to defraud to be retained in a recast statutory form.[44]

If one is prepared to go that far, there are benefits to be had in going the one step further and providing a general fraud offence unencumbered by the need to establish a conspiracy. The fraudulent conduct of individuals such as Maxwell, Nadir, Clowes and, from an earlier era, Eric Miller, demonstrates that individuals in command of organisations can loot its assets without necessarily involving any minions.[45] Whether such looting involves theft, deception or any other nominate offence or can only be dealt with by charging conspiracy to defraud (if any agreement with another can be established) may well depend on variables unrelated to the culpability of the fraudulent conduct. *Barlow Clowes* (No. 2)[46] makes this point graphically. Whether investors retained a proprietary interest in money advanced to an investment fund ultimately turned on whether the phrase in the investment deed 'and to place any uninvested funds with any bank, local authority or other body . . .' was auxiliary or substantive. It was held to be the former and therefore investors retained a proprietary interest in the monies they had entrusted to the fund. Consequently, the money Clowes abstracted for his own purposes was stolen by him. A reading of the case shows this point of construction to have been a pretty close run thing. One may muse whether the exercise would have come out the same way in less charged circumstances. Had it gone the other way, conspiracy to defraud would have foundered on the fact that Clowes perpetrated many abstractions of funds without involving anyone else. Either way, the substance of his wrongdoing—making dishonest abstractions of funds to the prejudice of the financial interests of others—remains precisely the same.

The economy of means implicit in a general fraud offence induces hesitation. Even if it is drafted in substantially narrower terms than the current offence, its sweep would still be considerable. All Theft Act offences save those with aggravating features of violence, threat or trespass could be threatened with extinction. To avoid this, *Andrew Ashworth suggested that procedural limitations could be devised to restrain recourse to a general fraud offence to circumstances where another nominate offence could not be charged. This writer has made suggestions to similar effect.[47] This cannot, however, be expected to appease those persons whose objection is based on lack of fair warning.[48] To them it would amount to little more than saying we will abide with principle when we can but depart from it when we must.

Thus the fair-warning question must be addressed directly. I have argued elsewhere that a general fraud offence proscribing dishonest conduct which is intended to achieve an economic gain and which is done in the knowledge that it would cause economic loss to another is acceptable provided that gains to which there is an indefeasible title/right at civil law are put beyond its ambit.[49] Arguably too, gains achieved by the non-performance of a contractual obligation, without more, should be excluded.[50] It has to be conceded that this proposed offence would penalise conduct in ways that may defy prediction. That, it is contended, is not objectionable provided the definitional elements of the offence ensure that

[39] E.g. *A-G for Hong Kong* v. *Reid* [1993] 3 W.L.R. 1143.

[40] [1984] A.C. 447.

[41] E.g. *Lloyd* [1985] Q.B. 829; *Hollinshead* [1985] A.C. 985.

[42] Criminal Justice Act 1987 section 12.

[43] *Law Commission Working Paper No. 104*, Criminal Law, Conspiracy to Defraud.

[44] Loc. cit., note 35 at 000.

[45] 'A powerful chairman or managing director, with a board of directors which is not able or willing to play an inquisitorial role into his transactions and expenditure, has immense scope for diverting company money to his own use over a long period of time': *Investigation into the affairs of the Peachey Property Corporation Limited*, HMSO (1979), para. 227.

[46] [1994] 2 All E.R. 316.

[47] 'Fraud and the Efficacy of the Criminal Law' [1985] Crim. L./R. 616; 'Framing an Acceptable General Offence of Fraud' [1989] J. Cr.L. 92.

[48] The Ashworth, Sullivan proposals are essentially conservatory.

[49] Loc. cit., note 47.

[50] It may be thought that Parliament should specifically determine whether or not the apparently growing practice of consistently delaying the payment of contractual debts should be brought within the criminal law rather than leaving the matter to be decided under the rubric of a general fraud offence.

conduct which falls within it is of a culpability commensurate with criminal sanctioning.[51]

For conduct *male in se*, the fair warning principle lacks sufficient moral purchase to stymie the creation of conceptually defined offences which make no reference to specifics of conduct. This point may be reinforced by reference to a decision from a very different part of the criminal law. As we know, the *House of Lords* in *R* v. *R*[52] removed the husband's immunity to a charge of raping his wife. Equally familiar is the controversy the case gave rise to in legal circles concerning judicial law-making in the criminal law. The matters of principle arising in *R* concern the judicial role in an uncodified system, essentially a separation of powers question. In terms of substantive justice to the defendant, or the lack thereof, it matters not a whit if he assumed he could act with legal impunity in such a fashion to his wife.[52a]

Those who would regard fair-warning as a more significant restraining factor commit themselves to more than a rejection of a general fraud offence. If a minimum condition for the acceptability of an offence is that it provides a measure of concretised detail as to what it is that may be punished (as is the case, for example, for offences such as false accounting or procuring the execution of a valuable security) any offence heavily reliant on an unfleshed out concept of dishonesty or fraud is equally unacceptable. On that basis theft in a large part of its current ambit is too vague. So too is the Law Commission's suggestion for an offence of fraudulent trading unconfined to those carrying on the business of companies.[53] In their breadth they are narrower[54] than a general fraud offence but within their ambit they may be just as opaque.

Conclusion

If the phrase may be permitted, there is something of a 'back to basics' movement on the part of some lawyers and politicians in relation to serious fraud. The major platform consists of the abolition of any form of self-incrimination and compelled defence involvement in preparatory hearings, a cut-back on the current ambit of theft and the abolition of conspiracy to defraud. Whatever gains in principle may be achieved by such a programme it would impair the effectiveness of response to serious fraud, an effectiveness which, even under current dispensations, is very questionable.

Such a loss of efficacy is proposed at a time when the market is the dominant force in society and when there is rising concern about the 'legitimate' rewards company directors, merchant bankers, brokers etc can achieve. For those in such positions who seek illegitimate rewards there are many devices which assist the creation and concealment of such gains: nominee shareholdings; cheap, immediate incorporation here and overseas, generating a myriad of companies which exist solely for the purpose of obfuscation; immediate electronic transfers of funds; discretionary trusts; complex financial instruments; tax havens; banking secrecy jurisdictions and so on.[55] To insist, in the light of this lawyer assisted sophistication and flexibility, on the classic virtues of mainstream criminal procedure and evidence is, perhaps, a little asymmetrical. At the very least, these matters go beyond lawyer's business and require informed, dispassionate public debate.

[51] The requirement of a jury finding of dishonesty appropriately links this question to current community sentiment under the ruling in *Ghosh* [1982] Q.B. 1053. That, of course, would be a ground of criticism for those who maintain that dishonesty is too vague a concept for definitional use and should play merely a residual, defeasing role in property offences: see the discussion in Smith, *loc. cit.*, note 36, at 000.

[52] [1992] 1 A.C. 599.

[52a] The European Commission of Human Rights has decided by a majority that the judicial abolition of the husband's immunity did not constitute an Article 7 violation: *CR* v. *UK* No. 20190/92; *SW* v. *UK* No. 20166/92.

[53] Working Paper No. 104, paras. 10.12–10.24.

[54] The Law Commission proposal, presented as an alternative to a general fraud offence, is of very considerable breadth given that the only 'trading' may consist of the fraudulent conduct itself (*Kemp* [1988] B.C.L.C. 217) and may consist of a single transaction (*Lockwood* [1986] Crim. L.R. 244).

[55] See the well informed discussion of these matters by Scott J (as he then was) in *Re London United Investments plc* [1992] 1 B.C.L.C. 91 at pp. 113–114.

PART III

FREEDOM OF EXPRESSION

10. Freedom of Speech in an Era of Mass Communication

ERIC BARENDT

I

ENGLISH free speech law seems at last to have abandoned the narrow, insular perspective, which received its classic expression in Dicey's treatment of civil liberties. It is no longer tenable to view freedom of speech as merely a residual liberty, recognised only in the gaps left by the law of blasphemy, libel, contempt of court and so on. The landmark ruling of the House of Lords in the *Derbyshire* case recognises that the freedom is a matter of legal principle, to which the courts will (and must) give appropriate weight. In that case it was held that to allow public authorities to sue in libel is 'contrary to the public interest because to admit such actions would place an undesirable fetter on freedom of speech.'[1] In effect a common law principle of freedom of speech was applied to disentitle a local authority from bringing an action which a (relatively) recent High Court decision, some Commonwealth rulings, and the basic rules of libel law would all have permitted. Most interestingly, the House of Lords, unlike the Court of Appeal, considered that the result could be reached by the common law, without recourse to the European Convention of Human Rights (ECHR). Indeed, Lord Keith was of the view, as had been Lord Goff in the second *Spycatcher* case,[2] that there is no real difference between the common law of free speech and Article 10 of the Convention.

It is of course far too early to predict how significant this ruling will prove to be. If the English courts take Lord Keith's broad statements of principle seriously, some of the fundamental rules of libel law may not survive without major modification. There must be doubts, for example, about the compatibility (at least in the context of actions by public officials) of the principle of strict liability and the presumption of falsity with freedom of political speech.[3] For the imposition of strict liability for statements presumed to be false undoubtedly deters, or to use the American term 'chills', political discourse, as the Supreme Court of the United States appreciated thirty years ago.[4] Further, the recognition of freedom of speech as a matter of legal principle may have a significant impact outside the area of libel. For example, the courts should be more prepared to depart from the American *Cyanamid* 'balance of convenience' test in deciding whether to grant interlocutory injunctions in breach of confidence cases where there is a serious free speech issue; it would generally be preferable to apply the libel rule, under which the courts will only grant such an injunction where the defendant does not plead justification or fair comment. And, as I have argued elsewhere, some of the reasoning, if not necessarily the result in the broadcasting ban case would surely have been different, had freedom of speech been recognised as a principle of English law.[5]

The *Derbyshire* case perhaps fully states a theme—that freedom of speech is a principle of the common law—the first notes of which can be detected in countless other judgements in libel law, contempt rulings and so on. There were intimations also in decisions such as *Brutus* v. *Cozens*,[6] interpreting the public order legislation restrictively in order to preserve so far as possible the freedom of peaceful protest. The theme has now been developed in other recent judgements. For instance, Laws J. said the libel rule in *Bonnard* v. *Perryman* was an instance of a general presumption against the imposition of judicial prior restraints.[7] In the recent *Central Television* case the Court of Appeal lifted an injunction which had been imposed to prevent the transmission of a television documentary about the Scotland Yard Obscene Publications Squad.[8] The programme contained pictures of a man, who had been convicted on two charges of indecency with young boys; this might have led to the identification of his 5 year old son and consequent distress. But the Court unanimously held that in this case, where the publication did not relate to the upbringing of a child over whose welfare it was exercising a supervisory role, it was inappropriate to balance his interests against that of freedom of speech.[9] Passages in the judgement of

[1] *Derbyshire County Council* v. *Times Newspapers Ltd.* [1993] 2 WLR 449, 458 per Lord Keith.

[2] *Attorney-General* v. *Guardian Newspapers (No. 2)* [1990] 1 AC 109, 283–4.

[3] See my article, 'Libel and Freedom of Speech In English Law', [1993] *Public Law* 449, 452–7, for a fuller exposition of this argument.

[4] *New York Times* v. *Sullivan* 376 US 254 (1964).

[5] See my discussion of *R.* v. *Secretary of State for the Home Department, ex parte Brind* [1991] 1 AC 696 in 'Libel and Freedom of Speech', 463.

[6] [1973] AC 854.

[7] *R.* v. *Advertising Standards Authority, ex parte Vernons Ltd.* [1992] 1 WLR 1289, 1293.

[8] [1994] 3 WLR 20.

[9] The Court of Appeal followed its earlier decision in *Re X (A Minor)* [1975] Fam. 47.

Hoffman LJ are particularly striking. In his view freedom of speech could only be subject to clearly defined exceptions which were already formulated by common law or statute, and which also met the standards of the ECHR. The courts had no jurisdiction to extend the established grounds of restraint, even when publication (as perhaps in the case itself) would lead to great distress: 'the principle that the press is free from both governmental and judicial control is more important than the particular case.'

It is tempting from these cases and pronouncements to argue that the High Court has become an effective guardian of freedom of speech (and for that matter, other civil liberties). The temptation should be resisted. Partly this is for the obvious reason that the courts cannot review legislation, such as the Obscene Publications Act, the incitement to racial hatred provisions in the Public Order Act 1986 or section 10 of the Broadcasting Act 1990, all of which arguably infringe the freedom. In the United Kingdom, Parliament is free to balance in its absolute discretion the interests of free speech against other private interests (such as the rights to reputation and confidentiality) or against competing public interests, such as national security and good order. Freedom of speech is, in Hohfeldian terms, almost always a bare liberty; in English law the freedom confers no immunities and only rarely positive or claim-rights.[10]

In this short paper, however, I do not wish to discuss the ways in which Parliament has exercised its unlimited legislative powers, nor for that matter how the courts have weighed free speech against other interests in those areas still largely governed by the common law. Instead, I want to discuss another aspect of freedom of speech, which seems to me of growing importance in the era of mass communications: how far should the freedom be regarded solely as a liberty *against the State*? Might it in some circumstances require the introduction of measures to promote freedom of speech against private concentrations of power? In countries which guarantee freedom of speech and of the press in a Bill of Rights, these arguments may take a constitutional form. It may be contended, for example, in the context of the mass media that rights of reply and access should be recognised or that legislation should be introduced to prevent the development of media oligopolies. Another context for argument, at least in the United States, is provided by campaign financing laws, introduced to achieve a level playing-field at elections, but viewed with disfavour by the Supreme Court.[11]

The second part of this paper offers some remarks about the importance of these difficult issues. My view is that we should no longer regard freedom of speech as solely a right against the state; we should recognise that it may also be endangered by private power, in particular by media concentrations. There are admittedly powerful arguments of principle against that conclusion, but it may be supported by a recent decision of the European Court of Human Rights, which I discuss in Part III. Finally, I argue, in the most straightforward part of this paper (Part IV) that the common law principle of freedom of speech is unable to offer much help in this context.

II

Freedom of speech has traditionally provided a set of liberties against state or public regulation. By far the most potent restraints were those at times imposed by official censorship, though licensing of the press ended as early as 1695. In the eighteenth and nineteenth centuries the freedom was generally asserted by individual writers and pamphleteers who were prosecuted under the laws of sedition and blasphemy, or who were prosecuted or sued for private libel (or their civil law equivalents). In this traditional account, therefore, the bearer of the right to freedom of speech was typically a persecuted dissenter, unable to communicate his beliefs in public, because of the harsh restraints of an oppressive government.

A second feature of this account is that the terms 'freedom of speech' and 'freedom of the press' (or 'media freedom') are used interchangeably; there is no suggestion that the former might be more fundamental than the latter. The rise of the political press in the nineteenth century did not for the most part affect this perspective. Admittedly, on occasion, press freedom was invoked in situations where it was difficult to see that any particular individual's freedom of speech was at stake, as in the successful campaigns to remove the stamp duty on newspapers. But generally the freedoms were regarded (as they still often are) as if they were identical;[12] it was clearly immaterial, for example, whether a newspaper editor, often also its owner, claimed that a sedition law infringed his freedom of speech or press freedom.

[10] However, an access or claim-right to freedom of speech is (rather anomalously) provided for speakers on university premises by the Education (No. 2) Act 1986.

[11] The leading case is *Buckley* v. *Valeo* 424 US 1 (1976), a decision which influenced a majority of the High Court of Australia to strike down legislative restrictions on political party advertising: *Australian Capital Television* v. *The Commonwealth* (1992) 177 CLR 106.

[12] A. V. Dicey, *Introduction to the Study of the Law of the Constitution* (10th ed., London, 1959), ch. VI treats the terms 'free expression of opinion', 'freedom of discussion' and 'liberty of the press' interchangeably.

The question is whether this account of freedom of speech remains adequate. Most speech may now be characterised as 'mass speech'.[13] Among the principal features of this phenomenon is that the communicator packages messages, which may or may not reflect his own personal beliefs, for distribution on the mass media. Typical forms of such expression are political or commercial advertisements and sound-bite interviews. Unlike the speech at the town-hall meeting, there is no invitation to dialogue. Moreover, most mass speech is heavily dependent on access to the press or broadcasting media, inevitably the privilege of a small minority; or it may involve the expenditure of large sums of money on newspaper or hoardings advertisements. Several United States cases concern, for example, the extent to which legislation may restrict expenditure and contributions to political or referendum campaigns; other cases touch on the question whether corporations enjoy the protection of the First Amendment in the same way as natural persons. (Although these issues have been litigated more fully in the United States than in Europe, much the same questions are equally relevant here. This is also true for the United Kingdom, though in the absence of a constitutional free speech provision the questions are more matters of political debate than for legal resolution.)

In the context of mass speech the right to freedom of speech is most often asserted by corporations and media giants, generally anxious to protect their ability to influence public debate from a right-wing or free market perspective. They argue, for example, that legislation, providing for a right of reply to personal attacks in the press or limiting the media outlets a particular corporation may control, is incompatible with the First Amendment.[14] Insofar as the courts have upheld these arguments and denied the government's competence to equalize the opportunities for speech, some commentators in the United States have concluded that there is now an inevitable conservative tilt to free speech jurisprudence. The 'market-place of ideas' is not so much a metaphor (so conceived by Holmes J. in his classic dissent in *Abrams*)[15] as an accurate description of public discourse.[16] It is no accident that right-wing thinkers and corporations are now so supportive of freedom of speech, a principle traditionally associated with radical dissenters and political liberals. Effective communication (with the exception of street protest) is dependent on large sums of money, so that unrestricted free speech disproportionately benefits the wealthy.

Naturally one may take the view that this does not matter very much. Conceivably the media might be dominated by left-wing magnates (in the United Kingdom Robert Maxwell and Lord Hollick), so the conservative tilt to freedom of speech, detected by United States commentators, is a matter of historical chance. It may also be said that the wealthy and powerful take more advantage of other freedoms, for example, to choose education 'in conformity with their own religious and philosophical convictions'.[17] Why should not the same be true of the right to freedom of speech? Moreover, to some extent free speech inequalities could be redressed by more progressive tax laws.[18] (It is, however, hard to envisage how such rules could do much to ensure, say, more equal access to the media, if that is thought a desirable objective.)

There is something to these arguments, but they fail to tackle the crucial point that in many, perhaps most, of these 'mass speech' cases the very significance and meaning of the right to freedom of expression is at issue. Take, for example, the controversy about rights of reply to the press, mandated by many continental European legal systems, but regarded as contrary to freedom of the press in the USA.[19] In this context there is a conflict between two views of the scope of freedom of speech: a potential letter-writer argues that the law recognises a positive free speech right to put her case to newspaper readers and that the press has become a public forum for the discussion of public issues, while the editor (or newspaper owner) claims that freedom of speech and of the press gives him a prerogative to determine the contents of his newspaper. Another issue related to the dispute is the relationship between freedom of speech and of the press. When an editor claims a prerogative to determine his newspaper's contents, is this a speech or a press right? Is the latter more or less identical to the former (the traditional view), or is it to be regarded, as media freedom is in German

[13] The term is used by L. A. Powe in his article, 'Mass Speech and the Newer First Amendment', [1982] *Supreme Court Review* 243.

[14] The Supreme Court has held a statute mandating a right of reply to personal attacks in a newspaper incompatible with freedom of the press (*Miami Herald* v. *Tornillo* 418 US 241 (1974), but upheld such a right to broadcast attacks: *Red Lion Broadcasting Co.* v. *FCC* 395 US 367 (1969). It has also upheld the constitutionality of cross-media ownership rules, including possible divestiture orders: *FCC* v. *National Citizens' Committee for Broadcasting* 436 US 775 (1978).

[15] 250 US 616, 630–1 (1919).

[16] See F. Schauer, 'The Political Incidence of the Free Speech Principle', 64 *Colorado Law Rev.* 935, 949 (1993).

[17] See First Protocol to the European Convention on Human Rights, Art. 2.

[18] See L. Powe, 'Mass Speech', 282–3.

[19] See the *Tornillo* case, n. 14 above. The classic exposition of the case for access rights to the media is J. A. Barron, 'Access to the Press—A New First Amendment Right', 80 *Harv. L. Rev.* 1641 (1967).

jurisprudence, as an instrumental freedom (*dienende Freiheit*), to be protected only insofar as this promotes the underlying values of freedom of speech?[20]

Similarly campaign financing and political advertising cases raise the question whether limitations on expenditure should be treated as equivalent to restraints on speech itself. In *Buckley* v. *Valeo* the Supreme Court concluded that they should be. It moved from the acceptable proposition that in the era of mass communications the effective dissemination of speech is dependent on money to the controversial conclusion that expenditure limits are subject to the same scrutiny as restraints on the substance of speech. But the latter are aimed at the contents of the speech itself and therefore suspect; in contrast expenditure limits are on their face and in application content-neutral. The US election expenditure cases do not show that there is a necessary connection between free market libertarianism and freedom of speech, only that for the last twenty years the Supreme Court has made that connection. It has done so, it seems to me, by avoiding serious reflection on the meaning of 'freedom of speech'.

Hard questions about the meaning and scope of freedom of speech can probably only be answered by reflection on why the freedom is (or should be) valued and why it enjoys a special place in most liberal constitutions. To some extent the text, not only of the free speech clause itself, but the constitution (or the European Convention) as a whole may provide assistance. In addition constitutional courts must interpret the freedom in the light of underlying philosophical principles and of the relevant political culture and tradition. This complex enterprise is, it seems to me, necessary for courts to resolve familiar free speech issues: for example, the coverage of pornography and commercial advertising, and the balancing of freedom of political speech against the right of human beings to the dignity and self-esteem which may be endangered by hate speech. It is hardly surprising that it is also essential to determine free speech rights in the era of mass communications.

A number of arguments support the special (constitutional) position of free speech: Mill's classic argument from truth, that free expression is crucial to individual autonomy and self-fulfilment, and the utilitarian case for its role in the promotion of an effective participatory democracy.[21] Characteristic also of much US jurisprudence and commentary is the distrust of government intervention in this area and, as already mentioned, a belief in the effective working of the 'market-place of ideas'.[22] As some US commentators have observed with varying degrees of enthusiasm, the Supreme Court has for the most part accepted that free speech is worthy of protection because it is an exercise of individual autonomy, the only enemy of which is the state.[23] Thus, the regulation of speech is likely to be struck down, as incompatible with the First Amendment, not only when it discriminates between types of speech on the basis of their content, but also when it is intended to promote speech or to equalize opportunities for its dissemination. This approach largely explains the Court's hostility to a right of reply to the press and to Congress's attempt to place limits on election expenditure—though in neither case had government shown any bias against any type of speech or viewpoint. What was crucial for the Court was the autonomy of the press editor (or owner) and of wealthy political candidates and their supporters.

There was of course nothing inevitable about these decisions. It is perfectly proper within the US constitutional tradition to ask whether the freedoms protected by the Supreme Court in the *Tornillo* case and in *Buckley* v. *Valeo* were not really property (or economic) rights rather than free speech rights. Moreover, in the 1960s and 1970s the Court emphasized another principle underlying freedom of speech: the promotion of vigorous public debate and the public's right to freedom of information. The land-mark decision in *New York Times* v. *Sullivan*, applying the First Amendment to the law of libel, was not taken in order to protect the autonomy of the press as such, but to encourage uninhibited discussion of the conduct of public officials.[24] On this approach, what is important is not necessarily that the speech of a particular individual is unregulated, but that a diversity of views (or a multiplicity of voices) should be heard. As Alexander Meiklejohn put it in a celebrated aphorism: 'What is essential is not that every-

[20] For the German view, see the ruling of the Constitutional Court in the *Third Television* case, 57 BVerfGE 295, 320 (1981), and for a full statement of this argument by an American commentator, see J. Lichtenberg, 'Foundations and Limits of Freedom of the Press', in *Democracy and the Mass Media* (ed. by J. Lichtenberg, Cambridge, 1990), 102–35.

[21] The classic modern summary of these and other philosophical and political arguments for free speech is that of F. Schauer, *Free Speech: A Philosophical Enquiry* (Cambridge, 1982).

[22] I have discussed the characteristics of US free speech jurisprudence in more detail in 'Free Speech in Australia: A Comparative Perspective', 16 *Sydney L. Rev.* 149 (1994).

[23] In support of this position, see R. Post, 'Meiklejohn's Mistake; Individual Autonomy and the Reform of Public Discourse', 64 *Univ. of Colorado L. Rev.* 1109 (1993), while a classic exposition of the critical case is by O. M. Fiss, 'Free Speech and Social Structure', 71 *Iowa L. Rev.* 1405 (1986).

[24] 376 US 254 (1964). Equally the decision to extend the coverage of the First Amendment to commercial speech was taken, not to protect the autonomy of advertisers, but to allow the public access to more information: see *Virginia State Board of Pharmacy* v. *Virginia Citizens Consumer Council* 425 US 748 (1976).

one shall speak, but that everything worth saying shall be said.'[25]

European jurists need not be unduly concerned with the correct interpretation of the First Amendment. For the American perspective on freedom of speech (or on other civil liberties or constitutional issues for that matter) does not possess a monopoly of wisdom. Constitutional interpretation is subject to political and cultural influences, which are not felt in equal degree on both sides of the Atlantic. Few Europeans share the suspicion of government which colours United States attitudes to free speech regulation. In contrast, both the French Conseil constitutionnel and the German Constitutional Court have accepted, for example, that it is legitimate for legislation to limit the freedom of broadcasters in the interests of plurality of the sources of information.[26] Indeed, the German jurisprudence requires the *Länder* legislatures to promote freedom of speech in the context of broadcasting; in effect they have a constitutional duty to guarantee the development of public broadcasting and to ensure that some programme standards are imposed on the private sector. (I will return to the position of freedom of speech in the broadcasting context in Part III of this paper.) In Germany, freedom of speech (and other basic rights) is not only a defensive liberty (*Abwehrrecht*) against the state, but a fundamental constitutional value which governs all legal relationships.[27]

There are a number of reasons for an English lawyer to prefer this broader view of freedom of speech to the individual autonomy perspective now largely favoured in the USA. For a start it explains more of our law. The Fair Trading Act 1973 requires the Monopolies and Mergers Commission to take into account the impact of a press merger on free expression of opinion when preparing its report on whether it is against the public interest.[28] The limited immunity from disclosing sources of information was granted to serve the public interest in freedom of the media and access to information, not primarily the rights of individual journalists.[29] A number of statutory rules ensure that political parties and candidates are able to communicate their platform at election times.[30] None of these rules is easily explicable in terms of the rights of individuals to free speech against the state. Secondly, it is not *necessarily* the case that the government poses unique, or even greater, dangers to a free and vigorous public debate than private power. Imagine a society in which there is no public broadcasting and in which all, or virtually all, private television channels, newspapers and magazines are under the control of one magnate with pronounced political opinions.[31] Could it then be seriously argued that the divesting of some of his titles, together with public subsidies to enable those of opposing political views to start up national newspapers, would be contrary to freedom of speech? Admittedly, government has usually posed greater dangers to free speech than private persons; but this is a matter of historical contingency, not inevitably the case.

Quite apart from this melodramatic scenario, there are more common place questions about the application of freedom of speech to private relations. These can be raised inter alia in privacy and libel cases, in the context of picketing and other employment disputes and of claims to use private property, such as shopping arcades, for the conduct of meetings and processions. In the United States there must be 'state action' for the First Amendment to be implicated; the issue, in some contexts at least, has given rise to a complex body of case law, while the Supreme Court of Canada in a well-known case rejected the application of the Charter to private labour disputes.[32] If, however, freedom of speech is to be regarded as a constitutional value, rather than solely an individual right against the state, there is no justification for a sharp dividing line between 'public' and 'private' cases. Our administrative law remedies and now European Community law (with regard to the scope of the principle of direct effect) highlight the difficulty in satisfactorily drawing lines between public and private bodies. Moreover, the characterization of an agency or a function as 'public' or 'private' is now largely a matter of political choice. In increasingly privatized societies, there are fewer circumstances for genuine 'state action', and, on the traditional perspective, fewer cases where fundamental rights might be at issue.

[25] *Political Freedom: The Constitutional Powers of the People* (New York, 1965), 26.

[26] See Conseil Decisions 82–141 of 27 July 1982, Rec. 1982, 48, and 86–217 of 18 Sept. 1986, Rec. 1986, 141; for the German Constitutional Court, see in particular, 12 BVerfGE 205 (1961) and 57 BVerfGE 295 (1981).

[27] The principle was established in the *Numerus Clausus* case, 33 BVerfGE 303, 330 (1972).

[28] S. 59(3).

[29] Contempt of Court Act 1981, s. 10. It is interesting that even in the USA this immunity has not been recognised as an integral aspect of the right to freedom of speech: *Branzburg* v. *Hayes* 408 US 665 (1972), while more recently the Court has denied the right of the press to waive a promise of confidentiality: *Cohen* v. *Cowles Media* 111 S. Ct. 2513 (1991).

[30] See Representation of the People Act 1983, ss. 93–6, Broadcasting Act 1990, s. 36.

[31] Observers of modern Italy might fear that country is alarmingly close to this dystopia.

[32] *RWDSU* v. *Dolphin Delivery* (1987) 33 DLR (4th) 174. Contrast remarks of Neill LJ in *Middlebrook Mushrooms* v. *TGWU, The Times* January 18, 1993 to the effect that freedom of speech under the ECHR should be borne in mind in resolving labour picketing cases.

There is also, however, a question of principle. A Canadian commentator, defending the refusal to apply the Charter to private disputes, has argued that constitutions are concerned to regulate the conduct of government institutions.[33] Only government has coercive power. A similar view has been expressed by Charles Fried in the United States: state restrictions are radically different from private restrictions on speech, since the state controls, or indeed is, the law.[34] But a constitution is also the expression of the fundamental values and ideals of a society. It may emphasize (as does the ECHR) the responsibilities as well as the rights of citizens, and its precepts may have legal significance for private institutions, such as political parties and the media, as well as the branches of government.

III

Most of the decisions of the European Human Rights Court on Article 10 have involved what may be termed traditional free speech issues: for example, how far does 'freedom of expression' cover non-political speech, particularly sexually explicit art and literature, or how should the freedom be weighed against the rights of reputation and to a fair trial? Recently the Court has decided three cases involving the application of the Article to the broadcasting media.[35] In the third, and most important, of these cases it held that the public broadcasting monopoly in Austria was incompatible with freedom of expression; the monopoly could not be justified under Article 10(2) in view of the number of frequencies now available for broadcasting and the fact that there are a number of other (more proportionate) measures to ensure pluralism in the broadcasting media, e.g., attaching conditions to the grant of private licenses. In other states pluralism was achieved by anti-trust measures designed to obviate the risk of private media monopolies.

The key paragraph in the Court's judgement reads as follows:[36]

> The Court has frequently stressed the fundamental role of freedom of expression in a democratic society, in particular where, through the press, it serves to impart information and ideas of general interest, which the public is moreover entitled to receive . . . Such an undertaking cannot be successfully accomplished unless it is grounded in the principle of pluralism, of which the State is the ultimate guarantor. This observation is especially valid in relation to audio-visual media, whose programmes are often broadcast very widely.

A number of points in this remarkable passage are worthy of emphasis. First, the Court envisages that freedom of expression has a social role, particularly where the press and broadcasting media are involved. This perspective is justified in view of the part the exercise of the freedom plays in democratic life and of the rights of members of the public to receive information and ideas. (It is worth pointing out that Article 10 of the Convention guarantees the right to receive information and ideas—the German *Informationsfreiheit*—as well as the right to impart them.) The Court would appear implicitly to reject the usual perspective in the United States, that what matters is only the autonomy of the speaker (or newspaper editor) and not the range and variety of ideas circulating in society.[37] Secondly, the Court invoked the principle of pluralism, as it had done in its earlier broadcasting rulings. In *Groppera* the Court had accepted the Swiss government's argument that it was entitled to prevent the retransmission in its territory of an unlicensed Italian radio station's broadcasts. This was acceptable in the interests of pluralism, in that case the interests of lawful Swiss and foreign stations and their listeners. The free expression of the applicant station, Groppera, was thus properly limited to protect 'the rights of others' to an orderly and varied broadcasting system.

The scope of the pluralism principle requires elaboration. It is to be found in the broadcasting jurisprudence of the French Conseil constitutionnel, and the German and Italian constitutional courts. In its important ruling of 1986, for example, the Conseill held that the principle was one of constitutional status, and respect for it one of the conditions of democracy. Without it, freedom of expression would be ineffective. In the context of broadcasting, pluralism requires that listeners and viewers are able to exercise some choice of programme; this should not be dictated by public or private interests, or left entirely to the market.[38] This principle underlay many of the provisions in the Chirac Bill which had been referred to the Council, for instances, those requiring a right of reply and limited access rights and also those imposing some programme standards;

[33] P. W. Hogg, *Constitutional Law of Canada* (3rd ed., Toronto, 1992), 848.

[34] 'The New First Amendment Jurisprudence: A Threat to Liberty' in *The Bill of Rights in the Modern State*, ed. by G. R. Stone, R. A. Epstein, and C. R. Sunstein (Chicago, 1992), 236–7.

[35] *Groppera* v. *Switzerland* (1990) 12 EHRR 321; *Autronic* v. *Switzerland* (1990) 12 EHRR 485; *Informationsverein Lentia and Others* v. *Austria* (1994) 17 EHRR 93.

[36] Ibid., para. 38.

[37] Admittedly the Supreme Court has not adopted this perspective in the context of broadcasting: see *Red Lion* v. *FCC* 395 US 367 (1969), but many commentators treat that as an aberrant decision, which might soon be overruled.

[38] Decision 86–217 of 1 September 1986, Rec. 1986, 141.

these were held legitimate, but under the pluralism principle the competition and cross-media ownership rules were found deficient in some respects.[39] The European Human Rights Court now clearly takes the view that a public broadcasting monopoly is incompatible with the principle. It might conceivably one day be called on to decide the question how far an unregulated (or lightly regulated) private broadcasting oligopoly met the pluralism requirement.

For the third point flowing from the Austrian decision is that the state must guarantee pluralism. It must take active steps to promote a variety of sources of information; in other words, freedom of speech in European jurisprudence is not merely a liberty against the state. The Human Rights Commission had already suggested that the states had a duty to prevent the development of press monopolies in *De Geillustreerde Pers* v. *Netherlands*.[40] Although in some situations an applicant may have difficulty in establishing that he is a 'victim' of a violation of the Convention,[41] it is now clear that Article 10 is not concerned merely with individual free speech rights. The European Court did not formulate a *right* to institute a private radio station, for that would depend on the grant of a licence by the state.[42] Instead, it asserted that freedom of expression is a fundamental constitutional value for parties to the ECHR, a value which requires the recognition of some private access to the broadcasting media under state regulation.[43]

It remains to be seen how significant this ruling will prove to be outside the broadcasting context. In particular, it is unclear how far states have, under the Convention, duties to promote pluralism and access to the traditionally unregulated (or less regulated) press sector. What is clear is that this case is in line with the Court's approach in related contexts. In another Austrian case it had emphasized that Article 11 requires states to take positive steps to guarantee an effective right to peaceful public assembly.[44] This might require the law to be formulated to prevent, so far as possible, such assemblies being broken up by a hostile audience—arguably, a private restriction on speech.

IV

Much of what is written in this paper may be controversial. In particular, I may not have given adequate weight to the strong arguments against the tolerance of government measures designed to promote speech or to equalize opportunities for its expression. There is, as history shows, a serious risk that government will promote what it likes to the cost of the views (and their holders) it finds unattractive or hostile. Although this risk can to some extent be reduced by leaving the ultimate decision to independent constitutional courts, it would be foolish to deny it exists. Moreover, the use of a free speech principle to regulate private legal relations would entail restrictions on individual liberties, though these might be property or privacy rights, in many circumstances of much less weight than freedom of speech. (A free speech principle capable of affecting private legal relations would, of course, be very welcome to the press, if a statutory right of privacy were introduced.)

What seems to me incontrovertible is that the common law cannot be expected properly to tackle these issue. Admittedly, it is no longer true that freedom of speech is solely a negative, residual liberty; the *Derbyshire* case shows that it may be used to limit other rights. such as the right to reputation. But the courts are unable (or at least unwilling) to consider freedom of speech properly when a statute gives central government broad discretionary powers.[45] More pertinently, it is inconceivable that an English court could intervene, as the German Constitutional Court and French Conseil have repeatedly done, to ameliorate broadcasting laws which failed to respect free speech values. Only the introduction of a constitutional provision would enable intervention of this character—though, of course, that possibility would not prove that such intervention was necessarily appropriate.

Recently two prominent judges have argued that the courts in this country can effectively protect fundamental rights even without the incorporation of the European Convention.[46] One reason for rejecting this argument is that it proceeds from a traditional view of freedom of speech (and other liberties) which sees the only threat to its exercise as that

[39] For details of the ruling, see E. Barendt, *Broadcasting Law* (Oxford, 1993), 17, 127.

[40] 5178/71, 8 D & R 5, 14 (para. 88).

[41] This poses no problem for prospective private broadcasters, as the Austrian case shows, but it might be much harder for, say, a listeners' and viewers' organization to challenge the adequacy of programme regulations or of cross-media ownership rules.

[42] This is supported by the refusal of the Court to award the applicants compensation under Article 50. It is not certain that licences would have been awarded.

[43] Paragraph 39 of the decision appears to suggest that pluralism might be satisfied by the recognition of independent producers' access rights.

[44] *Platform 'Arzte für das Leben'* v. *Austria* (1991) 13 EHRR 204.

[45] See the broadcasting ban case, *R.* v. *Secretary of State for the Home Dept., ex parte Brind* [1991] 1 AC 696.

[46] Lord Browne-Wilkinson, 'The Infiltration of a Bill of Rights', [1992] *Public Law* 397; Sir J. Laws, 'Is the High Court the Guardian of Fundamental Constitutional Rights?', [1993] *Public Law* 59.

posed by the state. The common law could not, for instance, compel the legislature to introduce, or revise, legislation to counter the dangers of private censorship. Nor will an English court be able to develop the new common law free speech principle along the lines suggested by the European Human Rights Court in the Austrian broadcasting case.

Incorporation of the Convention is, therefore, desirable, because it enables a legal argument to be made, which cannot be deployed at common law: that the government has affirmative responsibilities to promote freedom of speech. It would be better, in a way, if this were done as part of a major constitutional settlement. Many free speech questions (and I suspect other civil liberties issues) can best be resolved if they are understood in the context of a constitution, and its distinctive values, rather than solely in terms of the protection of individual rights. The meaning of political speech, the scope of the freedom for candidates and their supporters during election campaigns, and the application of basic principles to the media, are all matters which raise problems of a general constitutional character. Put shortly, freedom of speech has significance for the vitality of public life, as well as constituting a fundamental human right. That is why the common law, and perhaps even a Human Rights Convention, cannot do justice to its complexity.

11. Article 10 of the European Convention on Human Rights

DAVID PANNICK QC[1]

Introduction

FREEDOM of expression can injure reputations, outrage moral sensibilities, and, in extreme circumstances, endanger lives. These may be prices worth paying for the preservation and enjoyment of this fundamental right. Nevertheless, difficult judgments have to be made as to when the right to inform, and to be informed, should give way to competing duties and responsibilities.

English law lacks developed principles of freedom of expression which assist analysis of such questions. Courts readily issue injunctions to stop the publication of newsworthy articles which are said to be in 'breach of confidence'. An expanding law of contempt threatens journalists with imprisonment. Instead of a freedom of information law, we are patronised each year by the release of those 30 year old documents which officials are satisfied it is now safe to let out into the open. London is the libel capital of the world.

Article 10 of the European Convention on Human Rights[2] provides a helpful framework for consideration of the issues of principle raised by free speech. Most—not all—of the judgments of the European Court of Human Rights, and the decisions of the European Commission of Human Rights, in Strasbourg have rightly recognised the value of free speech and the strict scrutiny to which limitations on its scope should be subjected. Those judgments have, to a much greater extent than the decisions of English courts, understood the wisdom of the principle stated by James Madison (one of the founding fathers of the American Constitution):

> 'Some degree of abuse is inseparable from the proper use of every thing; and in no instance is this more true than in that of the press'.[3]

Article 10 begins by stating the extent of the right. It entitles everyone to the freedom to hold opinions and to receive and impart information and ideas without interference by public authority and regardless of frontiers. Then Article 10 defines the circumstances in which limitations on free expression are permitted. Such limitations are permissible only if they satisfy three tests. First, the restrictions must be prescribed by law, that is stated in reasonably accessible and clear domestic law.[4] Second, a restriction on free speech is valid only if it is designed to further one or more specified objectives. And third, a restriction on free speech is permissible only if it is 'necessary in a democratic society'.

The principles contained in Article 10

The jurisprudence of the European Court of Human Rights involves the repeated recognition and assertion of the importance and value of freedom of expression. The court has explained that freedom of expression is central to a liberal, democratic society. Only by exercising the right to discuss, to dispute and to dissent can we hope to understand what is true and to identify what is prejudice, confusion, or plain error. The Court has appreciated that free speech helps the truth to emerge. It aids the revelation of corruption, bias and mistakes. It assists

[1] Practising barrister and Fellow of All Souls College, Oxford.

[2] Article 10 provides:

'1. Everyone has the right to freedom of expression. This right shall include freedom to hold opinions and to receive and impart information and ideas without interference by public authority and regardless of frontiers. This Article shall not prevent States from requiring the licensing of broadcasting, television or cinema enterprise.

2. The exercise of these freedoms, since it carries with it duties and responsibilities, may be subject to such formalities, conditions, restrictions or penalties as are prescribed by law and are necessary in a democratic society, in the interests of national security, territorial integrity or public safety, for the prevention of disorder or crime, for the protection of health or morals, for the protection of the reputation or rights of others, for preventing the disclosure of information received in confidence, or for maintaining the authority and impartiality of the judiciary'.

[3] Cited in *New York Times Co.* v. *Sullivan* 376 US 254, 271 (1964).

[4] In *Muller* v. *Switzerland* (1988) 13 EHRR 212, 226 (paragraph 29) the Court emphasised in the context of Article 10

> 'the impossibility of attaining absolute precision in the framing of laws, particularly in fields in which the situation changes according to the prevailing views of society. The need to avoid excessive rigidity and to keep pace with changing circumstances means that many laws are inevitably couched in terms which, to a greater or lesser extent, are vague. Criminal law provisions on obscenity fall within this category'.

Similarly, in *Hodgson and others* v. *United Kingdom* (Applications 11553/85 and 11658/85, Admissibility decision of 9 March 1987) 51 D & R 136, 144, the Commission explained, in relation to Article 10(2), that

> 'The mere fact that a legislative provision may give rise to problems of interpretation does not mean that it is so vague and imprecise as to lack the quality of "law" in this sense'.

stability by permitting the articulation of grievances and by promoting the peaceful resolution of conflicts. Without the liberty to impart and receive information and ideas, we cannot take full advantage of our potential as autonomous beings. And it is futile to boast of democracy if we are prevented from learning and then criticising what those who govern us are doing on our behalf.

The Court has struck down a large number of restrictions on the freedom of citizens to receive and impart information. In 1979, the Court held that the House of Lords acted in breach of Article 10 by imposing an injunction to stop the *Sunday Times* from publishing information about the Thalidomide scandal. The Court was satisfied that damages claims against the Distillers company did not justify an injunction to stop publication of information on a matter of considerable public interest and concern.[5] In 1986, in the *Lingens* case, the Court held that Article 10 was breached by the imposition of a fine on a journalist in criminal proceedings for an article critical of Mr Kreisky, the Austrian Chancellor.[6]

In 1991, the Court held that the majority of the House of Lords had breached Article 10 by prohibiting the *Sunday Times* from publishing extracts from *Spycatcher* even after publication of the book in the United States of America and throughout the world. That the book was top of the bestseller list in the USA and Canada, that lengthy extracts had been published in newspapers throughout the world, that the book's author, Peter Wright, had sold the foreign language rights to publish *Spycatcher* in various translations, from Catalan to Icelandic, none of this impressed the majority of the Law Lords who prohibited newspapers from disclosing the book's contents in England. As Lord Bridge, one of the dissenting Law Lords, warned, the Government faced 'inevitable condemnation and humiliation' in Strasbourg.[7] The Government duly lost 11–0 before the Commission, and 24–0 before the European Court.[8]

In October 1992, the Court held that the Irish Republic was in breach of Article 10 by prohibiting organisations which counsel pregnant women from providing information about the identity and location of abortion clinics outside Ireland. If a pregnant woman in Ireland wished to consider the option of abortion, then arrangements were made by the counselling services to refer her to appropriate medical clinics in the United Kingdom. In March 1988, the Irish Supreme Court held that these activities were in breach of Article 40.3.3 of the Irish Constitution which recognises 'the right to life of the unborn'. Chief Justice Finlay concluded that the counselling organisations were 'assisting in the ultimate destruction of the life of the unborn'. An injunction was granted to prevent the provision of information about abortion services abroad.

The European Court of Human Rights held that the Irish ban on the provision of information was not 'necessary in a democratic society'. The ban was absolute, in that it applied regardless of the age or state of health of the pregnant woman, or her reasons for seeking counselling on the termination of her pregnancy. The Applicant organisations were not advocating abortion. They were providing objective information about reliable and lawful services in the United Kingdom. Such information would in any event be available to well-informed members of Irish society, through books and magazines, and so the ban was likely only to affect poorer women. The injunction had not reduced the numbers of Irish women having abortions in the United Kingdom, but had resulted in those women travelling at a later stage in their pregnancy. So the judgment of the Irish Supreme Court did not advance any interests of the foetus, but was damaging to the health and welfare of Irish women.[9]

In these and other cases, the basic principles of Article 10 have been established. In the 1979 *Sunday Times Case*, the European Court explained its philosophy:

> 'Freedom of expression constitutes one of the essential foundations of a democratic society; subject to paragraph 2 of Article 10, it is applicable not only to information or ideas that are favourably received or regarded as inoffensive or as a matter of indifference, but also to those that offend, shock or disturb the State or any sector of the population . . . These principles are of particular importance as far as the press is concerned . . . Not only do the media have the task of imparting such information and ideas: the public has a right to receive them'.

The Court added that it was faced 'not with a choice between two conflicting principles, but with a principle of freedom of expression that is subject to a

[5] *The Sunday Times Case (No. 1)* (1979) 2 EHRR 245.

[6] *Lingens* v. *Austria* (1986) 8 EHRR 407. See, similarly, *Castells* v. *Spain* (1992) 14 EHRR 445 (the conviction of a politician for insulting the Government because he wrote a critical magazine article was a breach of Article 10 as the Spanish court had ruled inadmissible evidence which he wished to adduce to establish the truth of his statements).

[7] *Attorney-General* v. *Guardian Newspapers Ltd and others* [1987] 1 WLR 1248, 1286G–H.

[8] *The Sunday Times* v. *United Kingdom (No. 2)* (1991) 14 EHRR 229. See, similarly, *Weber* v. *Switzerland* (1990) 12 EHRR 508 (the Court held that it could not be necessary in a democratic society to punish a journalist for revealing allegedly confidential information when the substance of it had already been publicly disclosed).

[9] *Open Door and Dublin Well Woman* v. *Ireland* (1992) 15 EHRR 244.

number of exceptions which must be narrowly interpreted'.[10]

Although States have a margin of appreciation in this context, the Commission and the Court have made it plain that *they* are empowered to give the final ruling on whether the State has justified the interference of which complaint is made. In particular, as the Court explained in the *Sunday Times Case*, the supervision by the Commission and the Court is not limited

'to ascertaining whether a respondent State exercised its discretion reasonably, carefully and in good faith. Even a Contracting State so acting remains subject to the Court's control as regards the compatibility of its conduct with the engagements it has undertaken under the Convention'.

The adjective 'necessary' (in 'necessary in a democratic society') is synonymous neither with 'indispensable' nor with the looser tests of ' "admissible", "ordinary", "useful;", "reasonable" or "desirable" '. Rather 'it implies the existence of a "pressing social need" '.[11]

The test to be satisfied by the Respondent State (and the burden is on it) is

'whether the interference complained of corresponded to a pressing social need, whether it was proportionate to the legitimate aim pursued, whether the reasons given by the national authorities to justify it are relevant and sufficient under Article 10.2'.[12]

A broad restriction on freedom of speech 'calls for a particularly close scrutiny of its "necessity" '.[13]

To assess whether the interference complained of was based on sufficient reasons which rendered it necessary in a democratic society, 'account must thus be taken of any public interest aspect of the case'. So where the issue upon which freedom of speech is restrained is 'a matter of undisputed public concern' upon which people have ' a vital interest in knowing' relevant information, then it is permissible to deprive them of that information 'only if it appeared absolutely certain that its diffusion would' have the adverse consequences legitimately feared by the State.[14]

Where there has been an interference with the exercise of the rights and freedoms guaranteed by Article 10.1,

'the supervision must be strict, because of the importance of the rights in question; the importance of these rights has been stressed by the Court many times. The necessity for restricting them must be convincingly established'.[15]

Article 10 recognises 'the pre-eminent role of the press in a State governed by the rule of law'. So

'Whilst the press must not overstep the bounds set, inter alia, for "the protection of the reputation of . . . others", it is nevertheless incumbent on it to impart information and ideas on matters of public interest. Not only does it have the task of imparting such information and ideas: the public also has a right to receive them. Were it otherwise, the press would be unable to play its vital role of "public watchdog" '.[16]

Where the publication 'bore . . . on a matter of serious public concern' and where a criminal penalty is 'capable of discouraging open discussion of matters of public concern' and where

'by bringing to light certain facts, the article might have served as a break on speculative and unenlightened discussion',

the State is unlikely to be able to pass the pressing social need test.[17]

All of these statements of principle are enlightened acknowledgements of the primacy of freedom of expression, and the strict scrutiny which must be applied to any interference with free speech. Unfortunately, there have also been a number of cases where the judgments of the Court and the decisions of the Commission have failed to accord freedom of expression the recognition which it deserves.

While the Court has been especially vigilant to control interferences with political speech, its record in relation to artistic and commercial speech is less impressive. In those contexts, the Court has displayed a greater reluctance to conclude that the decisions of domestic authorities have exceeded the margin of appreciation enjoyed by them. While it must always be remembered that the primary responsibility for securing the protection of fundamental freedoms lies with national authorities, and that the Court and the Commission do not express their own policy decisions, but merely decide whether national choices have exceeded the limits of the discretion of Contracting States, nevertheless some of the decisions in Strasbourg are disappointing failures to apply a strong concept of freedom of expression.

[10] (1979) 2 EHRR 245, 280 (paragraph 65).
[11] (1979) 2 EHRR 245, 275–276 (paragraph 59).
[12] (1979) 2 EHRR 245, 277–278 (paragraph 62).
[13] (1979) 2 EHRR 245, 278 (paragraph 63).
[14] (1979) 2 EHRR 245, 280–281 (paragraphs 65–66).
[15] *Autronic AG* v. *Switzerland* (1990) 12 EHRR 485, 502–503 (paragraph 61).
[16] *Thorgeirson* v. *Iceland* (1992) 14 EHRR 843, 865 (paragraph 63). See similarly *Lingens* v. *Austria* (1986) 8 EHRR 407, 418 (paragraph 41).
[17] *Thorgeirson* v. *Iceland* (1992) 14 EHRR 843, 866–867 (paragraphs 67–68) and *The Sunday Times Case (No. 1)* (1979) 2 EHRR 245, 282 (paragraph 66).

Criticism of the Judiciary

The 1989 *Barfod Case* concerned a fine imposed on a Danish citizen by the courts of Greenland for critical comments by him in a magazine article alleging a lack of impartiality by lay judges in particular cases. The European Commission concluded, by 14 votes to 1, that there had been a breach of Article 10. The Court took a different view and held that there was no violation of the Convention.

The Court's error was to focus on whether the complainant could justify the allegations he had made, and to conclude that because he could not, Greenland was entitled to protect the reputation of the lay judges. The Court should have given greater weight to the fact that to penalise people for comments critical of the judiciary will deter others from expressing their views of judicial conduct, and will thereby inhibit free expression on aspects of the legal system. Even if the punishment is confined to false statements of fact, this will inevitably have a chilling effect on others who will be inhibited from commenting lest they be faced by legal proceedings in which they need to show that their comments are true, or have a reasonable basis in fact. The Court should have concluded that those who sit in judicial office must be prepared to put up with criticism, even if it is unsubstantiated.[18] As the Commission held in that case, 'the general interest in allowing a public debate about the functioning of the judiciary weighs more heavily than the interest of the two judges in being protected against criticism of the kind expressed in the applicant's article'.[19]

Obscenity and indecency

The Court and the Commission have taken an unjustifiably narrow approach to freedom of expression relating to public morals.

In 1976, in the *Handyside Case*, the Court held that the conviction of the publisher of *The Little Red School Book* under the Obscene Publications Act was not a breach of Article 10.[20] More recently, in 1988, in *Muller*, the Court recognised that

> 'those who create, perform, distribute or exhibit works of art contribute to the exchange of ideas and opinion which is essential for a democratic society. Hence the obligation on the State not to encroach unduly on their freedom of expression'.

But the Court dismissed a complaint that there was a breach of Article 10 in Switzerland by reason of the criminal conviction of an artist for publishing obscene materials and by reason of the confiscation of his paintings. The paintings had been shown as part of an exhibition of contemporary art. The Court stated that, having inspected the paintings, it did not find unreasonable the view taken by the Swiss Courts that the paintings 'with their emphasis on sexuality in some of its crudest forms', were, as the Swiss Court had held, 'liable grossly to offend the sense of sexual propriety of persons of ordinary sensitivity'.[21] In the *Gay News Case*, the Commission rejected as inadmissible the complaint by the author who had been convicted of blasphemy for publishing a poem about Jesus Christ.[22]

These decisions indicate a fundamental failure to understand that (other than in very extreme cases, involving intrusion on the privacy of others) freedom of expression in relation to art and literature cannot properly be impeded because the contents of the material may offend others. I much prefer the principles stated by Mr Justice Stewart in an opinion in the US Supreme Court in 1966. As he explained,

> 'Censorship reflects a society's lack of confidence in itself. It is a hallmark of an authoritarian regime . . . [T]he Constitution protects coarse expression as well as refined, and vulgarity no less than elegance. A book worthless to me may convey something of value to my neighbour. In the free society to which our Constitution has committed us, it is for each to choose for himself'.[23]

Commercial Speech

In 1983, the Barcelona Bar Council gave a disciplinary warning to Mr Casado Coca, a Spanish lawyer, for publishing in local newspapers an advertisement stating his name, profession, address and telephone number. In a disappointing and surprising decision, the European Court of Human Rights recently rejected, by 7 votes to 2, Mr Casado Coca's complaint that he was the victim of a breach of Arti-

[18] See *Ambard* v. *Attorney-General for Trinidad and Tobago* [1936] AC 322, 335 (Lord Atkin for the Judicial Committee of the Privy Council).

[19] *Barfod* v. *Denmark* (1989) 13 EHRR 493.

[20] *Handyside* v. *United Kingdom* (1976) 1 EHRR 737.

[21] *Muller* v. *Switzerland* (1988) 13 EHRR 212. The European Commission had held that the confiscation of the paintings was a breach of Article 10. The Commission rightly explained that 'freedom of artistic expression is of fundamental importance in a democratic society. Typically it is in undemocratic societies that artistic freedom and the freedom to circulate works of art are severely restricted. Through his creative work the artist expresses not only a personal vision of the world but also his view of the society in which he lives. To that extent art not only helps shape public opinion but is also an expression of it and can confront the public with the major issues of the day'.

[22] (1982) 5 EHRR 123.

[23] *Ginzburg* v. *US* 383 US 463, 498 (1966).

cle 10.[24] The Court rightly accepted that, in principle, commercial speech is covered by Article 10.[25] But, the Court concluded, a balance had to be struck between competing interests, which include the dignity of the legal profession, and it could not be said that the approach of the Barcelona Bar in 1983 was unreasonable.

The basic principles of freedom of expression in this context were stated by the United States Supreme Court in 1977 in upholding the legality of advertising by lawyers in *Bates* v. *State Bar of Arizona*. Commercial speech 'serves to inform the public of the availability, nature and prices of products and services, and thus performs an indispensable role in the allocation of resources in a free enterprise system'. The Supreme Court rightly ridiculed the notion that advertising by lawyers was an erosion of true professionalism. Such an argument 'presumed that attorneys must conceal from themselves and from their clients the real-life fact that lawyers earn their livelihood at the bar'.[26]

As the United States Supreme Court observed, lawyers have always advertised their services, by social contacts, through members of their family, or even by writing for newspapers. It is difficult to understand what rational goal is served by penalising the provision of accurate information by advertising to assist those who may wish to make use of legal services. Indeed, one of the main problems faced by legal professions throughout Europe is the need to remove public ignorance of, and misunderstandings about, the legal services open to them.

Above all, prohibitions on advertising by lawyers are objectionable because they imply a contempt for the public: that lay people are so simple that they need to be protected from the provision of accurate information because otherwise devious attorneys will persuade them to bring law-suits against their loved-ones.

For those reasons, the United States Supreme Court has concluded that only false, deceptive or misleading commercial speech may be banned. Commercial speech that is not false, deceptive or misleading can be restricted, but only if the State shows that the restriction directly and materially advances a substantial State interest in a manner no more extensive than is necessary to serve that interest.[27]

Until the last few years, the Law Society and the Bar Council in England and Wales maintained prohibitions on advertising by lawyers similar to those at issue in the Spanish case. Lawyers lived in terror that they might be thought to have acted 'unprofessionally' in some minor respect, and suffer the consequence of professional disgrace. Until 1989, the *Code of Conduct* for the Bar was the object of ridicule for specifying what information could be contained on a barrister's visiting card, and for regulating the circumstances in which solicitors could be invited to chambers' parties. Now, barristers and solicitors in this country have been freed from most of the petty restrictions on advertising which previously applied. Advertising is permitted (subject to minor restrictions) where it is legal, decent, honest and truthful, the criteria laid down in the British Code of Advertising Practice. It is now recognised that the previous rules, so long retained as vital to the integrity of the legal system, were in fact pointless relics of a bygone age which damaged the image of lawyers and hindered their ability to serve the public.

The judgment of the European Court in *Casado Coca* approves a quaint principle that lawyers 'must be discreet . . . and dignified',[28] as well as honest. It fails to recognise the vital interests of legal consumers in knowing what services are available. It allows the imposition of a disciplinary penalty for an advertisement which it recognises did no more than state

> 'particulars that were wholly neutral (his name, occupation and business address and telephone number) and did not contain information that was untrue or offensive to fellow members of the Bar'.[29]

It panders to the prejudices of a conservative legal profession which has always been frightened by competition. It is troubling that the European Court, as the guardian of fundamental freedoms, should tolerate such arbitrary restrictions on free speech.

The broadcasting of terrorists and their supporters

In October 1988, the government of the United Kingdom issued directives which prohibited radio and television from broadcasting the voices of those who spoke on behalf of, or expressed words of support for, terrorist groups in Northern Ireland. The content of what such people say could be broadcast, but only in reported speech or if 'spoken by an actor'. (This policy was repealed in September 1994 in the light

24 *Casado Coca* v. *Spain* (1994) 18 EHRR 1.
25 See also *Markt Intern* v. *Germany* (1989) 12 EHRR 161.
26 433 US 350 (1977).
27 See, most recently, *Ibanez* v. *Florida Department of Business and Professional Regulation, Board of Accountancy* (U.S. Supreme Court, Decision of 13 June (1994).
28 (1994) 18 EHRR 1, 23 (paragraph 46).
29 (1994) 18 EHRR 1, 23 (paragraph 49).

of the ceasefire called by the IRA). The decision of the European Commission of Human Rights[30] dismissing a complaint under Article 10 of the European Convention on Human Rights is a disappointing end to a legal battle to remove an arbitrary and damaging interference with freedom of expression.

The Home Secretary, Douglas Hurd, announced the broadcasting ban in 1988 because the Prime Minister, Margaret Thatcher, wished to deny terrorists 'the oxygen of publicity'. The case against the ban was, and remains, overwhelming. If broadcasters cannot question the supporters of violence on camera, with the sound turned on, the public is denied information which will assist it to understand the intricacies of political debate, and the poverty of the political thinking of the terrorist cannot easily be exposed to the viewer.

The ban was based on an assertion which the Home Secretary was unable to substantiate in fact: that apologists for terrorism had previously been given easy access to the airwaves to intimidate others. The directives to the broadcasters unacceptably implied that those who watch television and listen to the radio need protection from free speech because they are unable to exercise their critical faculties to reject the feeble attempts of terrorists and their supporters to justify their evil conduct.

The reputation of our broadcasters for independence is harmed throughout the world by the imposition of government directives about the content of news bulletins. Dictators who are criticised for suppressing free speech now point with satisfaction to the restrictions imposed on the BBC and ITN. The directives imposing the ban inevitably caused broadcasters to avoid controversial issues of Northern Ireland policy because difficulties of application resulted in uncertain legal obligations. The integrity of news programmes was diminished by the manifest absurdity of actors speaking what we were not allowed to hear from the politicians themselves.

All of this might be tolerable if it saved lives. Free speech is not an absolute right. But no politician could seriously believe that the directives made any positive contribution to the efforts to stop the gunmen and the bombers of Northern Ireland.

A judicial review application challenging the introduction of the ban was brought by six broadcast journalists and a viewer of news programmes, Donald Brind, Fred Emery, Alexander Graham, Victoria Leonard, Scarlett McGwire, John Pilger and Thomas Nash. The House of Lords dismissed the claim in February 1991.[31]

The Law Lords concluded that public law does not require the Secretary of State to exercise discretionary powers consistently with the European Convention on Human Rights and that public law does not contain any concept of proportionality. These general principles are very likely to be reconsidered by the House of Lords before the end of the decade.

Donald Brind and his colleagues pursued the matter to Strasbourg. They argued that the broadcasting ban was a breach of the right to freedom of expression guaranteed by Article 10 of the European Convention. The European Commission of Human Rights has now decided, by a majority, to dismiss that complaint as inadmissible. The Commission concluded that because of 'the limited extent of the interference' with free speech and 'the importance of measures to combat terrorism', there was no breach of Article 10.

The reasoning of the Commission is unpersuasive. The Commission itself asserted the well-established principles of Convention case-law that freedom of the press 'affords the public one of the best means of discovering and forming an opinion of the ideas and attitudes of political leaders, and freedom of political debate is at the very core of the concept of a democratic society'.

It does not sit easily with those important values for the Commission to tolerate restrictions on how news and current affairs programmes may be presented to the public. The directives inevitably impeded the free flow of information on fundamental issues of political debate. Such an interference with editorial freedom by government demands a substantial justification. But it was impossible to regard the directives as playing any significant role in combatting terrorism. As the Commission itself stated, 'the logic of the continuation of the directions is not readily apparent when they appear to have little real impact on the information available to the public'.[32]

Racial abuse

One of the most difficult issues faced by the Commission is the extent to which freedom of expression should extend to those who wish to abuse racial minorities. The European Commission has concluded that Article 10 does not protect such 'hate

[30] *Brind and others* v. *United Kingdom* (Application No. 18714/91, decision of 9 May 1994).

[31] *R* v. *Secretary of State for the Home Department ex parte Brind* [1991] 1 AC 696.

[32] In 1991, the Commission rejected as inadmissible a similar application brought against the Republic of Ireland by sixteen radio and television journalists and producers: Application No. 15404/89, *Betty Purcell* v. *Ireland* (decision dated 16 April 1991).

speech'.[33] This decision can be contrasted with the approach taken by American constitutional law to the same issue. The American federal courts have applied to hate speech liberal criteria which combine the principled and the pragmatic.[34] For the State to have the power to prosecute people for the offensive content of racist abuse is, they have concluded, to adopt vague standards which will lead to arbitrary enforcement and will deter and so undermine free speech by others. To prosecute those who abuse free speech is to confer publicity on, and to create martyrs of, some of the most repellent elements in society. American law therefore proceeds on the premiss that to ignore racists, or to engage them in open debate, are much more effective means of reducing their support and demonstrating their poverty of thought, than prosecuting them in court.

All of this may be surprising and unfamiliar to lawyers brought up in the common law or continental tradition of European legal systems. No doubt because of the tragic history of Europe this century, freedom of expression is not so absolute in relation to hate speech on this side of the Atlantic. Laws such as the incitement to racial hatred provisions in the Public Order Act, and group libel laws in Europe, prohibit speech which abuses others by reason of their race or religion. For Europeans, the law is a statement of basic principles of civilized conduct, a means of educating society in what is decent and proper. European law agrees with Professor Alexander Bickel of Yale Law School that 'where nothing is unspeakable, nothing is undoable'. As memories of the Nazi Holocaust fade, and support for racism grows, society will be under increasing pressure to draw lines between permissible expression with which we may not agree and unacceptable hate speech which we are determined to prevent. Many commentators are suggesting that denial of the Holocaust should be made a criminal offence in the United Kingdom.

There are no easy answers to these complex and troubling issues. As in all cases where values conflict, any solution involves the paying of a price. It is painful to protect freedom of expression for those whose views we find repellent, especially when it involves tolerating the abuse of racial minorities. But the most persuasive principle is that adopted by the Anti-Defamation League of B'nai B'rith, the leading organisation opposing anti-semitism in the USA. It

> 'believes that the best answer to hate speech is not laws driving it underground, but decent people speaking out, society making such hatred unfashionable and unacceptable, and the power of education, of confronting prejudice by teaching children and adults that differences should be celebrated'.[35]

Conclusion

Some of the difficult cases heard in Strasbourg test the extent of our commitment to freedom of expression. But as Mr Justice Holmes explained in a 1925 judgment in the United States Supreme Court, 'every idea is an incitement'.[36] The question is whether we are really prepared to trust ourselves, and each other, to discuss and debate the most difficult problems which confront us, to challenge society with our thoughts and beliefs, to make up our own minds about the merits of what we hear, see and read, or whether we need protection by the State.

The European Court of Human Rights has produced many valuable judgments under Article 10, but there is some way to go before we are free, in Strasbourg and more so in England, from unjustified State interference with freedom of expression.

[33] *Glimmerveen and Hagenbeck* v. *Netherlands* (1979) 18 D & R 187. The Commission here held inadmissible a complaint by Dutch politicians concerning their conviction for distributing leaflets advocating racial discrimination and the repatriation of non-whites. The Commission relied on Article 17 which precludes reliance on the Convention in respect of 'any act aimed at the destruction of any of the rights and freedoms set forth herein or at their limitation to a greater extent than is provided for in the Convention'.

[34] See, for example, *R.A.V.* v. *City of St Paul, Minnesota* 112 S. Ct. 2538 (1992).

[35] See *Striking a Balance: Hate Speech, Freedom of Expression and Non-Discrimination* (1992, edited by Sandra Coliver), p. 327.

[36] *Gitlow* v. *New York* 268 US 652, 673 (1925).

12. Freedom of Speech and Racial Equality

CHRISTOPHER MCCRUDDEN[1]

THERE are several recent political and intellectual developments which have made a reassessment of the legal relationship between equality and freedom of speech a newly important topic in Britain in particular and Europe generally. The aim of this paper is modest: to map the contours of some of the emerging debate,[2] and to suggest that it challenges the way in which we might think about the theory of freedom of speech more generally. I shall concentrate in particular on the controversial issue of legislation which seeks to control speech and publications which are perceived to be racist.[3]

The context of the debate

In 1965 the first Race Relations Act attempted to deal with the problems of racial incitement in two ways. First, the Public Order Act 1936 was extended to make it illegal to publish threatening and insulting material with intent to provoke a breach of the peace. Second, incitement to racial hatred itself was also made unlawful by section 6(1) of the Act. When introducing the measure to the House of Commons, the Home Secretary explained that the clause was 'designed to deal with more dangerous, persistent and insidious forms of propaganda campaigns—the campaign which over a period of time engenders the hate which begets violence'.[4] No prosecutions might take place except by or with the consent of the Attorney General, and few prosecutions were in fact brought under the 1965 Act. Lord Scarman described Section 6(1) in his report on the Red Lion Square disorders in 1974 as 'an embarrassment to the police' and 'useless to a policeman on the street'.[5]

In 1975, after numerous calls for its revision, the Government reviewed the 1965 Act's provisions and concluded that changes were necessary: 'During the past decade, probably largely as a result of Section 6, there has been a decided change in the style of racialist propaganda. It tends to be less blatantly bigoted, to disclaim any intention of stirring up racial hatred, and to purport to make a contribution to public education and debate. Whilst this shift away from crudely racialist propaganda and abuse is welcome, it is not an unmixed benefit. The more apparently rational and moderate is the message, the greater is its probable impact on public opinion. But it is not justifiable in a democratic society to interfere with freedom of expression except where it is necessary to do so for the prevention of disorder or for the protection of other basic freedoms. The present law penalises crude verbal attacks if and only if it is established that they have been made with the deliberate intention of causing groups to be hated because of their racial origins. In the Government's view this is too narrow an approach. . . . It therefore proposes that it will no longer be necessary to prove a subjective intention to stir up racial hatred.'[6] Section 70 of the Race Relations Act put this policy into effect by amending section 6 of the 1965 Act and inserting the provision in the Public Order Act 1936. It was no longer necessary to prove that a person intended to stir up racial hatred: if his or her words or actions were objectively likely to stir up hatred in fact, then an offence was committed. It was still necessary, however, for any prosecution to be taken by or with the consent of the Attorney General.

Several criticisms were directed at Section 70 of the 1976 Act and its enforcement. On the one hand it was argued that the section went too far, both because the removal of a requirement of intention to incite racial hatred was 'contrary to the fundamental principles of British justice',[7] and on the ground that '[a]n increase in the rate of successful prosecutions might create the impression among the public that the sensibilities of ethnic minorities were being protected in a manner not extended to other groups in society'.[8]

[1] I am grateful to Mark Janis, Sandra Fredman, David Feldman, John Gardner, and Jane Hanna, and participants at the SPTL seminar, for reading and commenting on an earlier draft. They bear no responsibility for errors or interpretations.

[2] I do not attempt to assess the effectiveness of such legislation, for example, see generally, S. Coliver (ed.), *Striking a Balance: Hate Speech, Freedom of Expression and Non-Discrimination* (Article 19, 1992).

[3] There is, of course, an equally important debate involving similar issues in the context of feminist responses to pornography, but that issue is beyond the scope of this paper. While there has been considerable academic debate in Britain on the pornography issue, the theoretical issues surrounding race hate speech have been substantially ignored.

[4] Hansard, House of Commons, vol. 711, 3 May 1965, col. 941.

[5] Scarman Report on the Red Lion Square Disorders of 15 June 1974, Cmnd. 5919, 1975, p. 35.

[6] White Paper, Racial Discrimination, Cmnd. 6234, 1975, para. 126.

[7] Home Office, Review of the Public Order Act 1936 and related legislation, Cmnd. 7891, 1980, para. 105.

[8] House of Commons Home Affairs Committee, Fifth Report, Session 1979–80, The Law Relating to Public Order, HC 756, 1970–80, para. 99.

On the other hand it was argued that the section did not go far enough, since it did not confer on the police a power of summary arrest and required the Attorney-General's consent for prosecutions. Limiting prosecutions in this way, it was claimed, precluded proceedings other than in respect of the most blatant offences.[9] The Government replied that the law might be brought into disrepute, and harm might be done to race relations, if private prosecutions were allowed which were doomed to fail but gave additional publicity to the defendants by providing them with the opportunity to restate their views in court.[10]

Section 70 of the 1976 Act followed the 1965 Act in not penalising 'the dissemination of ideas based on an assumption of racial superiority or inferiority or facts (whether true or false) which may encourage racial prejudice or discrimination'.[11] Other countries have, however, outlawed racist propaganda of this type. Indeed Article 4 of the International Convention on the Elimination of All Forms of Racial Discrimination, which is in force and which the United Kingdom has ratified, appears to require states to go considerably beyond what the United Kingdom has so far been prepared to go. In addition, article 20(2) of the International Covenant on Civil and Political Rights states: 'Any advocacy of national, racial or religious hatred that constitutes incitement to discrimination, hostility or violence shall be prohibited by law.' Drawing on standards such as these, organisations in this country sought a wider scope for the British legislation. The Commission for Racial Equality, for example, proposed a new definition of incitement to racial hatred to the Home Affairs Committee. This would have made unlawful the uttering at a public meeting, or the publishing of words which having regard to all the circumstances, expose any racial group in Great Britain to hatred, ridicule or contempt. The CRE's aim was to remove the need to evaluate the subjective reactions of readers or audience; an objective test would be left to the jury. The Home Affairs Committee rejected the proposal.[12]

Extending the Act to include similar proposals had been considered in 1975 but the White Paper of that year announced: '[The Government is not] at this stage putting forward proposals to extend the criminal law to deal with the dissemination of racialist propaganda in the absence of a likelihood that group hatred will be stirred up by it . . . It is arguable that false and evil publications of this kind may well be more effectively defeated by public education and debate than by prosecution and that in practice the criminal law would be ineffective to deal with such material. Due regard must also of course be paid to allowing the free expression of opinion.'[13] A Home Office Green Paper in 1980 also stressed the effect of such a proposal on freedom of expression: 'It would make no allowance for genuine discussion and debate or for academic consideration of such proposals. To single out political proposals for proscription by law regardless of how they are expressed, and in what circumstances, and of the possible consequences would be a new departure. In the Government's view such a departure would be totally inconsistent with a democratic society in which—provided the manner of expression, and the circumstances, do not provoke unacceptable consequences—political proposals, however odious and undesirable, can be freely advocated.'[14]

However, attempts to make proof of an offence easier were enacted in Part III of the Public Order Act 1986, which was itself subsequently amended by the Broadcasting Act 1990 (section 164). Taken together, these provisions replaced the provisions in the Race Relations Act 1976. Part III, as amended, provides for several offences concerned with behaviour intended to or likely to result in the stirring up of racial hatred. Racial hatred is defined as hatred against a group of persons in Great Britain defined by reference to colour, race, nationality (including citizenship) or ethnic or national origins. As with the previous offences which it replaced, prosecutions may not be instituted except by or with the consent of the Attorney General.

The legislation is complex in its detail, and no attempt is made here to describe all of the complexity,[15] but an idea of certain elements is important for the purposes of this paper. The legislation is wide in its coverage, including the use of words or behaviour; the display of written material; publishing or distributing written material; public performance of a play; distributing, showing or playing a recording of visual images or sounds; including a programme in a television or radio broadcasting service; and possession of written material. Offences are committed if the words, behaviour, etc. are 'threatening, abusive or insulting' and if it is intended to stir

[9] House of Commons Home Affairs Committee, Fifth Report, Session 1979–80, The Law Relating to Public Order, HC 756, 1979–80, para. 97.

[10] United Kingdom, Sixth Periodic Report, Committee on the Elimination of Racial Discrimination, CERD/C/66 Add. 13, 1980, p. 11.

[11] White Paper, Racial Discrimination, Cmnd. 6234, 1975, para. 127.

[12] House of Commons Home Affairs Committee, 1979–80, paras. 96 and 99.

[13] White Paper, Racial Discrimination, Cmnd. 6234, 1975.

[14] Home Office, Review of the public Order Act 1936 and related legislation, Cmnd. 7891, 1980, para. 112.

[15] For a comprehensive discussion, see R. Card, *Public Order: the New Law* (Butterworths, 1987), chapter 5, and the entry 'Race Relations' in *Halsbury's Laws.*

up racial hatred, or if, having regard to all the circumstances, racial hatred is likely to be stirred up. There are several important exceptions. There are limited exceptions where the activity takes place inside a private house. There is a group of defences based on not intending the words or behaviour etc., to be threatening abusive or insulting, where there was also lack of awareness that they might be so. And the likelihood that a play may stir up racial hatred is to be judged having regard to all the circumstances *and* taking the performance as a whole.[16]

In recent years, however, there appears to have been a steady increase in racially motivated attacks in several inner-city areas. These have been seen as connected to, some say caused by, the activities of far-right groups and political parties, in particular the British National Party. These events have led to proposals from ethnic minority groups and others for amendment of the law in several respects, including (inter alia) a further tightening of the incitement to racial hatred provisions of the Public Order Act 1986, new offences of racial harassment and 'violence on racial grounds', a crime of group vilification and defamation.[17] Racial hatred would be redefined to mean 'hatred, hostility, violence or discrimination . . .'[18] A person would be guilty of an offence of racial harassment if on racial grounds, he 'uses words or behaviour or displays any writing, sign or other visual representation which is offensive on racial grounds within the hearing or sight of any person likely to be caused harassment, alarm or distress thereby'.[19] Civil remedies would be made available to individuals seeking to complain of racial harassment, and by the Commission for Racial Equality.[20,21] Recently, the Home Affairs Select Committee recommended the creation of a new offence of racially-motivated violence, further amendment of the incitement to racial hatred provisions of the Public Order Act, and further consideration of a new law relating to group defamation.[22]

To some limited extent these proposals echo legal developments which have already taken place. An important, comparatively recent, development in British and European anti-discrimination law interprets the concept of direct discrimination as now including within it a situation in which a person is racially or sexually harassed in an employment situation. It may include unwelcome behaviour which the recipient finds intimidating, hostile or offensive, ranging from unwelcome sexual advances, unpleasant or denigratory remarks, to the display of offensive material of an explicitly racist nature. Such conduct may be physical, verbal or non-verbal. In general, the starting point for the determination of what is offensive to he recipient will be the perceptions of the recipient of the alleged conduct. Sexual and racial harassment may also consist in the creation of a hostile work environment, where an indi- idual is intimidated by words or actions which may not be directed specifically at them. Several universities have also adopted provisions penalising harassment, including racial and sexual harassment.[23] All of these have considerable implications for freedom of speech, sometimes discussed, more often not.[24]

The countries of western Europe have, rather belatedly, become concerned at the extent to which social cohesion is threatened by the growth of fascist and racist groups which seek to use economic recession and unemployment as excuses for encouraging resentment against Jews and against immigrants from Turkey, eastern Europe and North Africa. Partly because of the growth of electoral support for such groups (in one German state, Hesse, the Republican vote in the March 1993 election was nearly 8 per cent;

[16] In addition to these restrictive provisions, which form the basis for the following discussion, there are several others which are connected. Section 5 of the Public Order Act 1986, the Malicious Communications Act 1988, Part II of the Public Order Act dealing with processions and demonstrations, and section 3 of the Football (Offences) Act 1991, which criminalises racist chanting at football matches. In addition, the Public Order (Northern Ireland) Order 1987 (1987 NO. 463 (NI 7)), Part II provides for several offences of stirring up religious hatred or arousing fear.

[17] All but the last are included in the proposed Racial Hatred and Violence Bill 1993. See on this G. Bindman, Fighting Hatred, *Law Society Gazette* 91/4 26 January 1994. In addition some have gone further urging the banning of racist political groups. At its 1993 Annual Conference, the Labour Party called for a ban 'on all organisations which pursue policies and actions which constitute an incitement to racial hatred and violence.' *Financial Times*, 1 October 1993 (;The Labour Party Conference: Delegates call for banning of NBP').

[18] Clause 2.

[19] Clause 10(1)(b).

[20] Clause 11.

[21] Its draftsman, Geoffrey Bindman, argues that such legislation is closely tied in with the purposes of the race relations legislation, 'supplying the sense of security and equal treatment to ethnic minorities which is surely the right of every citizen.' G. Bindman, Fighting Hatred, *Law Society Gazette* 91/4 26 January 1994.

[22] House of Commons, Home Affairs Committee, Racial Attacks and Harassment, Session 1993–4, 25 May 1994, HC 71.

[23] See, for example, Oxford University, *Code of Practice on Harassment*.

[24] A notable feature of British political life is the relative lack of public attention paid to freedom of speech issues when these issues are discussed. More often the conflicts are discussed in smaller groups where the conflicts can, of course, be extremely tense, see the discussions involving the issue of whether the NCCL as it was, should give advice to racist organisations, see S. Sedley, 'The Spider and the Fly: A Question of Principle', in L. Gostin, *Civil Liberties in Conflict* (Routledge, 1988), 136. A notable exception to the absence of public debate occurred when several university student unions adopted a 'no-platform' policy for speakers who were regarded as racist. This resulted in the provisions of section 43 of the Education (No. 2) Act 1986 guaranteeing 'freedom of speech' in universities, polytechnics and colleges.

in France candidates for the party of M. Le Pen attracted 12 per cent in the first-round vote of the March 1993 election[25]), and partly because of a substantial increase in racially-motivated attacks, the relationship between European social policy and the role of immigrants in western Europe is currently under reconsideration. How best, for example, can we retain adherence to values such as freedom of speech, while at the same time encouraging respect and tolerance for groups which may feel excluded from civil society by the exercise of such freedoms by others? The debate over the publication of *Satanic Verses* is one recent example of such an issue, stimulating consideration of how far, if at all, grave offence to the religious sensibilities of ethnic minority groups, should be justification for restricting what is published.

The European Community has been struggling with how to approach these issues on a European level for some years.[26] Recently, the European Parliament agreed to two particularly relevant resolutions. In May 1993, the Parliament considered that certain specific legal and institutional measures were essential,[27] in particular that there should be a Council Directive on the introduction of national legislation designed to 'combat racism, xenophobia and anti-semitism on the basis of the most stringent measures' existing in the Member States. Such legislation must 'acknowledge that racist acts are in fact criminal offences' and the Directive and the Member State's legislation must be 'effective as regards groups and associations which incite racial, religious or ethnic hatred'. The Resolution further considers that Member States should adopt legislation 'condemning any denial of the genocide perpetrated during the Second World War and any justification and attempt at rehabilitation of the regimes and institutions which were responsible for and parties to it'. A further Resolution in December 1993, reiterated the need for 'incitement to racism to be treated as a real offence' and called on all the Member States 'to adjust their legal measures accordingly against those who commit racist acts.'[28] More interestingly, perhaps, the Resolution sets out in general terms the justification for such a legal approach. The Parliament considered that the European Union 'has a duty to protect democratic values and that the principles of tolerance and solidarity are fundamental in a Europe which has always claimed to be an open society and a guarantor of diversity.'[29]

The fall of the Berlin Wall, and the collapse of the Communist governments of central and eastern Europe has resulted in the unleashing of nationalistic and ethnic chauvinism of a type which threatens to engulf several of the fledgling democracies struggling for stability, and has already led to the bloody Balkan conflict. The role of speech in whipping up these ethnic tensions has been seen by some as important. Since several of these countries are parties to the European Convention on Human Rights, and several are actual, or likely candidates for membership of the European Union, we need to assess how we would view action taken by these countries to suppress speech which was thought likely to generate, or contribute to, ethnic tensions.

In each of these areas the European Convention on Human Rights is likely to play an increasingly important role in legal consideration of policy proposals in both Britain and at the Western European level, not least because of the extent to which the European Court of Justice and the British courts have (partly) embraced its principles, and the Treaty on European Union has underpinned its importance. It is appropriate therefore, to examine the conformity of recent proposals to curb racist speech in western Europe against the requirements of freedom of expression guaranteed by Article 10 ECHR.

This debate is likely to be influenced by approaches taken in the United States to issues of freedom of speech.[30] The intellectual and legal influence of the United States and its approach to freedom of speech remains for many of profound

[25] See J. Rogaly, 'Racists' Protective Blanket', *Financial Times*, 23 October 1993.

[26] For a brief account, see McCrudden, 'Racial Discrimination', in C. McCrudden and G. Chambers (eds.), *Individual Rights and the Law in Britain* (OUP, 1993), 409, at 444–6.

[27] European Parliament, Resolution on racism, xenophobia in Europe and the danger of right-wing extremist violence, OJ C 150, 31.5.93, p. 127, para. 12.

[28] European Parliament, Resolution on racism and xenophobia, OJ C 342, 20.12.93, pp. 19–23, para. 10.

[29] Id at E. See further report of the Committee on Civil Liberties and Internal Affairs of the resurgence of racism and xenophobia in Europe and the danger of right-wing extremist violence. Rapporteur: Mr. Cesare De Piccoli, A 3–0127/93.

[30] In *Democracy and the Problem of Free Speech* (Free Press, 1993), Cass Sunstein has usefully summarised the current orthodox approach to free speech adopted by the United States Supreme Court. His view, which I will adopt for the purposes of this discussion, is that the United States Supreme Court requires two questions to be asked: (i) 'Does the speech at issue classify as "low-value"?' (ii) 'Has government regulated the relevant speech in a sufficiently neutral way?' (at 8) The first question distinguishes between low value and high value speech. Although the standard it uses to distinguish between the two is unclear, ordinary political speech belongs to the core of the notion of high value speech. The closer to the core, the stronger the showing of harm which must be demonstrated by government for it to be allowed to regulate it. Low value speech 'may be regulated if the government can show a legitimate, plausible justification.' (at 9) Some speech is regarded as outside the scope of protection on a per se rule, such as 'obscenity'. The second question involves 'not the value of the speech, but the particular method by which government regulates speech'. (p. 11). The United States Supreme Court distinguishes between three different types of restrictions on speech: 'content-neutral restrictions; viewpoint-based restrictions; and consent-based restrictions'. (at 11). Viewpoint-based restrictions are 'almost automatically unconstitutional' (at 13). Content-

importance for the way in which we conceptualise problems and structure our assessments. On the one hand, United States courts have, in several decisions, adopted increasingly broad notions of what freedom of speech requires. On the other hand, several American intellectual movements have recently challenged the current United States judicial approaches. The debate which has been generated has, to some extent, begun to enter mainstream British intellectual discourse. We need to rethink how far the United States judicial approach to freedom of speech should influence the European issues sketched out above.

David Feldman's argument

To focus the discussion, and provide a European context for it, it will be useful to consider an argument recently put forward by David Feldman in his magnificent recent book, *Civil Liberties and Human Rights in England and Wales.*[31] Following a brief discussion of the incitement to racial hatred provisions in British law, he writes as follows: 'In terms of the European Convention on Human Rights, [presumably under Article 10] there is a question mark over whether there is a pressing social need for such legislation, and whether it is proportionate to the legitimate aim pursued (the prevention of disorder), but it does not on its face discriminate against any one viewpoint more than others. In order to prevent the state from acting as censor of points of view, this is important.'[32] Then, after a discussion of recent American case law, he concludes, 'the significance of the way in which interferences with freedom of expression operate against advocates on particular subjects, or with particular viewpoints, in a discriminatory way, emphasises the importance to civil liberties of political neutrality in the drafting of rules which restrict the liberty.'[33]

When I first read this passage, alarm bells started ringing. It is a somewhat opaque discussion, but the impression left is that provisions such as the existing incitement to racial hatred provisions are of questionable conformity with Article 10 of the ECHR, but that they are saved due to the lack of overt ('on its face') viewpoint discrimination. If this is correct then it raises considerable questions about existing British legislation, and the suggested reforms to that legislation discussed above, as well as the European Community legislation proposed by the European Parliament. European social policy in the area of race relations would be subject to greater constraints than had hitherto been thought to be the case. Thinking about the implications further, the emerging picture seemed even more worrying. If Feldman's view was correct, was it not also the case that the important part of anti-discrimination law restricting workplace racial and sexual harassment was also questionable?[34]

I will argue that Feldman's concerns are misplaced. The legislation *is* justified by a pressing social need, but the legitimate aim pursued should *not*, however, be seen as the prevention of disorder. The legislation is justified also despite the fact that it *does* discriminate against particular viewpoints. I shall suggest, in addition, that Feldman's use of United States Supreme Court approaches to these topics is not only highly controversial and needs to be *argued*, it is also misguided. My argument will be that while the approach adopted there is, so to speak, a useful barium meal (helping us to identify previously unnoticed elements in one's own jurisdiction's approach), it is a doubtful litmus test for the acceptability of our approach.

These will be my conclusions, but this is not to say that Feldman's argument does not have considerable weight behind it. It is, indeed, that weight which makes it a serious issue. His position and approach is supported by other leading academics and some judicial authority in Britain, and by the United States Supreme Court; powerful allies, indeed. Let us consider these issues in turn.

Academic and judicial approaches in Britain

British academic discussion of the legislation has been relatively limited, but David Feldman is far from being alone in his reservations about its justifiability.[35] Though few go so far as to call the

neutral restrictions are often accepted, with the Court adopting a balancing test looking at the 'extent of the effects on speech and at the nature and strength of the government's claim that its interest is sufficient to justify content-neutral restrictions.' (at 13) Content-based restrictions 'face a strong, though not irrebutable, presumption of unconstitutionality.' (at 13) In a few well-defined areas, content-based restriction are perfectly acceptable. 'For example, government may regulate obscenity, false or misleading commercial speech, and private libel, even though all these restrictions are content-based.' (at 13).

31 OUP, 1993.

32 p. 813.

33 at 814.

34 Feldman does not himself make this connection.

35 That said, several academics and other legal writers have strongly supported such legislation, S. Sedley, 'The Spider and the Fly: a Question of Principle', in L. Gostin, *Civil Liberties in Conflict* (Routledge, 1988) 136, urged further tightening up of enforcement, G. Bindman,Fighting Hatred, *Law Society Gazette* 91/4 26 January 1994 at 23, and extension in its coverage, S. Poulter, 'Towards Legislative Reform of the Blasphemy and Racial Hatred Laws', 1991 *Public Law* 371 and R. Wintemute, Sexual Orientation Discrimination, in McCrudden and Chambers, *Individual Rights and the Law in Britain* at 503. Some have also expressed their reservations about reliance on what they see as the peculiarities of American jurisprudence on the issue. A. W. Bradley, 'Free Expression and Acts of Racial Hatred', 1992 *Public Law* 357 at 359: 'In this area at least, the United Kingdom and many other countries are fortunate to be without the full rigours of First Amendment jurisprudence.'

provisions into question under the European Convention, several academic and legal writers in the United Kingdom are at best neutral and worried about such legal restrictions on hate speech,[36] at worst downright hostile.[37] Robertson and Nicol's discussion in their impressive and sensitive book is fairly typical of civil libertarian unease.[38] They have several concerns about the current legislation. First, the legislation has 'a potential for punishing the expression of genuine political statements, albeit couched in crude or insulting terminology'.[39] Second, the legislation may have a chilling effect on public discussion of racism. The offence of inciting racial hatred by the transmission of television or radio programmes 'will make it more hazardous to produce programmes about racism'.[40] Third, those who may suffer most may be oppressed minorities themselves whose activists may use 'rhetoric . . . designed to jolt what they perceive as white complacency'.[41] Fourth, where those prosecuted are acquitted, an element of encouragement is given to those who use such speech, and prosecutions may then be counterproductive. In their scepticism, several of those worried or hostile also appear, like David Feldman, to be heavily influenced by their interpretation of the constitutional position in the United States.[42]

Several also support Feldman's view that the purpose of the legislation lies in safeguarding public order, on the basis that there is a serious threat to public order inherent in the conduct proscribed.[43] Tony Bradley regarded the earlier legislation as justifiable only 'because there is considered to be a serious threat to public order inherent in certain forms of political and social expression.'[44] Geoffrey Robertson agrees, distinguishing between the hurt caused by racist speech from that caused by speech denigrating other groups: '[R]acism is a special case because of its particular propensity to cause public disorder . . .'[45] But if that is the rationale,[46] then the drafting of the legislation seems ill-suited. None of the offences under Part III, as Card points out,[47] requires 'an intent to provoke a breach of the peace, or the likelihood of such a breach (let alone that public disorder resulted)'. Nor is the rationale that there is an inherent public order threat applicable to the offence of possessing racially inflammatory material.[48] Undermining the public order rationale undermines the justifiability of the legislation, as Feldman has argued.

Can the incitement legislation be seen, instead, as drawing support from its race relations legislation origins? Several in the sceptical tradition seek to separate what they see as the dubious incitement provisions from enthusiastically-supported anti-discrimination law provisions. In one of the earliest, and most influential, commentaries on the 1965 and 1968 Race Relations Acts,[49] Anthony Lester and Geoffrey Bindman argued with vigour that the inclusion of the incitement provisions in legislation dealing with racial discrimination was a mistake, leading to confusion between the criminal offence of incitement and the civil regulation of discrimination, impairing the enforcement of the latter. The provisions were related to each other in 'a wider sense. Where racial hatred is stirred up, it is obviously much harder to reduce racial discrimination against the victims of such hatred; conversely, where racial discrimination is prevented, the conditions in which racial hatred flourish are likely to be removed.'[50] However, the racial incitement provisions raise 'controversial issues both of principle and practical expediency which do not apply to the law against racial discrimination.' The 'wiser course' would be to extend the incitement provisions 'to include incitement to group hatred (rather than racial hatred) and incorporate it in a separate statute where it cannot be confused—and in conflict

[36] For example, D. Pannick, 'Article 10 of the European Convention on Human Rights', 4 *King's College Law Journal* 44 at 50 (1993–4): 'There are no easy answers to these complex and troubling issues' but 'the most persuasive principle' is 'decent people speaking out' and 'the power of education'.

[37] For example, J. Gardner, 'Freedom of Expression' in C. McCrudden and G. Chambers (eds.), *Individual Rights and the Law in Britain* at 219: 'The incitement-to-racial-hatred laws, as drafted, carry an alarming element of life-style censorship . . .'

[38] *Media Law* (Penguin, 3rd ed. 1992).

[39] at 169.

[40] at 168.

[41] at 169.

[42] See, for example D. Pannick, 'Article 10 of the European Convention on Human Rights', 4 *King's College Law Journal* 44.

[43] *Brownlie's Law of Public Order and National Security*, 2nd ed., p. 17.

[44] A. W. Bradley, *Constitutional and Administrative Law* (9th ed., 1979, Longman, at 477.

[45] G. Robertson, *Freedom, the Individual and the Law* (Penguin, 6th ed., 1989).

[46] Academic British legal writing about these provisions also diverges remarkably on what the purpose and justification of these provisions are. Rodney Brazier, for example, regards 'the gist of these offences [as lying in] the opprobrious nature of the words or conduct in question and the feelings of disgust they are likely to arouse. To this extent the offence is more akin to the old common law of obscenity than to other modern limitations imposed by the criminal law on freedom of expression' (Stanley de Smith and Rodney Brazier, *Constitutional and Administrative Law* (6th ed., Penguin 1989, p. 502). Woolfe considers at least seven possible justifications, but concludes: 'Such issues were not satisfactorily considered or dealt with 'during the passage of the legislation. (W. J. Woolfe, 'Values in Conflict: Incitement to Racial Hatred and the Public Order Act 1986', 1987 *Public Law* 85 at 95).

[47] Card, *Public Order: the New Law*, at para. 5.11, p. 97.

[48] Ibid.

[49] A. Lester and G. Bindman, *Race and Law* (Penguin, 1972), p. 343–4.

[50] Op cit. at 344.

with—the use of law to combat racial discrimination.'[51] Indeed, this approach was to some extent adopted in the Public Order Act 1986 which removed the offence from the Race Relations Act 1976. It is notable that none of the main texts on the law of racial discrimination include consideration of incitement to racial hatred.

With such a weight of sceptical reaction, can the legislation on incitement to racial hatred survive? My concerns were increased further by recent judicial developments. There has been very little occasion[52] for British courts to consider free speech arguments in the context of the incitement to racial hatred provisions. In only one case, indeed, has the potential clash between anti-racist policies and freedom of speech been, to my knowledge, explicitly raised and this did not concern the incitement to hatred legislation. In *Wheeler* v. *Leicester City Council*[53] the courts considered the statutory duty of a local authority to have 'due regard' to the need to eliminate unlawful racial discrimination, and to promote equality of opportunity, and good relations, between persons of different racial groups.[54] The council had a policy of withholding support for and discouraging sporting links with South Africa because of the then practice of apartheid. The English Rugby Football Union decided to send a team to play in South Africa and selected three members of the team from a local club. The local club had, over a period of years been permitted to use one of the city's recreation grounds for matches and training. The Council required the club to support opposition to the tour, press for its cancellation, and press its own players not to participate in the tour. The club in response condemned apartheid but recognised that there were differences of opinion over the way in which apartheid could be broken down. Its members had the choice of whether or not to go on the tour, but it agreed to circulate to its members a memorandum prepared by the anti-apartheid movement to the players and asked them to consider the contents seriously before deciding whether to play in South Africa. After the three players had gone on the tour, the Council banned the club from using the recreation ground for twelve months. Judicial review was sought. The Court of Appeal, by a majority, Browne-Wilkinson LJ (as he then was) dissenting, upheld the club's decision. The House of Lords unanimously struck down the Council's decision on the grounds that the decision was unreasonable, and unfair.

The interest of the case from our point of view lies in the use of freedom of expression argument by Browne-Wilkinson, LJ in dissent in the Court of Appeal, an argument which was not supported either by the other members of the Court of Appeal, or by the House of Lords, but one which nevertheless is one of the few circumstances in which freedom of speech has been explicitly considered by the senior judiciary in the context of anti-racist activity. For Browne-Wilkinson LJ, the case 'raises a conflict between two basic principles of a democratic society; viz., on one hand, the right of a democratically elected body to conduct their affairs in accordance with their own views and, on the other, the right to freedom of speech and conscience enjoyed by each individual in a democratic society.'[55] He regarded the punishment of the club as being for the failure 'publicly to endorse the views of the council on this issue . . . As it seems to me, there is no doubt but that the club was punished for its failure to speak and act in the particular way required by the council.'[56] In his view, the value of freedom of speech was inherent in the common law and remained in force unless Parliament explicitly took it away. The Race Relations Act 'does not expressly authorise existing powers to be used so as to discriminate against those who hold lawful views on racial matters. Therefore . . . I would hold that section 71 did not authorise such views to be taken into account in exercising . . . discretionary powers . . . It is noteworthy that at no stage does the Race Relations Act declare racially discriminatory views or words to be unlawful. The Act renders unlawful only discriminatory *action*.'[57]

What is worrying about the judgment is its potential implications for the interpretation of unlawful direct discrimination under anti-discrimination law as including sexual and racial harassment which in practice *does* declare racially and sexually discriminatory words to be unlawful in certain contexts. Is there here the seeds of a substantial challenge to these interpretations?

American constitutional law and race-hate speech

In 1952, when the United States Supreme Court first considered state legislation outlawing race-hate speech, the majority took a broadly sympathetic approach. In *Beauharnais* v. *People of the State of Illinois*[58] the Supreme Court was asked to consider the constitutionality of a state criminal provision

[51] At 374.
[52] Since the *Jordan* case, see infra, note 124.
[53] [1985] 1 AC 1054.
[54] Section 71 Race Relations Act 1976.

[55] At 1062.
[56] At 1063.
[57] At 1066.
[58] 343 U.S. 250, 72 S. Ct. 725 (1952).

which provided that publications or exhibitions which portray 'depravity, criminality, unchastity, or lack of virtue of a class of citizens, of any race, color, creed or religion which said publication or exhibition exposes the citizens of any race, color, creed or religion to contempt, derision, or obloquy or which is productive of breach of the peace or riots.' In downtown Chicago, a leaflet was extensively distributed by the President of the White Circle League, a White supremacist organization. The leaflet contained a petition calling on the Mayor and City Council 'to halt the further encroachment, harassment and invasion of white people, their property, neighborhoods and persons, by the Negro . . .' Below this there was a call for 'One million self respecting white people in Chicago to unite . . .' The leaflet continued: 'If persuasion and the need to prevent the white race from becoming mongrelized by the negro will not unite us, then the aggressions . . . rapes, robberies, knives, guns and marijuana of the negro, surely will.' Attached, was an application form for membership in the White Circle League of America, Inc. Beauharnais was prosecuted, found guilty and fined $200.00. The United States Supreme Court upheld the constitutionality of the provision, with four members of the Court dissenting. The opinion of the Court was given by Frankfurter, J.

Frankfurter J. construed the statute as akin to a prohibition of criminal libel against groups. His view was that 'certain well defined and narrowly limited classes of speech'[59] did not raise any Constitutional problems. These included 'the lewd and obscene, the profane, the libellous, and the insulting or "fighting" words—those which by their very utterance inflict injury or tend to incite an immediate breach of the peace.'[60] There was no constitutional problem with restricting such speech, because they 'are no essential part of any exposition of ideas, and are of such slight social value as a step to truth that any benefit that may derived from them is clearly outweighed by the social interest in order and morality.'[61] He would be prepared to deny the state the power to regulate such speech, only if 'we can say that this is a wilful and purposeless restriction unrelated to the peace and well-being of the State.'[62] The history of race relations in Illinois was such as to show 'that wilful purveyors of falsehood concerning racial and religious groups promote strife and tend powerfully to obstruct the manifold adjustments required for free, ordered life in a metropolitan, polyglot community.'[63]

On the other hand, Frankfurter J. acknowledged strong arguments against the desirability of such legislation: 'It may be argued, and weightily, that this legislation will not help matters; that tension and on occasion violence between racial and religious groups must be traced to causes more deeply embedded in our society than the rantings of modern Know-Nothings.' Given the arguments on both sides, he argued, 'Only those lacking responsible humanity will have a confident solution for problems as intractable as the frictions attributable to differences of race, color or religion.'[64] This being so, he concluded, 'it would be out of bounds for the judiciary to deny the legislature a choice of policy, provided it is not unrelated to the problem and not forbidden by some explicit limitation on the State's power. That the legislative remedy might not in practice mitigate the evil, or might itself raise new problems, would only manifest once more the paradox of reform. It is the price to be paid for the trial-and-error inherent in legislative efforts to deal with obstinate social issues.'[65]

Given the constitutionality of state laws restricting libel directed at an individual, Frankfurter J. was unwilling to condemn restrictions on libel when directed against a group. The Court was not in a position to deny that the legislature 'may warrantably believe that a man's job and his educational opportunities and the dignity accorded him may depend as much on the reputation of the racial and religious groups to which he willy-nilly belongs, as on his own merits.'[66] To do so, would be 'arrant dogmatism' quite outside the scope of judicial authority'.[67] 'This being so, we are precluded from saying that speech concededly punishable when immediately directed at individuals cannot be outlawed if directed at groups with whose position and esteem in society the affiliated individual may be inextricably involved.'[68]

There were dissents from Black, J., Douglas, J., Reed J., and Jackson J. The opinion of Black J. was the most forthright in condemning the legislation as contrary to free speech principles, producing one of his classic statements that the First Amendment meant what it said. In particular, Frankfurter J's use of the 'fighting words' doctrine in support of his decision, was strongly contested, on the ground that

[59] At 256.
[60] Ibid.
[61] At 257.
[62] At 258.
[63] At 259.
[64] At 262.
[65] At 262.
[66] At 263.
[67] At 263.
[68] At 263.

the law upheld in that case related to words directed 'at an *individual* on a public street',[69] words which were 'not an essential part of the exposition of ideas.'[70] The publication at issue in this case was not only not 'addressed to or about *individuals*',[71] the publication was 'but part of arguments on questions of wide public interest and importance.'[72] Such laws 'present a constant overhanging threat to freedom of speech, press and religion. . . . Moreover, the same kind of state law that makes Beauharnais a criminal for advocating segregation in Illinois can be utilised to send people to jail in other states for advocating equality and nonsegregation. What Beauharnais said in his leaflet is mild compared with usual arguments on both sides of racial controversies.'[73]

Douglas J., as well as joining the dissent of Black J., produced his own opinion, emphasising the need for any restrictions on free speech to be justified on the basis of a 'clear and present danger': 'the peril of speech must be clear and present, raising no doubts as to the necessity of curbing speech in order to prevent disaster.'[74] What the Court had done in this case, in his view, was to adopt a much less rigorous test of reasonableness, and this was 'an ominous and alarming trend'[75] which could well rebound on the minorities themselves: 'Today a white man stands convicted for protesting in unseemly language against our decisions invalidating restrictive covenants. Tomorrow a negro will be hailed before a court for denouncing lynch law in heated terms. Farm laborers in the west who compete with field hands drifting up from Mexico; whites who feel the pressure of orientals; a minority which finds employment going to members of the dominant religious group—all of these are caught in the mesh of today's decision.'[76] Contesting the view that his position reflected a naive view of politics, Douglas J. concluded: 'The Framers of the Constitution knew human nature as well as we do. They too had lived in dangerous days; they too knew the suffocating influence of orthodoxy and standardized thought. They weighed the compulsions for retrained (sic) speech and thought against the abuses of liberty. They chose liberty.'[77]

The dissent of Jackson J. was particularly interesting, in light of his experience before the Nuremburg War Crimes Tribunal. In general, he was not unfavourably disposed to such legislation: 'Group libel statutes represent a commendable desire to reduce sinister abuses of our freedoms of expression—abuses which I have had occasion to learn can tear apart a society, brutalize its dominant elements, and persecute, even to extermination, its minorities. While laws or prosecutions might not alleviate racial or sectarian hatreds and may even invest scoundrels with a specious martyrdom, I should be loath to foreclose the States from a considerable latitude of experimentation in this field. Such efforts, if properly applied, do not justify frenetic forebodings of crushed liberty. But these acts represent most difficult policy and technical problems . . . No group interest in any particular prosecution should forget that the shoe may be on the other foot in some prosecution tomorrow. In these, as in other matters, our guiding spirit should be that each freedom is balanced with a responsibility, and every power of the State must be checked with safeguards.'

In this case, however, there were insufficient safeguards. In particular, Jackson J. commented on two restrictions which were not, and should have been, placed on the statute. First, there was insufficient protection for those commenting on matters of public interest. 'When any naturally cohesive or artificially organized group possesses a racial or sectarian solidarity which is or may be exploited to influence public affairs, that group becomes a legitimate subject for public comment. Of course, one can only deplore the habitual intemperance and bitter disparagement which characterizes most such comment. While I support the right of a State to place bounds upon it, I am not ready to hold that group purposes, characteristics and histories are to be immunized from comment or may be discussed only at the risk of prosecution free of all usual standards.'[78] Nor was there any requirement to 'find any injury to any person, or group, or to the public peace, nor to find any probability, let alone any clear and present danger, of injury to any of these. Even though no individuals were named or described as targets of this pamphlet, if it resulted in a riot or caused injury to any individual Negro, such as being refused living quarters in a particular section, house or apartment, or being refused employment, certainly there would be no constitutional obstacle to imposing civil or criminal liability for actual results. But in this case no actual violence and no specific injury was charged or proved.'[79] The leaflet here was held punishable on the basis of 'judicial attribution of a likelihood of evil

[69] At 272.
[70] At 272.
[71] At 273.
[72] Ibid.
[73] At 274.
[74] At 285.
[75] At 285.
[76] At 286.
[77] At 287.
[78] At 301.
[79] At 302.

results',[80] a tendency to cause a breach of the peace, but there was no finding of a 'clear and present danger'. Such a test 'is the most just and workable standard yet evolved for determining criminality of words whose injurious or inciting tendencies are not demonstrated by the event but are ascribed to them on the basis of probabilities.' One of the merits of such a test 'is that the triers of fact would take into account the realities of race relations and any smouldering fires too be fanned into holocausts.'[81]

Had the majority opinion survived, then a position supportive of European approaches would be the current American orthodoxy. However, over the next twenty years, the approach taken by Frankfurter, J. became increasingly seen as out of date and not in keeping with the emerging approach to freedom of speech being developed by the United States Supreme Court. By the mid 1970s, the dissents in *Beauharnais* came closer to representing the new orthodoxy than the majority opinion. More technically, the post-*Beauharnais* decisions limiting substantially state libel laws were seen as undermining one of the central planks of the Frankfurter judgment.

The effects of this change in approach can be be seen in *Collin* v. *Smith*[82] in which the United States Court of Appeal for the Seventh Circuit considered the constitutionality of several local town ordinances enacted to deal with a proposed march by the American Nazi party.[83] One ordinance prohibited 'the dissemination of any material within the Village of Skokie which promotes and incites hatred against persons by reason of their race, national origin, or religion, and is intended to do so.' A second ordinance prohibited public demonstrations by members of political parties while wearing 'military style' uniforms. Both ordinances provided for criminal penalties in the event of violations. The Village conceded the unconstitutionality of the second provision. The court held that both ordinances were unconstitutionally in violation of free speech and assembly protection.

Several concessions were made by the town council which eliminated the possibility of sustaining the constitutionality of the first of the two contested provisions 'on the basis of some of the more obvious exceptions to the rule against content control'.[84] The Village did not rely on a fear of violence in response to the demonstration to justify the ordinance, and did not suggest that there would be any physical violence if the march was held. In particular, this concession took out of consideration any justification of the ordinance on the basis of 'fighting words'.

Instead, the Village put forward four arguments in support of the constitutionality of the ordinance. None of these did the court find convincing. First, it was argued that the activity prohibited was totally lacking in social content and consisted of false statements of fact in which there was no constitutional value. The court however dismissed this argument on the basis that 'The asserted falseness of Nazi dogma, and, indeed, its general repudiation, simply do not justify its suppression.'[85] Second, the Village relied on *Beauharnais*. The court, however, did not regard that case as supportive, for two reasons. In its interpretation of the case, the court considered that 'the rationale of that decision turns quite plainly on the strong tendency of the prohibited utterances to cause violence and disorder',[86] but the concession by the Village that no violence was anticipated meant that *Beauharnais* did not assist. However, the Village's interpretation of the *Beauharnais* case was that speech which invoked racial or religious hatred even without reference to fears of violence was unprotected. The court did not agree that this was the correct interpretation of the case, but held that, even if it were, it was an open question whether the case would then be good law, given the intervening Supreme Court decisions limiting considerably the constitutionality of libel laws generally.[87] Third, the Village argued that the dissemination of racially defamatory material could undercut the Village's policy of fair housing. This argument, too, was rejected on the basis that 'the effective exercise of

[80] At 302.

[81] At 304.

[82] 578 F. 2d 1197 (1978, 7th Cir.), *cert den.* 439 U.S. 916, 99 S. Ct. 291 (1978).

[83] A political group, the National Socialist Party of America, believed that black people are biologically inferior to white persons, and should be expatriated to Africa as soon as possible. American Jews have 'inordinate . . . political and financial power' in the world and are in the forefront of the international communist revolution. The members of the group were a uniform similar to German Nazi uniform and carry swastikas on various paraphernalia that they carry. They announced plans to march through a suburb north of Chicago which has a large Jewish population, including several thousand survivors of the Nazi holocaust.

[84] At 1202.

[85] At 102.

[86] At 1204.

[87] In a partly dissenting opinion, however, Judge Sprecher was more willing to leave open the question of the current status of *Beauharnais*, quoting portions of Frankfurter J's opinion for the Court with evident approval. He disagreed that the subsequent decisions of the Supreme Court which limited libel laws undercut the authority of the case, and noted that the case had never been overruled. He concluded: 'It appears to me that the plaintiffs' proposed activities, under the circumstances presented here, might reasonably be viewed as not within the area of constitutionally protected activity. At least the question seems close enough to warrant serious concern and analysis within the factual situation presented.' At 1218.

First Amendment rights may undercut a given government's policy on some issue',[88] and indeed that is 'one of the purposes of those rights'.[89] Fourth, the Village argued that the march 'will create a substantive evil that it has a right to prohibit: the infliction of psychic trauma on resident holocaust survivors and other Jewish residents.'[90] The court rejected this argument on the basis that it would then be permissible to prohibit offensive speech generally. But, constitutionally, those who found speech offensive could only be protected 'where the speaker intrudes on the privacy of the home, or a captive audience cannot practically avoid exposure.'[91] Neither situation was the case here.

The United States Supreme Court refused certiorari, accompanied however by a dissent from the refusal from Blackmun J. He pointed to the conflict between, on the one hand, 'precious First Amendment rights'[92] as against 'evidence of a potentially explosive and dangerous situation, enflamed by unforgettable recollections of traumatic experiences in the second world conflict.'[93] Regarding the status of *Beauharnais*, he noted that the case 'has not been overruled or formally limited in any way.'[94] He argued, therefore that certiorari should have been granted to resolve any possible conflict between the decision by the Court of Appeals in this case and the *Beauharnais* case. '[T]he present case affords the Court an opportunity to consider whether, in the context of the facts that this record appears to present, there is no limit whatsoever to the exercise of free speech. There indeed may be no such limit, but when citizens assert, not casually but with deep conviction, that the proposed demonstration is scheduled at a place and in a manner that is taunting and overwhelmingly offensive to the citizens of that place, that assertion, uncomfortable though it may be for judges, deserves to be examined.'[95]

In *RAV* v. *City of St Paul, Minnesota*,[96] the US Supreme Court did take up the opportunity of considering these issues further in the context of judging the constitutionality of a city ordinance. The ordinance provided that 'Whoever places on public or private property a symbol, object, appellation, characterization or graffiti, including, but not limited to, a burning cross or Nazi swastika, which one knows or has reasonable grounds to know arouses anger, alarm or resentment in others on the basis of race, color, creed, religion or gender commits disorderly conduct and shall be guilty of a misdemeanor.' In an appeal against a conviction[97] the Minnesota Supreme Court interpreted the ordinance as reaching only conduct which amount to 'fighting words', i.e. 'conduct that itself inflicts injury or tends to immediate violence' and this interpretation was accepted by the US Supreme Court. Nevertheless, the US Supreme Court held *unanimously* that the ordinance was unconstitutional under the First Amendment. The Court was internally divided, however, as to the reasons why the ordinance was unconstitutional.

Justice Scalia delivered the opinion of the Court in which four other Justices joined. In the majority's view, the First Amendment jurisprudence of the Court should be interpreted as generally preventing government from proscribing speech and expressive conduct because of disapproval of the ideas expressed (viewpoint discrimination). Content-based restrictions were also presumptively invalid, and could only be justified if the government demonstrated a 'compelling state interest'. However, restrictions were more broadly permitted on the content of speech in certain recognised areas such as obscenity, defamation and 'fighting words', although the scope of such permitted restrictions had been narrowed since the 1960s.

These exceptions to the general principle did not mean, however, that government might regulate these areas (obscenity, etc.) without any constitutional restriction. In particular, government may not regulate 'based on hostility—or favoritism—towards the underlying message expressed.'[98] Thus, in an example cited by Scalia, J, 'the government may proscribe libel; but it may not make the further content discrimination of proscribing *only* libel critical of the government.'[99] The fear, which this further limitation on content discrimination is meant to address, is the 'realistic possibility that official suppression of ideas ["viewpoint" discrimination] is afoot.'[100]

Where there is no such realistic possibility, however, content discrimination within the area of obscenity, etc. may be permissible. Two particular

88 At 1205.
89 At 1205.
90 At 1205.
91 At 1206.
92 At 292.
93 Ibid.
94 At 293.
95 At 293.
96 112 S Ct. 2538 (1992).
97 During a summer night a group of teenagers assembled a cross by taping together broken chair legs. They then went across the road to the house of a black family, enter the fenced-in area in front of the house, and set fire to the cross. Cross-burning was, of course, a practice adopted for much of the first part of this century by the Ku Klux Klan, the white supremacist organisation, to intimidate black Americans.
98 At 2545.
99 At 2543.
100 At 2547.

examples were given where content discrimination may be permissible: (i) when 'the basis for the content discrimination consists entirely of the very reason the entire class of speech at issue is proscribable', and (ii) where the sub-class of speech being proscribed 'happens to be associated with particular "secondary effects" of the speech'. The first example would permit the Federal Government to criminalize only those threats of violence directed against the President; the second would permit a State to allow all obscene live performances except those involving children, or prohibit various kinds of sexual harassment (even where such harassment consisted of speech), where it would produce a violation of a law prohibiting employment discrimination.

Applying these principles to the ordinance, the majority held that it was unconstitutional under the First Amendment for two main reasons. First, it was clear, according to Scalia, J., that although the ordinance applied to 'fighting words' it applied to only a narrow category of fighting words, viz. those that insulted or provoked violence 'on the basis of race, color, creed, religion or gender.'[101] Other types of fighting words, however, were permissible under the ordinance. 'Those who wish to use "fighting words" in connection with other ideas—to express hostility, for example, on the basis of political affiliation, union membership, or homosexuality—are not covered. The First Amendment does not permit St Paul to impose special prohibitions on those speakers who express views on disfavoured subjects.'[102]

The second reason for its unconstitutionality was that, 'in its practical operation',[103] the ordinance fell foul of the prohibition of 'viewpoint discrimination' itself, since it seemed to disprefer speech that communicated messages of 'racial, gender, or religious intolerance'.[104] Indeed one of the justifications put forward by the City of St Paul to support the ordinance was that such a measure would communicate to *minority groups* that racist speech was unacceptable to the majority. Scalia, J. concluded that St Paul 'had no . . . authority to license one side of a debate to fight freestyle, while requiring the other to follow Marquis of Queensbury Rules.'[105]

The ordinance came within neither of the two specific examples of the exception to First Amendment suspicion of content discrimination. In the case of the ordinance, the basis for the content discrimination did not consist entirely of the very reason the entire class of speech at issue was proscribable, viz. that it consisted of 'fighting words'. Nor did the subclass of speech being proscribed 'happen to be associated with particular "secondary effects" of the speech'; the 'emotive impact of speech on its audience is not a "secondary effect".'[106]

Nor could the ordinance be upheld on the basis that, even if the ordinance regulated expression based on hostility towards its protected ideological content, this discrimination was nonetheless justified because it was 'narrowly tailored to serve compelling state interests'.[107] The City of St Paul argued that 'the ordinance helps to ensure the basic human rights of members of groups that have historically been subjected to discrimination, including the right of such group members to live in peace where they wish'.[108] Although Scalia, J. agreed that the interests were 'compelling' and that the ordinance could be said to promote them, the danger of censorship was such that content-neutral alternatives must be used if they are available. 'An ordinance not limited to the favored topics, for example, would have precisely the same beneficial effect. In fact the only interest distinctively served by the content limitation is that of displaying the city council's special hostility towards the particular biases thus singled out. This is precisely what the First Amendment forbids.'[109]

[101] At 2547.
[102] At 2547.
[103] At 2547.
[104] At 2549.
[105] At 2548.
[106] At 2549, quoting *Renton* v. *Playtime Theatres, Inc.*, 475 U.S. 41 (1986).
[107] At 2549.
[108] At 2549.
[109] At 2550. Those who refused to join the majority opinion put forward several reasons. The main 'dissent' was that of White J., in most arguments joined by three other members of the Court. The principal objection to the majority judgment, as applied to the instant case, appeared to lie in his disagreement that the words and conduct prohibited by the ordinance fell within the 'fighting words' doctrine. The state Supreme Court misconstrued the doctrine viewing it as permitting the restriction of expression that ' "by its very utterance" causes "anger, alarm or resentment".' At 2559. This was incorrect since 'the mere fact that expressive activity causes hurt feelings, offense, or resentment does not render the expression unprotected.' At 2559. Since the state Supreme Court interpreted the ordinance as extending to include such expression within the reach of the ordinance's prohibition, the ordinance was overbroad and invalid.

However, the main objection to the majority's judgment was based on more far reaching reasoning, viz. his view that the majority was attempting to rewrite First Amendment jurisprudence. He argued, first, joined by two other members of the Court, against the majority's view that categories of speech such as obscenity, libel and 'fighting words' were still constitutionally protected to the extent that content discrimination by the government within the category was suspect. His view was that not only did this element of the majority's decision go against recent precedent, but also that it served no desirable function. In particular, he was concerned that the approach of the majority, in undermining the rigor of the distinction between protected and unprotected speech was likely to lead to a reduction in the level of protection accorded protected speech. Second, White J., joined by three other members of the court, argued that the application by the majority of the 'compelling state interest test' was misguided in this case since it appeared from the majority opinion that 'a narrowly drawn, content-based ordinance could never pass constitutional

Interestingly, however, in the subsequent case of *Wisconsin* v. *Mitchell*,[110] the US Supreme Court considered the constitutionality of a statute which provided for enhanced sentences for racially motivated crimes. Under the relevant state law, ordinarily, aggravated battery carried a maximum sentence of two years' imprisonment. But because the jury found that Mitchell had intentionally selected his victim because of the boy's race, the maximum possible sentence for Mitchell's offence was increased to seven years.[111] In fact he was sentenced to four years' imprisonment. Purportedly applying *RAV*, the Wisconsin Supreme Court held that the statute violated the First Amendment 'directly by punishing what the legislature has deemed to be offensive thought'[112] and unconstitutionally overbroad. It reasoned that, in order to prove that a defendant intentionally selected his victim because of the victim's protected status, the State would often have to introduce evidence of the defendant's prior speech, such as racial epithets he may have uttered before the commission of the offence. The evidentiary use of protected speech would have a 'chilling effect' on those who feared the possibility of prosecution for offences subject to penalty enhancement. The Court distinguished anti-discrimination laws on the ground that the Wisconsin statute punishes the 'subjective mental process' of selecting a victim because of his protected status, whereas anti-discrimination laws prohibit 'objective acts of discrimination'.[113]

The United States Supreme Court appeared to have had little difficulty in disposing of the case, unanimously reversing the decision of the Wisconsin Supreme Court. The Court recognised the wide range of factors which judges traditionally took into account in sentencing and considered the defendant's motive 'one important factor',[114] while accepting that 'a defendant's abstract beliefs, however obnoxious to most people, may not be taken into consideration by a sentencing judge.'[115] That apart, 'the primary responsibility for fixing criminal penalties lies with the legislature.'[116] Nor did the Court agree with the argument that the role of motive was different in anti-discrimination law to its role in the penalty enhancement statute; indeed, it played 'the same role' under both statutes.[117] *RAV* was distinguished on the ground that whereas the ordinance struck down in that case was 'explicitly directed at expression . . . the statute in this case is aimed at conduct unprotected by the First Amendment.'[118] In addition, the Court accepted that the purpose of the penalty enhancement statute was to single out conduct 'thought to inflict greater individual and societal harm.'[119] Several examples had been presented to the Court: 'bias-motivated crimes are more likely to provoke retaliatory crimes, inflict distinct emotional harms on their victims, and incite community unrest.'[120] The desire to redress these perceived harms provided 'an adequate explanation for its penalty-enhancement provision over and above mere disagreement with offenders' beliefs or biases.'[121] The Court, finally, rejected the chilling argument on two grounds: first, that the chilling was 'simply too speculative',[122] and second, that in any event the First Amendment 'does not prohibit the evidentiary use of speech to establish the elements of a crime or to prove motive or intent'.[123]

On the basis of these decisions, David Feldman's assessment seems, if anything, *too* optimistic. True, those proposals which contemplate enhanced sentences for racially motivated crimes would pass muster but relatively little else, for at least two reasons. First, neither the incitement to racial hatred provisions in British law, nor the proposals for reform,

muster if the object of that legislation could be accomplished by banning a wider category of speech.' At p. 2554. The use of the First Amendment to prevent political discrimination (as the majority appeared to want to use it) was appropriately dealt with under the Fourteenth Amendment. Under that approach and assuming that the ordinance was restricted to 'fighting words', there 'is no question that it would pass equal protection review' at 2556. Third, White J. was withering on the examples selected by Scalia, J. to illustrate the general exception to First Amendment suspicion of content discrimination where there was no danger of viewpoint discrimination emerging, viewing the categories as merely ad hoc and confusing; the first exception would apply to the ordinance in this case, the second would not protect the sexual harassment currently prohibited under employment discrimination provisions in part at least since a general harassment provision (not limited to gender) would be feasible.

[110] 113 S. Ct. 2194 (1993).

[111] A group of young black men and youths gathered at an apartment complex. Several members of the group discussed a scene from the film *Mississippi Burning* in which a white man beat a young black boy who was praying. The group moved outside and one of the group, Mitchell, asked them: 'Do you feel hyped up to move on some white people?' Shortly after, a young white boy approached the group on the opposite side of the street where they were standing. As the boy walked by, Mitchell said: 'You want to fuck somebody up? There goes a white boy, go get him.' Mitchell counted to three and pointed in the boy's direction. The group ran towards the boy, beat him severely, and stole his tennis shoes. The boy was rendered unconscious and remained in a coma for four days.

[112] 495 N.W. 2d 807, 811 (1992).

[113] At 817.

[114] At 2199.

[115] At 2200.

[116] At 2200.

[117] At 2200.

[118] At 2201.

[119] At 2201.

[120] At 2201.

[121] At 2201.

[122] At 2201.

[123] At 2201.

nor the European Parliament's proposals are limiting to 'fighting words', as interpreted by the United States Supreme Court in *RAV*. Second, despite Feldman's implication that the absence of viewpoint discrimination 'on its face' would save the British legislation, the Supreme Court's approach would seem to condemn the British legislation as viewpoint discriminatory on the ground that it prohibited incitement to *racial* hatred only, and implied a *preference* for non-racist as opposed to racist speech.

In addition, Scalia J's attempted protection of the prohibition of sexual and racial harassment seems very thin indeed. As White J. argued in *RAV*, Scalia J's judgment in *RAV* would call these prohibitions into direct question since they are limited in the United States, as in Britain, to prohibition of racial and sexual harassment. A general harassment provision was a feasible alternative. Therefore these provisions betrayed viewpoint discrimination as well. Increasingly, the Feldman argument that the lack of viewpoint discrimination in the British legislation is its saving grace seems less and less reassuring.

Hate speech and the European Convention on Human Rights

One line of defence to the increasingly powerful (but increasingly worrying) Feldman approach is just to dismiss his argument on the ground that at the time of the publication of his book, the institutions of the European Convention on Human Rights had been entirely supportive of such legislation when it had been challenged by individuals as contrary to Article 10 of the Convention. I shall consider first those decisions of the European Commission on Human Rights which have not reached the Court.

So far as I have been able to ascertain, the first such unsuccessful challenge to reach the Commission arose, indeed, from the United Kingdom. The challenge was made by Colin Jordan, who had been sentenced to eighteen months imprisonment under the incitement to racial hatred legislation. His argument using freedom of speech was made both in the domestic courts and under the Convention machinery. In *R.* v. *Jordan*,[124] he applied for legal aid to apply for a writ of habeas corpus on the ground that the Race Relations Act 1965 was invalid as being a curtailment of free speech. The Queen's Bench Division dismissed the application on the ground that Parliament was supreme and there was no power in the courts to question the validity of an Act of Parliament. The ground of the application was completely unarguable. He pursued the issue further, however, arguing the same issue before the Commission on Human Rights, which rejected the complaint as manifestly ill-founded.[125]

Further cases had taken the same robust approach. In *Glimmerveen and Hagenbech* v. *the Netherlands*,[126] the complaint was made by the president of a party whose basic principles were described by one of the applicants to be 'a world conception which grants each nation a proper State, as well as the belief that the general interest of a State is best served by an ethnically homogeneous population and not by racial mixing.' He was convicted for possessing leaflets inciting racial discrimination by urging the removal of immigrants from the Netherlands. The applicants then sought to participate in municipal elections but were refused as the party was proscribed. They complained to the Commission under Article 10 and Article 3 of the First Protocol guaranteeing the right to free elections. The Commission declared the applications inadmissible, relying heavily on Article 17 of the Convention.[127] The policy advocated by the applicants was motivated by the aim of removing all non-white people from the country. It contained elements of racial discrimination prohibited under the Convention. The applicants were attempting to use Article 10 to establish a right to engage in activities which were contrary to the text and spirit of the Convention. If granted, such a right would contribute to the destruction of the rights and freedoms of others.

In two other cases, national legislation which penalised the publication of propaganda which disputed the historical truth of the extermination of the Jews, particular at Auschwitz, was challenged by those convicted under it. In these cases, the applicants argued that their rights under Article 10 had been infringed, but in both cases the Commission refused to hold that the laws were in any way contrary to the Convention. In a case from Belgium[128] the Commission relied on the ground that the legislation was justified as being necessary in a democratic society for the prevention of disorder. In a case from Germany[129] the legislation was held to be necessary under Article 10(2) for the protection of the reputation of others.

124 [1967] Crim L.R. 483.

125 *Yearbook of the European Convention on Human Rights*, 1969, p. 288.

126 Application nos 8348/78 and 4806/78, 18 Decisions and Reports (DR) 187 (1979).

127 'Nothing in this Convention may be interpreted as implying for any State, group or person any right to engage in any activity or perform any act aimed at the destruction of any of the rights and freedoms set forth herein or at their limitation to a greater extent than is provided for in the Convention.'

128 *T.* v. *Belgium*, DR 34 (1983), p. 158.

129 *Künen* v. *Germany*, Application No. 9235/81, DR 29 (1982), p. 194.

In another German case[130] a German journalist who was a leader in an organisation allegedly attempting to reinstitute the National Socialist party in Germany was convicted of preparing and disseminating material relating to an unconstitutional organisation. Referring to the *Glimmerveen* case, the Commission relied on Article 17. A similar case from Austria[131] led to a similar conclusion, relying on an Article 10(2) justification based on 'the interests of national security and territorial integrity as well as the prevention of crime' and an Article 17 justification, since 'National Socialism is a totalitarian doctrine incompatible with democracy and human rights and . . . its adherents undoubtedly pursue aims of the kind referred to in Article 17.'[132]

Turning now to the European *Court* of Human Rights, there was only one relevant judgment, and in that the issue we are concerned with was touched only tangentially. In *Kosiek* v. *Germany*,[133] the Court considered whether the termination of the employment of a temporary civil servant was contrary to the Convention. The applicant complained that his appointment was terminated partly on the ground of his political views, contrary to Article 10. He was a member of a far-right party and had published books which were considered to be racist. Since the Court, by a majority, considered that there was no Convention right of access to a national civil service, his case failed. Nor was there any violation of Article 10. The Land's decision not to accord him access to the civil service took account of his opinions and activities 'merely in order to determine whether he had proved himself during his probationary period and whether he possessed one of the necessary personal qualifications for the post in question.' There was therefore no interference with the right guaranteed by Article 10 and therefore no need to consider Article 10(2). While there were several dissenting and concurring judgments concerning this issue, only one judge, Judge Spielmann, upheld the complaint relying on Article 10. He regarded the actions of the Land not only as contravening the freedom of expression guaranteed in Article 10(1), but also as unnecessary in a democratic state under Article 10(2).

With the exception, therefore, of the arguably disproportionate action against the civil servant in *Kosiek*, the Commission and the Court on Human Rights had taken a robust view of the Convention protections, varying the grounds on which it has upheld legislative prohibitions, but consistently doing so. Apart, therefore, from one dissenting judgment in the Court, the judicial evidence on which one could have argued that the British legislation may be contrary to the Convention seems to have been non-existent.

It is very tempting, on the basis of this analysis, to say that we need go no further in seeking to reject Feldman's argument, and with it any doubt as to the compatibility of the actual and proposed British and European legislation with the Convention. It would, however, be wrong to do so, for several reasons. It is important to note that all the Commission decisions were on the issue of the admissibility of the complaint, and such decisions are notoriously uneven in quality. However, even allowing for this, the very variety of the grounds adopted by the Commission for upholding the challenged legislation, and the lack of consideration given to scrutinising how justified they were, is worrying. The level of scrutiny adopted by the Commission in these cases is so lacking in strictness as to be almost non-existent. The approach taken seems too cavalier in its dismissal of freedom of speech arguments. There is a justified fear that if casualness of approach is adopted in this context, then the Commission might well adopt a similarly casual approach in other contexts, allowing too little content to freedom of speech protection, and too much latitude to the state. And this concern seems to be borne out by the fact that on the same day as *Kosiek* was decided, the Court also rejected (in the *Glasenapp* case) an application brought by a German woman removed from a temporarily civil service post on the ground that she was a Communist Party supporter.[134]

The American approach in context

If the consequence of denying speech to racists is to permit the state to deny speech to Communists, then perhaps the approach of the United States Supreme Court is justified after all, and we just have to live with the consequences. But how appropriate *is* the United States Supreme Court approach for the British and European context? The answer, it seems to me, is quite plain: not very. To understand why, we must first appreciate somewhat more the context of the decisions and the intellectual assumptions which influence them, whether or not they are articulated. Nor do we *need* to make do with the United States Supreme Court approach if we reject the

[130] Application No. 12194/86.

[131] Application No. 12774/87, *H. W. P. and V.* v. *Austria*.

[132] Quoted in H. C. Krüger, 'Use of the Media to Promote and Infringe Human Rights', in K. E. Mahoney and P. Mahoney, *Human Rights in the Twenty-first Century* (Martinus Nijhoff, 1993) 743 at 753.

[133] Series A, volume 105 (1986).

[134] *Glasenapp* Case, 104 Series A, 28 August 1986. The Court will soon have the opportunity of reconsidering some of these issues in the forthcoming *Vogt* case.

European Convention institutions approach because there is a much more appropriate alternative to hand, that of the Supreme Court of Canada.

The United States Supreme Court decisions cannot be taken at face value and must be understood as a product of their time and context. These have two particular features of importance. First, the decisions reflect a particular, and contested view of how best the state and the law can protect racial minorities, and ensure a society which treats them equally. In other words, the decisions are as much to do with the racial politics of the United States as they are to do with principled decision-making in the area of free speech. Second, the decisions such as *RAV* are based on a notion of democratic government and politics which is highly contested; however right it may be for the United States, it is a dubious model for other countries to adopt without careful consideration. Hidden in the orthodox approach to the First Amendment, in other words, is a conception of democracy which may be highly contingent on a specific view of the role and function that freedom of speech plays, and should play in political life that may not be generalisable to other western states, let alone beyond. I shall examine both these points in somewhat greater detail.

The protection of minorities and the role of the state

As Robert Cover has argued,[135] the regulation of hate speech may best be seen as involving a more general debate over the protection of minorities. Seen in this context the question becomes not the limited, though important one of what limitations on freedom of speech are justified, but the more general question of what is the appropriate *strategy* for inclusion of minorities in the political process, the securing of an equal status, and the securing of their freedom from discrimination. In this light legislation against incitement to racial hatred may be seen as an attempt to remove certain forms of debate from orthodox political activity on an anti-discrimination rationale. This recognises the strength of such speech as an incitement not just to hatred but, looking beyond the formation of hatred, to the likely results of such hatred: discrimination, segregation, apartheid, holocaust, ethnic cleansing. This justification is based on the argument that statements inciting hatred foster or contribute to the prejudice, bigotry and mistrust between groups. These attitudes give rise to discrimination and improper exclusion from access to employment, and other civil, political, social and economic benefits.

Cover argues that the question faced by the United States after the Second World War was whether to attempt to cleanse the political process of the speech which was thought to lead to discrimination or whether to intervene against discrimination by opening up the political process, rather than restricting it. In some cases the restrictive approach was taken and this is reflected in the *Beauharnais* case. For Cover the United States Supreme Court decision upholding its constitutionality illustrates that at that time these two strategies of protection were still being kept open. '[O]n the eve of *Brown* [v. *Board of Education*], the possibility that a sanitized politics might be the only or the best hope for protecting minorities yet seemed reasonable. Black direct action had not yet begun, and Black participation in electoral politics, though in hindsight expanding, appeared to have reached a plateau.'[136]

Cover argues that ultimately the latter course of opening up the political process (in particular, through the expansion of speech and associational freedoms against the state) rather than restricting it was chosen. On balance, he regards this as the correct decision in context, in particular perhaps, because of the extent to which it empowered, rather than disabled vigorous Black protest politics. This model of politics rested on a claim by Black Americans 'to be essential participants in the public choices of the day'.

And, indeed, we can say that in several senses the current United States approach to freedom of speech serves egalitarian ends. Indeed, equality has been said to be the 'central meaning' of the First Amendment.[137] First, the hostility to content and viewpoint regulation attempts in its neutrality to treat different viewpoints in a non-discriminatory and formally equal way. Adopting this approach, it may be said, lessens the extent to which government will be able to discriminate against arguments with which it disagrees. The value served is one of formal political equality through political neutrality. A second way in which equality may be said to be served by the orthodox approach is as follows. The speech which government is likely to be most hostile to is speech which disturbs the status quo. Egalitarian arguments are of this type. Disabling government from restricting speech enables egalitarian arguments to be put more effectively. This in turn is more likely in practice to lead to egalitarian policies being adopted. The orthodox approach is therefore not only formally

[135] R. Cover, 'The Origins of Judicial Activism in the Protection of Minorities', 91 *Yale L.J.* 1287 (1982).
[136] At 1311.

[137] K. Karst, 'Equality as a Central Principle of the First Amendment', 43 *U. Chi Law Rev.* 20, 21 (1975).

egalitarian in the first sense, but egalitarian in a more substantive, if indirect sense in establishing a political process by means of which substantially egalitarian results are more likely to be brought about.

Several authors have pointed to the fact that much of the jurisprudence of the United States Supreme Court during the 1950s and 1960s in which the Court expanded the meaning and protection of the First Amendment took place in cases in which the civil rights movement's activities were being threatened by (usually) state governments. In protecting the National Association for the Advancement of Colored People to engage in activity aimed at bringing about equality, the Court used the First Amendment. As Tribe has written, 'the advance in First Amendment protection sprang from the commitment and the choices [the civil rights movement] represented, not from eternal principles or adherence to precedent, which in truth functioned more as an obstacle than as a source of protection.'[138]

Europe at present, however, seems about to embrace a somewhat different model of race relations policy, combining a mixture of 'sanitized political discourse' with traditional anti-discrimination legislation in the areas of employment, etc. It is by no means clear to me that many (if any) of Europe's racial and ethnic minorities are in the position of black Americans in the 1950s and 1960s. In few European countries does it currently seem likely that a strong self-help movement is likely to embark on effective political protest politics of the type which eventually changed racial politics in the United States. If this is correct, are we wise to foreclose a strategy which relies in part on 'sanitized political discourse'? Cover acknowledged an ambivalence to the course taken in the United States: 'It may be, of course, that a sanitized political discourse—one free of racist incentive—and a hygienic principle of political organization that would not tolerate racial exclusion at any level would produce at least as good a political system as we now have.'[139]

The 'free marketplace in ideas' approach to freedom of speech: neutrality as inequality

This point leads into a second problem with the transfer of the United States Supreme Court approach to Europe. The American approach is heavily influenced by the 'free marketplace in ideas' approach to freedom of speech. In this approach, the State's role is to provide a level playing field on which the battle of ideas takes place. From this perspective, Government must not prefer or disable any particular views. From the point of view of the state, all speech is in a sense the same. It is in the marketplace of ideas that the good will flourish and the bad will be defeated. The solution to bad speech is more speech.

Cass Sunstein has recently launched a sustained attack on the current United States Supreme Court approach precisely because it appears to him to place the marketplace of ideas at the heart of the ideal of the First Amendment. Neutrality in the sense demanded by that conception of free speech, he argues, may well not have neutral effects. 'Rules that are content-neutral can, in light of an unequal status quo, have severe harmful effects on some forms of speech.'[140] In some contexts, 'some content-based or even viewpoint-based restrictions might plausibly be seen as corrective to a content-based status quo.'[141] For Tribe similarly, such a conception of equality as neutrality is consistent with decisions which *in their effect* impact considerably more adversely against groups which, for example, do not have access to financial resources. Thus, for example, a ban on putting leaflets in letterboxes without using the postal service appears neutral as regards viewpoint, in that it applies to all irrespective of their views, but is anything but neutral in its impact. '[T]he regulation, by restricting the favored means of communication of the less wealthy people, augments the voice of the rich.'[142] Tribe regards the unwillingness of the United States Supreme Court to 'take account of background institutions of power and the costs of participation in public dialogue' as giving rise to a serious threat to the rights of expression of the less advantaged.

[138] L. H. Tribe, *Constitutional Choices*, at 191 (Harvard, 1985). A good example of the continuing strength and vitality of the orthodox free speech principle in providing protection for egalitarian social movements occurs in a 1980s case, *NAACP* v. *Claiborne Hardware Co.*, 458 US 886 (1982). In that case the United States Supreme Court overturned as unconstitutional an award of over $1,000,000 damages against several defendants, including the NAACP, for its part in a boycott of white owned businesses in Mississippi aimed at persuading the business and political leaders of the area to comply with several demands for equality and racial justice. Provided there was no violence, the activities were protected activity. Only those losses brought about by unlawful activity could be compensated. Justice Stevens made clear the connection between the protection accorded and the aim pursued: 'through exercise of these First Amendment rights, [the NAACP] sought to bring about political, social, and economic change. Through speech, assembly, and petition—rather than through riot or revolution—petitioners sought to change a social order that had consistently treated them as second-class citizens.'

[139] Cover, 'Origins of Judicia Activism', op. cit., at 1313.

[140] Sunstein, *Democracy and the Problem of Free Speech*, at 178.

[141] Sunstein, ibid., at 179.

[142] Tribe, *Constitutional Choices*, at 195.

Restricting statements inciting hatred may *improve* the quality of political debate by reducing the political temperature. The removal of the most provocative and offensive public statements may end a particular source of hostility and encourage *more* debate. Cover observes, surely correctly, that 'organized baiting of minorities has been one of the levers for manipulating masses since the advent of modern politics. . . . There are ways to block a message besides arresting the speaker, and one of them is to cry nigger.'[143] In a footnote, Cover expands on this observation, drawing on experiences in the American South: 'The history of Southern populism is replete with observations of the deflection of innovation via a quite conscious, manipulated reversion to racism to incite the white masses and prevent a political coalition of Blacks and Whites from advancing to power.'[144]

An insensitivity to the dynamics of inequality, therefore, seems to inhere in the current orthodox First Amendment approach. For some authors, this insensitivity is best illustrated by the refusal of the judgment for the Court in *RAV* even to mention the Fourteenth Amendment. Indeed, its absence from the discussion does seem astonishing, an almost studious refusal to acknowledge the obvious context for the legislation being contested. For those in particular who consider themselves adherents of Critical Race Theory, it is the importance of equality which is crucial to questioning whether the state should remain neutral in the face of race-hate speech. Equality requires a committed non-neutral approach against racial hatred. Viewpoint discrimination is precisely what is necessary if the ideal of equality is to be furthered.[145]

The approach of the Canadian Supreme Court

The Canadian Supreme Court has strongly adhered to an equality-sensitive approach in recent cases. In *R.* v. *Keegstra*[146] a teacher was charged under a provision[147] of the Canadian Criminal Code with wilfully promoting hatred against an identifiable group (meaning any section of the public distinguished by colour, race, religion or ethnic origin) by communicating anti-Semitic statements to his students. Prosecutions could not be instituted without the consent of the Attorney General. The Criminal Code provided that the offence was not committed if the statements were communicated in private conversation, or if the accused established that the statements communicated were true, or if the accused expressed or attempted to establish by argument an opinion on a religious subject, provided it was in good faith, or if the statements were relevant to any subject of public interest, the discussion of which was for the public benefit, and if on reasonable grounds the accused believed them to be true, or if, in good faith, the accused intended to point out for the purpose of removal, matters producing or tending to produce feelings of hatred towards an identifiable group in Canada. As none of these defences were established in this case, Keegstra was convicted after a jury trial. Keegstra challenged his conviction on several grounds, the primary one being that the provision of the Criminal Code under which he was convicted unjustifiably infringed his freedom of expression guaranteed under the Charter. The Supreme Court of Canada, by a majority, upheld the constitutionality of the contested provisions.

The constitutional question divided into two main issues. First, did the provision infringe freedom of expression as guaranteed by section 2(b) of the Charter which provides that 'Everyone has the following fundamental freedoms: . . . freedom of thought, belief, opinion and expression, including freedom of the press and other means of communication'? Both the majority and minority opinions of the Court agreed that Keegstra's expression of his views was protected under section 2(b), and their suppression therefore constituted a prima facie infringement the Charter. The majority and minority both considered that the speech sought to be prohibited had expressive content and conveyed meaning and was therefore protected. Both agreed that other provisions of the Charter, such as those which deal with equality or multiculturalism, and international agreements, such as those prohibiting racist statements, should not be used to interpret the scope of the protection accorded by section 2(b).[148]

[143] At 1296–1297.

[144] At 1297, fn. 28.

[145] See in general M. Matsuda, C. R. Lawrence, R. Delgado, K. W. Crenshaw, *Words that Wound* (Westview, 1993).

[146] [1990] 3 SCR 697 (Supreme Court of Canada).

[147] S. 319(2) of the Criminal Code of Canada, RSC 1985, c. C-46) In a small town in Alberta, Canada, a high school teacher taught anti-semitism to his pupils. He described Jews to his pupils as 'treacherous', 'subversive', 'sadistic', 'money-loving', 'power hungry' and 'child killers'. He taught that Jewish people seek to destroy Christianity and are responsible for depressions, anarchy, chaos, wars and revolution. According to the teacher, Jews 'created the Holocaust to gain sympathy'. The pupils were expected to reproduce these teachings in class and in examinations, otherwise their marked suffered.

[148] The majority and minority diverged on the first question primarily on the issue of whether violent speech and threats of violence were excluded from the ambit of protection accorded by section 2(b). The minority considered that both were excluded from the scope of section 2(b) protection, but that the speech in issue here was neither violence, nor threats of violence. The majority left open the question whether there was a possible limitation on the protection accorded by section 2(b) relating to violent expression, but considered that, in any

The second question was much the more controversial of the two and was the issue which primarily brought about the dissent. The issue raised was whether, if the provisions did constitute an infringement of section 2(b), they could be upheld under section 1 of the Charter as a reasonable limit on freedom of expression prescribed by law and demonstrably justified in a free and democratic society. The majority considered that they could. The minority disagreed. Two interrelated issues were considered as part of this second question. First, was Parliament's objective in passing the legislation of such 'pressing and substantial concern in a free and democratic society'[149] to warrant overriding freedom of expression? Second, were the means chosen to attain the objective reasonably and demonstrably justified in a free and democratic society, or, in the words of the majority judgment, is the relationship between the objective and the impugned measure 'proportionate'?[150]

Regarding the first issue, both the majority and minority considered that the Parliamentary objective of preventing the harm caused by hate propaganda was of sufficient importance to warrant overriding freedom of expression. For the majority, there were two main objectives sought to be attained. First, there was the objective of protecting members of the groups targeted from being humiliated and from being degraded. 'The derision, hostility and abuse encouraged by hate propaganda . . . have a severely negative impact on the individual's sense of self-worth and acceptance.'[151] The second objective was that of preventing the majority from exposure to such materials, with the 'possibility that prejudiced messages will gain some credence, with the attendant result of discrimination, and perhaps even violence, against minority groups in Canadian society.'[152] The contested provision served to illustrate the society's disapproval of the content of the speech, and was also a means by which the values of equality and individual dignity could be publicised. These values were given expression to through Canada's adherence to various international treaty obligations, which included requirements to prohibit various forms of racist speech, and in those Charter provisions which express a strong commitment to the values of equality and multiculturalism. The majority explicitly agreed with the argument that the public and wilful promotion of group hatred 'is properly understood as a practice of inequality'.[153] 'The message of the expressive activity covered by [the impugned legislation] is that members of identifiable groups are not to be given equal standing in society, and are not human beings equally deserving of concern, respect and consideration. The harms caused by this message run directly counter to the values central to a free and democratic society, and in restricting the promotion of hatred Parliament is therefore seeking to bolster the notion of mutual respect necessary in a nation which venerates the equality of all persons.'[154] These Parliamentary objectives were supported 'not only by the work of numerous study groups, but also by our collective historical knowledge of the potentially catastrophic effects of the promotion of hatred'.[155] There was, for these reasons, therefore, a strong and legitimate purpose sought to be furthered.

The disagreement between the majority and minority concentrated on the issue of proportionality, which involved the consideration of three further elements: the measures adopted must be 'rationally connected'[156] to the objective in question; the means chosen should impair the freedom 'as little as possible';[157] and there must be proportionality between the effects of the measures and the objective identified.[158] The majority considered the contested provision to be an acceptably proportionate response; the minority did not. The majority and minority disagreed on each of the three elements of proportionality.

However, this disagreement on the specific application of the three elements of the test was strongly affected by the disagreement between the majority and the minority about the value of the speech which the statutory provisions made criminal. It was this disagreement which affected the different views as to the application of the three-part proportionality test. For the majority the expression at issue lacked real value. The expression at which the provision was aimed was only tenuously connected with the values underlying the guarantee of freedom of expression. '[H]ate propaganda contributes little to the aspirations of Canadians or Canada in either the quest for truth, the promotion of individual self-development or the protection and fostering of a vibrant democracy where the participation of all individuals is accepted and encouraged.' For these

event, such as exception would not apply since the speech which Parliament seeks to suppress by this provision is not analogous to violence. The majority considered that threats of violence are not excluded from the ambit of protection accorded by section 2(b).

149 At 735, Dickson CJ.
150 At 735, Dickson CJ.
151 At 746, Dickson CJ.
152 p. 748, Dickson CJ.
153 p. 756, Dickson CJ.
154 At 756, Dickson CJ.
155 At 758, Dickson CJ.
156 p. 735, Dickson CJ.
157 Ibid.
158 Ibid.

reasons restrictions on such speech 'might be easier to justify than other infringements' of the Charter's protection of freedom of expression.[159] For the minority, on the other hand, 'restrictions which touch the critical core of social and political debate require particularly close consideration because of the dangers inherent in state censorship of such debate.'[160] Speech on social and political issues was not only fundamental itself, it was also unique in underpinning 'all the other rights and freedoms guaranteed by the Charter.'[161] The contested provision 'touches on values vital to the preservation of democratic government and our fundamental rights and freedoms, as well as our right to individual self-actualization. And its broad sweep makes the infringement it effects not only serious in nature, but in extent. An infringement of this seriousness can only be justified by a countervailing state interest of the most compelling nature.'[162]

Turning now to consider the approach to the three elements within proportionality, we can see how the different starting points concerning the value of the speech affects the way in which the different elements of the test are applied to the speech in question. For the majority, there was a rational connection both in theory and in effect between the criminal prohibition of such speech and the objective of protecting members of the groups targeted, and fostering harmonious social relations. The contested provision served to illustrate the society's disapproval of the content of the speech, and was also a means by which the society's commitment to the values of equality and individual dignity could be publicised.

The minority, on the other hand, while agreeing that it was Parliament's intention to link the means and the objective carefully, considered the connection between the contested provision and its goals to be tenuous in *effect*, as there is not 'a strong and evident connection between the criminalization of hate propaganda and its suppression.'[163] Legitimate expression may be adversely affected. Use of the criminal process may give extra publicity to the accused and his views, and may even bring him sympathy as a martyr. Suppression of such views may fuel allegations of a 'grand conspiracy' to suppress the truth.[164]

The majority and minority also disagreed whether the provision constituted a minimal interference with freedom of expression. The majority considered that the provision was neither too vague, nor overbroad. The terms of the offence included definitional limits which restricted the ambit of the offence to address the harms which concerned Parliament. 'Wilfully' imported a stringent standard of mens rea. 'Hatred' reduced the scope of the offence still further. Private communications were excluded from the coverage of the offence, and there were several important defences available which created a narrowly defined offence.

The minority, on the other hand, was unpersuaded that the terms used or the defences incorporated did in fact significantly narrow the scope of the offence. In addition, there was a significant danger of chilling legitimate speech. For the minority, too, the use of the criminal law was arguably unnecessary given the availability of alternative and more appropriate and effective remedies, such as the use of anti-discrimination legislation imposing civil penalties on discriminators. For the majority, however, while other non-criminal methods of combating the harms were available, 'it is eminently reasonable to utilize more than one type of legislative tool in working to prevent the spread of racist expression and its resultant harm.'[165]

Lastly, the majority and minority disagreed on whether any benefit brought about by the contested provision was outweighed by its deleterious effects on freedom of expression. For the majority, the infringement was not one of the most serious kinds. The 'expressive activity at which this provision aims is of a special category, a category only tenuously connected with the values underlying the guarantee of freedom of speech.'[166] For the minority, however, the chilling effect on legitimate speech, and the tenuous nature of the benefits claimed for the contested provision, meant that the balance between benefits and harms clearly went against the provision.

In *Taylor* v. *Canadian Human Rights Commission*[167] decided the same day as *Keegstra*,[168] the same majority as in *Keegstra* upheld the constitutionality of a provision of the Canadian Human Rights Act, section 13(1) of which made it a discriminatory practice to communicate by telephone any matter likely to expose a person or a group to hatred or contempt, inter alia, on the basis of race or religion. The same minority as in *Keegstra* dissented. Both the majority and minority in *Taylor* followed their approaches in *Keegstra* closely.

[159] At 766, Dickson, J.
[160] McLachlin, J., at 849.
[161] Ibid., at 849.
[162] McLachlin, J., at 864.
[163] McLachlin, J., at 854.
[164] Ibid. at 853.
[165] At 786, Dickson, CJ.
[166] At 787, Dickson CJ.
[167] (1991), 75 DLR (4th) 577 (Supreme Court of Canada).
[168] *R.* v. *Andrews* [1990] 3 SCR 870 (Supreme Court of Canada) was a third companion case to *Keegstra*, decided on the same day by the Supreme Court of Canada on the basis of the decision in *Keegstra*.

Only two important new issues were canvassed, both relevant to the consideration of 'proportionality'. The first of these issues involved the question whether the absence of an 'intent' requirement in the statute rendered it more at risk of unconstitutionality, particularly given the emphasis of the majority in *Keegstra* that the statute at issue in that case was very narrowly tailored in part because of a strong intent requirement. The second issue different from *Keegstra* involved the relevance of the statute at issue being a traditional anti-discrimination statute, of the type which the minority in *Keegstra* seemed to find more acceptable than a criminal provision. To what extent should this modify the minority's objection to the regulation of hate speech? In fact, neither issue swayed either the majority of the minority to depart from the approach adopted by them in *Keegstra*.

For the majority, the absence of an intent requirement in the statute at issue in *Taylor* was acceptable. The majority accepted that the absence of such a requirement was relevant in assessing proportionality, as it 'increases the degree of restriction upon the constitutionally protected freedom of expression'[169] because there may then be more of a tendency to exercise caution via self-censorship, but it was not determinative. The majority considered that the purpose of the statute at issue was to eradicate discriminatory practices. 'The preoccupation with effects, and not with intent, is readily explicable when one considers that systemic discrimination is much more widespread in our society than is intentional discrimination. To import a subjective intent requirement into human rights provisions, rather than allowing tribunals to focus solely upon effects, would thus defeat one of the primary goals of anti-discrimination statutes'.[170] Furthermore, the majority drew attention to the context of the restrictions, viz. that they were to be found in a 'human rights statute': 'The chill placed upon open expression in such a context will ordinarily be less severe than that occasioned where criminal legislation is involved, for attached to a criminal conviction is a significant degree of stigma and punishment, whereas the extent of opprobrium connected with the finding of discrimination is much diminished and the aim of remedial measures is much more compensation and protection of the victim. . . . [T]he purpose and impact of human rights codes is to prevent discriminatory effects rather than to stigmatize and punish those who discriminate.'[171]

For the minority, the different procedure for enforcing the restrictions was indeed relevant. After discussing the emphasis placed by the Human Rights Act procedures on voluntary compliance, negotiation and conciliation as the primary means of enforcement, and the extent to which penal sanctions are only a very last resort, the minority argue: 'For establishing the necessary balance between promoting harmony and dignity on the one hand, and safeguarding freedom of expression on the other, the process of this Act is exemplary. It is well designed to minimize many of the undesirable aspects of curbing free expression. This approach to curbing hate propaganda is far more appropriate than the all or nothing approach inherent in criminalization of such expression.' However, given the over-breadth of the provisions, even this acceptable process could not save the statute from unconstitutionality.

In *R.* v. *Zundel*[172] a person was charged with the offence contrary to section 181 of the Criminal Code as a result of his publication of a pamphlet entitled 'Did Six Million Really Die?' which denied the fact of the Holocaust during the Second World War. The section provided that 'everyone who wilfully publishes a statement, tale or news that he knows is false and that causes or is likely to cause injury or mischief to a public interest' is guilty of an indictable offence and liable to imprisonment for a term not exceeding two years. The issue which the Supreme Court of Canada considered was whether the provision violated the protection for freedom of expression in the Charter. The Court held (by a majority of four to three) that the provision was unconstitutional. McLachlin J., who wrote the dissent in *Keegstra* gave the opinion of the majority in *Zundel*.

On the basis of *Keegstra*, it was clear that the publication was protected by section 2(b) of the Charter, and that the primary issue was the question of whether the provision could be upheld as a reasonable limit under section 1 of the Charter. An argument that the falsity of the publication should take it outside the protection accorded by section 2(b) was rejected. Regarding the question of the reasonableness of the limitation, the majority found two points fatal to upholding the constitutionality of the provision. The first related to the lack of a clear objective of such pressing and substantial concern as to war-

169 At 931, Dickson CJ.

170 Dickson CJ at 931.

171 Dickson, CJ at 932–3. For a relatively straightforward application of *R.* v. *Taylor* see *Saskatchewan Human rights Commission* v. *Bell*, (1992), 88 DLR (4th) 71 (Saskatchewan Court of Queen's Bench) in which the court upheld the constitutionality of a similar provision in a provincial anti-discrimination statute which had been applied to a shop-owner selling small stickers depicting caricatures of persons of black, oriental and East Indian origin with a 'not allowed' symbol over each caricature.

172 [1992] 2 SCR 731 (Supreme Court of Canada).

rant overriding the Charter guarantee of freedom of expression. The majority rejected an argument, accepted by the minority, that the purpose of the provision should be regarded as encouraging racial harmony. This was an unconvincing explanation of the intentions of Parliament when it was enacting the offence. Even if that were the objective, a second fatal flaw was deemed determinative of its unconstitutionality, viz. its overbreadth. The section went much further than was necessary in order to achieve this objective, encompassing a broad range of historical and social speech. There was considerable danger, in addition, to legitimate speech being 'chilled' by the provision.[173]

Equality based approaches and the European Convention on Human Rights

The Canadian Supreme Court approach discussed above seems to me to provide the *beginning*[174] of an answer for how we might begin to develop a more appropriate approach to the interpretation of Article 10 of the ECHR. The Canadian approach is one which we could worse than emulate in Europe. It avoids the pitfalls of blinkered 'neutrality'. It places freedom of speech squarely in its primary political context. It is sceptical of a naive view of the free market place of ideas. At the same time it is principled. It has real bite when necessary in protecting appropriate freedom of speech. It is sensitive to the race relations policy context. It adopts a view of the role of equality in freedom of speech which is consistent with developments in anti-discrimination law. It is sensitive to history, and to the context of power relations. Above all it gives to a substantive view of equality a place at the heart of civic life.

Since David Feldman's book was published, and after the decisions of the Canadian Supreme Court discussed above, there are some indications that the European Court of Human Rights may be moving in a very similar direction to the Canadian Supreme Court in *Keegstra*. On the 23 September 1994 the Court delivered its important judgment in *Jersild* v. *Denmark*,[175] in which the Court decided that the conviction of a *journalist* of aiding and abetting the dissemination of racist statements was contrary to Article 10 of the Convention. A Danish radio news magazine programme broadcast an interview as part of a programme describing the attitudes to race issues in Denmark of a group of young people ('Greenjackets'). During the course of the broadcast several of those interviewed spoke in abusive and derogatory terms about immigrants and ethnic groups in Denmark, including allegations that such groups were responsible for illegal drug dealing. One said: '. . . Niggers . . . are not human beings, they are animals. Just take a picture of a gorilla, man, and then look at a nigger, it's the same body structure and everything, man, flat forehead and all kinds of things. A nigger is not a human being, it's an animal, that goes for all the other foreign workers as well, turks and Yugoslavs, and whatever they're called.'[176] These comments had been obtained by the journalist during the course of an extended interview in which the youths were encouraged to express their racist viewpoint, and the comments were broadcast without any explicit balancing adverse comment. Several of the Greenjackets were convicted for disseminating racist statements. The journalist who made the programme was convicted of aiding and abetting the dissemination of racist statements. The journalist contended that the purpose of the programme was to highlight the problem of racism. The Danish government argued that the programme did not have such news or information value that it could justify, in relation to the protection against racial discrimination, the dissemination of the racist statements. In July 1993, the Commission declared the case admissible, and in its report expressed the opinion that there had been a violation of Article 10 (by twelve votes to four). The Court held, by twelve votes to seven, that there had been a violation of the Convention. It was common ground between the parties that the measures constituted an interference with the journalist's right to freedom of expression, that the interference was 'prescribed by law', and that the interference pursued a legitimate aim, namely the 'protection of the reputation or rights of others.' The point in issue, and on which the Court concentrated, was whether the measures were 'necessary in a democratic society'.

[173] In *Ross* v. *Moncton Board of School Trustees*, District 15, (1994), 110 DLR (4th) 241, the New Brunswick Court of Appeal considered whether orders made under provincial anti-discrimination legislation were unconstitutional as contrary to the Charter's protection of freedom of expression and religion. The orders required a School Board to remove a teacher from class teaching on the basis of his anti-Jewish writings and public statements outside the class room, and ordering the School Board to terminate his employment even after he had been removed from the class room if at any time during his employment he published or distributed anti-Jewish writings. It was argued that his writings and statements contributed to a poisoned environment within the class-room. The court held that the order removing him from the class room was unconstitutional. The court emphasised that the basis for his removal was his activities outside the class room. To uphold the order would have the effect of condoning the suppression of views that are not politically popular at any given time.

[174] There are, of course, a multitude of issues which this approach generates. For some, see the recent interesting problems raised throughout R. Abel, *Speech and Respect* (Hamlyn Lecture, Stevens, 1994).

[175] Judgment, 23 September 1994, Series A, vol. 298.

[176] Transcript, at 10.

The Court emphasised 'at the outset' that 'it is particularly conscious of the vital importance of combatting racial discrimination in all it forms and manifestations.'[177] The Court regarded 'the object and purpose' pursued by the UN Convention on the Elimination of all Forms of Racial Discrimination to be 'of greater weight in determining whether the applicant's conviction, which . . . was based on a provision enacted in order to ensure Denmark's compliance with the UN Convention, was "necessary" within the meaning of Article 10(2).'[178] The Court considered that its interpretation of Article 10 'is compatible with Denmark's obligations under the UN Convention'.[179] The Court decided that the conviction was not 'necessary' and that the means adopted by Denmark were disproportionate to the aim of protecting 'the reputation or rights of others', given several significant features of the case: the applicant was acting in his capacity as a television journalist responsible for news; the safeguards to be afforded the press are of particular importance; the purpose of the broadcast was not to propagate racist views, but rather to expose those views; the programme was part of a serious news programme; the punishment of a journalist for participating in an interview of the type broadcast would seriously hamper discussion of matters of public interest. However, in a significant statement, the Court went out of its way to make clear its support for the approach taken by the European Commission in previous cases: 'There can be no doubt that the remarks in respect of which the Greenjackets were convicted . . . were more than insulting to members of the targeted groups and did not enjoy the protection of Article 10.'[180]

The seven dissentient judges wrote two dissenting opinions. In the first (by Judges Ryssdal, Bernhardt, Spielmann and Loizou), the Court's majority decision was regarded as 'attributing much more weight to the freedom of the journalist than to the protection of those who have to suffer from racist hatred.'[181] Their view was that a clear statement of disapproval should have been added by the journalist to the programme, and the decision by the Danish courts was 'within the margin of appreciation which must be left to the Contracting States in this sensitive area.'[182] The UN Convention 'supports the opinion that the media too can be obliged to take a clear stand in the area of racial discrimination and hatred.'[183] The second dissent (by Judges Gölcüklü, Russo and Valticos) added another argument against the majority's approach, and in favour of a requirement that a statement of disapproval should have been added: 'it has been sought to defend the broadcast on the ground that it would provoke a healthy reaction of rejection among the viewers. That is to display an optimism, which to say the least, is belied by experience. Large numbers of young people today, and even of the population at large, finding themselves overwhelmed by the difficulties of life, unemployment and poverty, are only too willing to seek scapegoats who are held up to them without any real word of caution.'[184]

Thus, although the majority held the conviction of the journalist to be in violation of the Convention, it did so on relatively narrow grounds, and in the face of a weighty group which was willing even to countenance the jailing of *bona fide* journalists under incitement to hatred legislation. We can see, then, the clear emergence of a Canadian Supreme Court—European Convention on Human Rights challenge to the free speech orthodoxy of the United States Supreme Court, a challenge based on the need for an approach to the issue which gives equality its due, but without abandoning the need for effective scrutiny of state restrictions on political speech in particular.

Conclusion

The notion of equality, particularly substantive equality between ethnic groups and between men and women, will, I suspect, be seen in retrospect as having brought about a paradigm shift in social thought during the Twentieth Century. The powerful nature of the concept is one which we have yet fully to realise. The concept has within it a series of unexploded time-bombs which will disrupt settled structures and settled modes of thought for a considerable time to come. Just as concepts such as 'merit', 'justice' and what is 'reasonable' have had to be reinterpreted, re-invented, reimagined even, so too what freedom of speech is, what it requires, and what it does not require, is rightly challenged from an equality perspective. One of the important insights of equality law is the need to challenge the reasonable, and scrutinise the traditional. What is reasonable and traditional have often been the vehicles by which racial and gender exclusion have been perpetuated. The same scrutiny applied to institutional practices (the usual context of equality law) should also be applied to such values as freedom of speech. The unsettling and destabilizing nature of equality

[177] Transcript, at 19.
[178] Transcript at 19.
[179] Transcript at 20.
[180] Transcript, p. 23.
[181] Transcript, p. 26.
[182] Transcript, at 27.
[183] Ibid.
[184] Transcript, p. 28.

may increasingly require a reconsideration, then, of one of the *other* most powerful ideas of twentieth century civil liberties, freedom of speech.

Why should the notion of equality destabilize freedom of speech? Instead of the principled, neutral, universalist approach adopted by many who most closely identify themselves with the value of freedom of speech, those viewing the concept through the lens of equality suggest a concept of freedom of speech which is committed, contextualized and historically sensitive. If the traditional American approach to freedom of speech remains unchanged, instead of a bulwark of civil liberties and the means by which the oppressed can achieve their rights, it may increasingly be seen as in opposition to equality, a barrier to justice, a problem rather than an opportunity. It would be the height of folly for Europe to follow the current American approach.

Thus, despite arguments which could be made in favour of his position, and sketched out above, Feldman is misguided in his assessment of the incitement to racial hatred legislation, for several reasons. First, the European Convention on Human Rights institutions were remarkably sympathetic to such legislation, even before publication of his book. Second, and most importantly, the Canadian Supreme Court (and the European Court of Human Rights since the book's publication) has convincingly rejected, and provides a coherent and principled alternative to, current United States Supreme Court orthodoxy.

13. Emergence of a European Conception of Freedom of Speech

PAUL MAHONEY*

I. Introduction

THE reporter's task is presumably not simply to summarise the written papers and accompanying discussion but, if possible, to inject some added value. All three papers were essentially forward-looking, in that they were seeking to identify how the 'law'—be it national law in the United Kingdom or European human rights law under the European Convention on Human Rights ('ECHR')—should be developed so as best to secure freedom of speech. The present report will try to review the problem areas that have been spotlighted and to identify any significant strands running through the papers and today's discussion.

We are all prisoners of our own environment, and so not unnaturally the following presentation is coloured by its author's background in the ECHR. Furthermore, it has taken as a working assumption that British law on freedom of speech needs to measure up to the standards laid down in Article 10 of the ECHR. This is not a question of preferring the ECHR approach to other approaches available on the market: the United Kingdom, as a Contracting Party, is bound by the ECHR. That is not to say that ECHR law may not have taken a few wrong turnings in its short life and that guidance is not to be sought in other systems that are wrestling with the same problems.

The main conclusion arrived at was a general recognition of the appropriateness of asserting a conception of freedom of speech in keeping with European society, culture and aspirations.

II. Common Points

A. *Rationale of freedom of speech*

One of the messages to be detected in today's contributions is that questions such as whether this or that restriction on free speech can be regarded as acceptable, or this or that legal framework as appropriate, depend not so much on legal reasoning as on one's (or the country's) understanding of the rationale of free speech. What purpose do you want it to serve in your society? This policy choice must be the starting point for any debate on free speech. As Professor Barendt put it, 'hard questions about the meaning and scope of freedom of expression can probably only be answered by reflection on why the freedom is (or should be) valued and why it enjoys a special place in most liberal constitutions'. Likewise, Dr McCrudden was not convinced that in relation to hate literature the US model of free speech was appropriate for Europe precisely because of the notions on which it is based—notions of democratic government, politics and the function of free speech in political life.

Whether in relation to international human rights law or the protection of fundamental rights under national constitutional law, the central role of freedom of expression in a democratic society is always stressed. Four major purposes of freedom of expression were adverted to:

- providing participation in decision-making by all members of society; this covers, evidently, the political process as well as matters of general concern or interest;
- advancing knowledge and discovering truth, by facilitating a 'free market place of ideas'; this involves allowing an open competition of a plurality of opinions;
- (what is sometimes called the 'emotive role' of freedom of expression) ensuring individual and group self-fulfilment, in particular in the fields of culture and the arts;
- and, generally, achieving a stable yet adaptable community, by maintaining the balance between healthy difference of opinion and necessary consensus.

The common thread running through these various rationales, which may come into play jointly or individually, is the belief that human progress depends on people questioning the established order and on the existence of a diversity of views. But evidently privileging one aspect over the others will influence the scope and level of protection afforded in different contexts.

Did any consensus emerge today as to what should be the rationale of free speech for us—for Europe and for the United Kingdom in particular? My perception was that there was a large degree of agreement—to begin with, no one put in question the Strasbourg Court's underlying philosophy as spelt out in the

* Official in the registry of the European Court of Human Rights. Any views expressed are personal.

1976 *Little Red Schoolbook* case against the United Kingdom[1] (which was analysed in greater depth by David Pannick):

'Freedom of expression constitutes one of the essential foundations of [a "democratic society"], one of the basic conditions for its progress and for the development of every man. . . . [It] is applicable not only to "information" or "ideas" that are favourably received or regarded as inoffensive or as a matter of indifference, but also those that offend, shock or disturb the State or any sector of the population. Such are the demands of that pluralism, tolerance and broadmindedness without which there is no "democratic society".'

From 1976 onwards 'the argument that free speech is an integral aspect of each individual's self-fulfilment may be found in several judgments, alongside the more frequently cited argument derived from citizen participation in the democratic process. The latter is doubtless the weightiest rationale for free speech in the Court's case-law'.[2] The free-market-place-of-ideas doctrine, which has influenced much of the thinking in the US, has hardly figured, if at all, in the Strasbourg Court's scheme.

B. Relevance of the US approach[3]

As Dr McCrudden demonstrated, the US Supreme Court has based its decisions—in the racist-speech area but the point is a general one—on quite specific values and notions not so prevalent in European thinking. Similarly, Professor Barendt observed: 'Constitutional interpretation is subject to political and cultural influences which are not felt in equal degree on both sides of the Atlantic.' There appeared to be no serious dispute with his opinion that a broader, more community-oriented view of freedom of speech was to be preferred for the United Kingdom to the individual-autonomy perspective now largely favoured in the USA. He cited the 'social role' that the Strasbourg Court has ascribed to freedom of expression under Article 10 of the ECHR.

In this connection one can note that the wording and structure of the safeguard under the ECHR differ from those of the US counterpart. Article 10 ECHR expressly contemplates that restrictions on an individual's exercise of freedom of expression may be justifiable in a democratic society for the common good. Indeed Article 10 states explicitly that the exercise of freedom of expression 'carries with it duties and responsibilities'. There is not the same brutal dichotomy between protected and unprotected speech.[4] The area of freedom guaranteed is vast and speech is a powerful weapon: as David Pannick observed in his opening remarks, it can do harm as well as good, it can promote human rights or it can be a source of abuse of human rights, it can be used to propagate truth or lies. It is therefore a freedom that carries risks. The second paragraph of Article 10 is unique in the ECHR, in that it is the only clause that speaks explicitly of the duties and responsibilities of the holder of the right or freedom guaranteed. It is those duties, owed to democratic society as a whole as well as to other citizens as individuals, which place limits on the liberty to say what one wishes. The Strasbourg Court has recognised that freedom of expression as safeguarded under Article 10 involves a balance of interests between the liberty of the individual to impart and receive information, on the one hand, and the need to protect the community and other individuals against the perceived harm that can be inflicted by speech, on the other hand.

The position under ECHR law is not singled out in an endeavour to sell Strasbourg wares but because it can be seen as reflecting the significant difference in mentality between Europe and the USA to which Professor Barendt and Dr McCrudden drew attention.

C. Equality

Both Professor Barendt and Dr McCrudden emphasised that, when working out what should be the constraints and requirements of freedom of speech, the notion of equality should figure largely in the equation: equal access to the media and equalising the opportunities for free speech in relation to problems posed by private—especially monied—power over means of public expression, and the necessary recognition of equality as lying at the heart of civil life in relation to legislation directed against the evils of racist speech and discrimination.

Again, the ECHR also allows regard to such civic human values as equality to be incorporated in its

[1] *Handyside* v. *United Kingdom*, 7.12.1976, Series A vol. 24, § 49.

[2] Quoted from 'Freedom of Expression under the European Convention on Human Rights', public lecture given by Rolv Ryssdal at University College Galway, Ireland, 11 April 1994.

[3] For a recent survey of the American case-law, see Henry J. Bourguignon, 'The United States Supreme Court and Freedom of Expression—October Term 1992', 15 *Human Rights Law Journal* 137 (1994).

[4] 'As a result, the European Court has not been faced with the same difficulties as the US Supreme Court, which has been torn between, on the one hand, a doctrine of absolute protection of any speech covered by the notion of "free speech" and, on the other hand, the need to develop, without having the benefit of constitutional guidance, a process of balancing between free speech and other compelling interests. . . . The very existence of the limitation clause in paragraph 2—and the balancing of interests for which it provides—may well explain why the European Court has not often been drawn into difficulties of distinguishing between protected and unprotected forms of "expression" under paragraph 1. . . . [E[ven admitted interferences with a protected form of expression may be legitimately justified under paragraph 2.'—per *Ryssdal*, *supra* note 2.

protection of freedom of expression, in that the justifiability of restrictions is conditioned by the notion of 'necessity in a democratic society'.

D. Diversity of views on freedom of speech

What also emerged was the remarkable diversity of views—among politicians, legislators, citizen groups, lawyers, academics, constitutional judges, social commentators—on many aspects of freedom of speech as to what should be permissible and what should, or could legitimately, be prohibited under the law.

Human rights such as the prohibition of torture and inhuman treatment, the prohibition of slavery and compulsory labour, the right to liberty, the right to a fair trial do not give rise to such wide ranges of disagreement on the scope and level of protection that should be afforded. There is perhaps in this an indication of what freedom of speech involves as a constitutional or human right binding even on the national legislature. There is clearly no blueprint—certainly not in the ECHR. The conclusion to be drawn was pithily expressed by Justice Frankfurter in the *Beauharnais* case,[5] now apparently discredited in the US:

'Only those lacking responsible humanity will have a confident solution for problems as intractable as the frictions attributable to differences of race, colour or religion.' This being so, he concluded, 'it would be out of bounds for the judiciary to deny the legislature a choice of policy, provided it is not unrelated to the problem and not forbidden by some explicit limitation on the State's power. That the legislative remedy might not in practice mitigate the evil, or might itself raise new problems, would only manifest once more the paradox of reform. It is the price to be paid for the trial-and-error inherent in legislative efforts to deal with obstinate social issues.'

The fact that there is this range of differing opinions in democratic society as to how to deal with racist speech, pornography, press concentrations, escalating spending on electoral campaigns, minority cultures being stifled by media-market domination, and so on, is in itself a powerful argument in favour of leaving some discretion to democratically elected parliaments to decide where the line is to be drawn for their community. This does not mean that there is *carte blanche*. What constitutionally protected freedom of speech serves to do in such a scheme is to set the boundaries of the area of legitimate democratic choice left to the legislator. A question of degree, you might say, but one that will be critical in borderline cases. The disquiet felt by Julian Rivers—of judges being drawn outside their hitherto recognised judicial role by being empowered to strike down any (social) legislation which they consider to offend some vaguely worded constitutional value—is a real one, but it could be answered if this notion of legitimate democratic choice were to be incorporated by the judges into their principles of interpretation, at least in free-speech cases. And it is not unreasonable to deduce that the greater the disparity of opinion within the community on social issues, the wider the area of policy choice that should be left to the elected legislator.

III. Problem Areas

A. Adequacy of British law

Professor Barendt, citing the *Derbyshire* case,[6] opened his paper by saying that English free-speech law seems at last to have abandoned the narrow, insular perspective which received its classic expression in Dicey's treatment of civil liberties. He saw *some* nascent signs that English common law is perhaps moving towards becoming a *more* effective guardian of freedom of speech than it has been in the past—subject of course to the inherent limitation on the role of the courts in our system to review legislation. But, having said that, both he and David Pannick concluded that the common law as it stands is not up to the job of coping with contemporary freedom-of-speech issues. Other participants such as Maurice Mendelson and Colin Warbrick spoke of the immaturity of British law in this respect or the lack of sophistication of British judges in general in dealing with constitutional or civil-liberty issues.

The notion of freedom of speech as being a negative, residual liberty is certainly strange for outsiders. More worrying though: to say that British law lacks the tools for addressing current issues of free speech adequately and that therefore we should look to the ECHR machinery in Strasbourg is to turn the logic of the ECHR system on its head. The Strasbourg system of protection is meant to be *subsidiary* to protection at national level. It is primarily for the national authorities—the legislature, the executive and the courts—to secure within the national legal order the guaranteed rights and freedoms. The Strasbourg safety-net should only come into play exceptionally. It is not there to take the place of national law or national judges. So there is more than a suspicion that if British judges are being prevented from ensuring a desirable level of protection of freedom of expression because of the state of the law, then the

[5] *Beauharnais* v. *People of the State of Illinois*, 343 U.S. 250 (1952)—as quoted in Dr McCrudden's paper.

[6] *Derbyshire County Council* v. *Times Newspapers Ltd.* [1993] 2 Weekly Law Reports 449.

law needs to be adapted in some way or another. In answer to Conor Gearty's question: 'who should deliver the recommended new manifesto for freedom of speech, the legislature or the courts?', Professor Barendt advocated a partnership between the two. A sensible and attractive model indeed: the legislature to provide the legal framework within which this or that aspect of freedom of speech is to be secured, the courts having a more circumscribed role of implementing the legislation (both the letter and the spirit) and, where judicial constitutional review is possible, of verifying whether the legislature has remained within its 'free' area of legitimate democratic choice. This is the ideal; for Conor Gearty and others, on the basis of past experience, harboured a fear that British judges might in practice undermine any innovative legislative agenda for free speech at variance with the traditional British (or even American) approach.

B. Protection of freedom of speech against non-State actors

The main question addressed by Professor Barendt was whether it is still appropriate to analyse freedom of expression in its traditional terms, that is exclusively or even primarily in terms of rights against the State and of protection against State interference. It is not necessarily the case in our society, in this era of 'mass speech' through means of communication controlled by media giants, that government poses greater dangers to a free and vigorous public debate than private power. Effective public communication, he noted, is dependent on large sums of money, so that unrestricted free speech disproportionately benefits the wealthy. For this reason he preferred the German constitutional characterisation of freedom of speech as being not only a defensive liberty against the State but a fundamental constitutional value which governs all legal relationships—and this in contrast to the individual-autonomy perspective now largely favoured in the USA.

Whilst his enthusiasm for the German model was not shared by all participants, most appeared convinced by his thesis that there should be no impermeable dividing line between public interferences (protected) and private interferences (unprotected).

To make this report's usual parenthesis about the ECHR: cases can only be brought in Strasbourg against a Contracting State, not against a legal or private person, so that in this sense cases are always about exercise of State power. But it should not be forgotten that what is in issue is the State's responsibility on an international level and in that context the State is responsible for its legislation—not only the rules governing how its own agents act but also rules governing relations between private individuals. This was the basis on which the United Kingdom was held responsible for the closed shop legislation which allowed an employer to dismiss an established employee for refusal to join a designated trade union.[7] Professor Barendt also referred to the Austrian broadcasting case, where the Strasbourg Court affirmed that the State is ultimate guarantor of the principle of pluralism—in other words, so it can be inferred, the State may be obliged, by virtue of its adherence to the ECHR, to take positive steps—perhaps against concentrations of private power—in order to secure pluralism in the field of broadcasting.[8]

C. Balance-sheet of the ECHR

We learnt from David Pannick's extremely clear presentation of ECHR law (text and interpretative case-law) that there are unifying principles but varying levels of protection—with political speech somewhere at the top of the sliding scale and commercial speech somewhere near the bottom. In judgments where a violation was held to have occurred, he found 'enlightened acknowledgements of the primacy of freedom of expression', whereas in cases of non-violation he talked of the Strasbourg Commission and Court 'having failed to accord freedom of expression the recognition it deserves'. This is not the occasion to express agreement or disagreement as to his appraisal of individual judgments. His comments of disapproval do however, as David Feldman stressed, pinpoint some interesting issues in the process of international review of human rights (and indeed national constitutional review, if ever it comes to the United Kingdom).

For example, his assertion that the Court and the Commission have taken an unjustifiably narrow approach to freedom of expression relating to morals goes beyond a mere querying whether the right balancing of interests was accomplished in the particular circumstances: as David Feldman argued, it poses the problem of the degree of discretion that the ECHR leaves to the different societies that make up the Convention community to introduce *their* conception of morals into their laws on obscenity and artistic freedom: legislating morality. Europe, it should not be forgotten, stretches from the Protestant north to the Catholic south (passing through Ireland), and then to Orthodox Greece and Islamic Turkey, and now to the emerging democracies of the former Communist bloc.

[7] *Young, James and Webster* v. *United Kingdom*, 13.8.1981, Series A vol. 44—case concerned freedom of association under Article 11 ECHR.

[8] *Informationsverein Lentia and Others* v. *Austria*, 24.11.1993, Series A vol. 276, § 38.

In addition, as Dr McCrudden urged, we should not forget that feminist responses to pornography are now querying orthodox liberal attitudes to treatment of freedom of speech under the criminal law.[9]

There was however no ambiguity in David Pannick's answer: the Strasbourg decisions 'indicate a fundamental failure to understand that (other than in very extreme cases, involving intrusion on the privacy of others) freedom of expression in relation to art cannot properly be impeded because the contents of the material may offend others'. Thus, the Salman Rushdie affair caused him and several other speakers to criticise the recent Strasbourg judgment holding that the Austrian courts had not violated freedom of expression in banning and confiscating a film found to be blasphemous under Austrian law.[10] Yet, as the chair of the meeting, Mr Ryssdal, pointed out, blasphemy also remains a punishable crime in the United Kingdom if not in his own country, Norway—the latest legislative attempt to have the criminal offence of blasphemy abolished having been withdrawn by Lord Lester this summer because he judged, in the light of the debate in the House of Lords, that the time was not yet ripe.

As regards the Spanish lawyer's inability to advertise his services,[11] David Pannick railed at the Court for having tolerated 'such arbitrary restrictions on free speech'. The problematical issue raised by this case is the desirability or not for the Strasbourg Court to go faster in introducing social or legal reforms than the democratic societies from which it draws its legitimacy. Is it evident that the judges in Strasbourg should have held that in 1983 it was no longer 'necessary in a democratic society' for a bar association to maintain its traditional ban on lawyers' advertising when at that time most of the Convention countries (unlike the US)[12] still regarded professional conduct rules of this kind as acceptable? Surely, to draw a parallel with the test of reasonableness in the tort of negligence, there would have to be exceptional circumstances before a State could be held liable for a breach of human rights by adhering to a generally recognised and well established practice? The wording of the judgment indicates that now, in 1994, in view of the radical evolution that has occurred in this domain in Europe, strict bans on purely factual advertising by lawyers would probably no longer be considered justifiable restrictions on free speech under the ECHR.

Behind the particular problem of lawyers' advertising looms the larger issue of the legitimacy of judicial human rights review, that is the legitimacy of the power of judges to disable democratic action. Some clear doctrine is needed—especially in a country as attached to the virtues of parliamentary sovereignty as ours—to provide the assurance that judicial human rights review does not mean the making and re-making of social policy by judges, the overturning of democratic decisions merely because the judges would have decided otherwise had they been in the decision-maker's place. A bad or less than ideal way of implementing the ECHR, for example is not keeping pace with more enlightened approaches in some of the ECHR countries, will not necessarily amount to a failure to implement.

The weakness that David Pannick sees in the Commission decision on the complaint about the broadcasting ban on direct reporting of terrorist speech[13] echoes a point made by Professor Barendt. He, Pannick, stresses that, along with the individual speaker's right to be allowed the maximum degree of freedom to express himself or herself, the public's right to know, to be fully and intelligently informed about matters of concern for society, also lies at the heart of freedom of speech. 'It does not fit easily with those important values for the Commission to tolerate restrictions on how news and current affairs programmes may be presented to the public.' Such reasoning underlies the ratio of last month's *Jersild* judgment,[14] where the Strasbourg Court, in the context of journalistic reporting of racist speech by skinheads in Denmark, placed much reliance on the notion of editorial freedom in the presentation of news and current affairs. It is not unreasonable to infer from *Jersild* that the performance by journalists of their normal job of informing the public about significant (and, in particular, disturbing or dangerous) phenomena in society such as racism cannot, without more, constitute a breach of freedom of expression under the ECHR.

D. Racist speech

Finally, David Pannick dealt with racial abuse. He asked: where are the lines to be drawn between permissible expression with which we may disagree and unacceptable hate speech which is liable to poison the life of communities and individuals? The passage quoted at the close of his paper is an argument of

[9] See, for example, 'Destruction of Women's Rights Through Mass Media Proliferation of Pornography', Kathleen E. Mahoney, in *Human Rights in the Twenty-first Century: A Global Challenge*, Kathleen E. Mahoney and Paul Mahoney, eds. (Martinus Nijhoff, 1993).

[10] *Otto-Preminger-Institut* v. *Austria*, 20.9.1994, Series A vol. 295-A.

[11] *Casada Coca* v. *Spain*, 24.2.1994, Series A vol. 285-A.

[12] *Bates* v. *State Bar*, 433 U.S. 350 (1977)—discussed in *Bourguignon*, *supra* note 3.

[13] *Brind and Others* v. *United Kingdom*, application no. 18,714/91, admissibility decision of 9.5.1994.

[14] *Jersild* v. *Denmark*, 23.9.1994, Series A vol. 298.

policy in the debate whether or not it is desirable for a country to legislate against hate speech: 'the most persuasive principle', 'the best answer'. Other speakers today also argued against laws driving hate speech underground. But can it be said that if a democratically elected parliament prefers to choose another route and does decide to eradicate racism by prosecuting those who actively espouse it in speech (leaving aside the *Jersild* situation of 'objective' reporting by journalists), this inevitably involves a breach of human rights? Can a parliament legitimately consider it 'necessary in a democratic society'—to use the terms of Article 10 ECHR—to outlaw racist speech? 'There are no easy answers to these complex and troubling issues', said David Pannick. But Dr McCrudden—very lucidly—did endeavour to provide some answers.

It is not easy to encompass in a few words the terrain covered by Dr McCrudden. He situated the requirements of freedom of speech in a conceptual framework where the law is also required to promote racial equality. There appeared to be no real disagreement that, whatever might be happening in the USA, this was one of the fundamental considerations underlying the appropriate rationale for freedom of speech in Europe. Where you start from in this context dictates where you end up.

Dr McCrudden's review of the US Supreme Court's jurisprudence was instructive. In Justice Frankfurter's 'broadly sympathetic approach' in the 1952 *Beauharnais*[15] case we can recognise many of the general principles later adopted by the Strasbourg Court in relation to freedom of speech under Article 10 of the ECHR: the margin of appreciation (i.e. the choice of policy) that is to be allowed to the legislature in dealing with 'intractable problems' where there is no obvious solution, the need to balance conflicting societal interests, and the principle of proportionality. This is perhaps why it can be characterised as 'broadly sympathetic'. The *Skokie* case, on the other hand, which came 25 years later, would appear to have placed a lot less reliance on such considerations.[16] This tendency being confirmed in the *R.A.V.* judgment of 1992, where legislation on racist speech was held to be unconstitutional because it involved 'viewpoint discrimination'.[17] On such reasoning, Dr McCrudden feared, not much of the mooted anti-racist legislation in Europe would pass muster. The prevailing US Supreme Court doctrine of free speech is based, he said, on underlying philosophies which may be 'right' for US society now but which constitute a dubious model for other countries.

As far as the treatment of hate speech under the ECHR was concerned, Dr McCrudden found the variety of grounds adopted by the Commission and its lack of in-depth scrutiny 'worrying'. In defence it should be said that these were admissibility decisions which are traditionally very summary in their reasoning. They are victims of the tension between the need for quality and speed in processing applications. Likewise the *Kosiek* and *Glasenapp*[18] judgments—referred to by Dr McCrudden and several speakers—have not been well received by commentators, but they deal with the marginal issue of access to the civil service and can probably be read as not having any serious implications beyond the particular facts. More pertinent is the *Jersild* judgment, delivered subsequent to Dr McCrudden's paper, where his fears of a 'cavalier' approach were not materialised.

Being unconvinced by the US philosophy and finding little succour in the Strasbourg case-law, Dr McCrudden turned to the Canadian Supreme Court, which 'has strongly adhered to an equality-sensitive approach'. After considering the *Keegstra* and *Zundel* cases,[19] he opined that the Canadian Supreme Court seems to have provided 'the beginning of an answer for . . . a more appropriate approach to the interpretation of Article 10 of the ECHR'. He described this 'new' Canadian approach as being principled, having real bite, being sensitive to the race-relations policy context and above all according a rightful role to equality at the heart of civil life.

If one does not stop one's analysis of the ECHR case-law short at the purely 'racist speech' cases, it can be seen that the Canadian Supreme Court and the Strasbourg Court plough the same furrow. One cannot but be struck by the similarities between the account given by David Pannick of the principles contained in Article 10 of the ECHR and Dr McCrudden's review of the Canadian Supreme Court's judgments. Most importantly perhaps, in interpreting and applying Article 10, as any other Article of the ECHR, regard must be had to the underlying ideals and values of a democratic society.[20] These have been identified in judgments as including pluralism, tolerance and broadmindedness, as well as protec-

[15] *Supra* note 5.

[16] *Collin* v. *Smith*, 439 U.S. 916 (1978).

[17] *R.A.V.* v. *City of St Paul, Minnesota*, 112 S.Ct. 2538 (1992).

[18] *Glasenapp* and *Kosiek* v. *Germany*, 28.8.1986, Series A vol. 104.

[19] *R.* v. *Keegstra*, [1990] 3 SCR 697; and *R.* v. *Zundel* [1992] 3 SCR 731.

[20] Any interpretation of the guaranteed rights and freedoms must be consistent with 'the general spirit of the Convention, an instrument designed to maintain and *promote* the ideals and values of a democratic society' (*Danish Sex Education* case, 7.12.1976, Series A vol. 23, § 53).

tion of minorities and equality.[21] The 'equality-sensitive approach' and the principled tools which Dr McCrudden so admires in the Canadian Supreme Court's application of the Canadian Charter have already figured in the Strasbourg Court's application of the ECHR. It could well be argued that there is no bar in the ECHR on content-based restrictions on freedom of speech if the content can be convincingly shown to be such as to undermine the democratic process or fundamental democratic values.

That this is so is confirmed by the very recent *Jersild* judgment, which declared: 'There can be no doubt that the remarks in respect of which the Greenjackets were convicted'—racist remarks—'were more than insulting to members of the targeted groups and *did not enjoy the protection of Article 10*' (emphasis supplied).[22] The *Jersild* judgment lays to rest fears that constitutional acceptance of the legitimacy of legislation outlawing racist speech carries the danger of stifling debate on matters of public interest. *Jersild* distinguishes—albeit without much accompanying explanation—between criminalisation of racist speech, which does not in principle run counter to freedom of expression, and good-faith journalistic reporting on phenomena in society such as expression of racist feelings, reporting which must be allowed to flourish. This is not to overlook that any piece of legislation on racist speech needs to satisfy the normal conditions in order to constitute a justifiable interference with freedom of expression—for example, it must not be 'disproportionate' in its repressive effects.

In his conclusion, Dr McCrudden spoke of the notion of equality as 'destabilising' freedom of speech, and he asked the seminar to suggest some higher principle to resolve the conflict. At first sight, it is a destabilising notion because it appears to be arguing against extensive freedom. But, if one looks deeper, the contradiction can be seen to be more apparent than real. The Strasbourg Court, for example, has made it clear that the concrete content of the Convention's loosely-worded freedoms in specific contexts is to be arrived at by giving full effect to the aim and object of the safeguard (that is, the chosen rationale of free speech), by identifying the relevant values of democratic society, and by balancing the general interest of the community against the interest of the individual to enjoy the maximum degree of liberty. On this basis, to take account of the dictates of equality—or, as Professor Barendt put it during the discussion, respect of human dignity—in the context of racist speech would not be destabilising but an inherent facet of the process of interpreting and applying freedom of speech.

Having said that, the foregoing qualifications of Dr McCrudden's paper are rather in the realm of quibbling. From the perspective of the ECHR it is difficult to argue with the substance of his far-ranging analysis or with his presentation of the principles that should guide the constitutional legitimacy of legislation outlawing racist speech.

IV. Conclusion

To conclude with what was taken to be the starting point of the three authors: the reach of the right to freedom of speech will in large measure be determined by what is deemed to be the underlying purpose or rationale of the safeguard provided. And here we return to what was discerned as the core of the Barendt and McCrudden theses: the central role that freedom of speech should play in furthering not only democracy, the political process and democratic debate in the narrow sense but also the democratic health, ideals and values of the community. If we espouse this more community-oriented and value-oriented philosophy, we in Europe would part company with the Americans and their 'content-neutral' approach, if not with the Canadians.

Next, as Professor Barendt and Dr McCrudden implicitly told us, in determining principles we should never lose sight of the impact in practice in the community of freedom of speech. Freedom of speech should not become irrelevant to those on the marges of society, and freedom of the press and freedom to debate in the political or public arena should not become freedom of property. The legal framework should be such that we do not get to the stage where we ask: who can afford freedom of expression? It is proper to try to reduce the gap between the law and reality and, therefore, to take some account of results in formulation and interpretation of the law.

Finally, if the conclusion is, like Professor Barendt's and David Pannick's, that the common law cannot be expected properly to tackle the demands of free speech in the United Kingdom today, then we should consider joining Professor Barendt in his support for the incorporation of the ECHR into British law and perhaps even in his recommendation for a major constitutional settlement that would embrace freedom of speech as well as other civil liberties.

[21] See the passage quoted above from the *Little Red Schoolbook* case as regards Article 10 (note 1). See also, e.g., the British *Closed Shop* case, *supra* note 5, §§ 58–65, where (in relation to freedom of association) the Court stated that although individual interests must on occasion be subordinated to those of a group, democracy does not simply mean that the views of the majority must always prevail: a balance must be achieved which ensures the fair and proper treatment of minorities and avoids an abuse of a dominant position.

[22] *Loc. cit.*, § 35.

The manufacturer's authorised representative in the EU for product safety is Oxford University Press España S.A. of el Parque Empresarial San Fernando de Henares, Avenida de Castilla, 2 – 28830 Madrid (www.oup.es/en or product.safety@oup.com). OUP España S.A. also acts as importer into Spain of products made by the manufacturer.

www.ingramcontent.com/pod-product-compliance
Ingram Content Group UK Ltd.
Pitfield, Milton Keynes, MK11 3LW, UK
UKHW050221160926
475595UK00015B/350
9780198260424